Serenity, Courage, and Wisdom

Niebuhr in retirement

Serenity, Courage, and Wisdom

*The Enduring Legacy
of Reinhold Niebuhr*

Henry B. Clark

*The Pilgrim Press
Cleveland, Ohio*

The Pilgrim Press, Cleveland, Ohio 44115
© 1994 by Henry B. Clark

The following publishers have generously given permission to use extended quotations from copyrighted works: From Harry Davis and Robert C. Good, eds., *Reinhold Niebuhr on Politics,* copyright © 1960 Charles Scribner's Sons, used by permission of Charles Scribner's Sons, an imprint of Macmillan Publishing Company; from Reinhold Niebuhr, *The Nature and Destiny of Man,* vol. 1, copyright 1941, © 1964 by Charles Scribner's Sons, copyright renewed 1969 by Reinhold Niebuhr, used by permission of Macmillan Publishing Company, a division of Macmillan, Inc.; from Reinhold Niebuhr, *The Nature and Destiny of Man,* vol. 2, copyright 1943, © 1964 by Charles Scribner's Sons, copyright renewed 1971 by Reinhold Niebuhr, used by permission of Macmillan Publishing Company, a division of Macmillan, Inc.; from Donald Meyer, *Protestant Search for Political Realism,* © 1988 by Donald Meyer, Wesleyan University Press, used by permission of University Press of New England.

Biblical quotations are from the New Revised Standard Version of the Bible, © 1989 by the Division of Christian Education of the National Council of the Churches of Christ in the U.S.A., and are used by permission

Photos courtesy of The Burke Library, Union Theological Seminary, New York, except for "Niebuhr in his seventies," which is courtesy of Ronald Stone.

99 98 97 96 95 94   5 4 3 2 1

Library of Congress Cataloging-in-Publication Data

Clark, Henry B. (Henry Balsley), 1930–
    Serenity, courage, and wisdom : the enduring legacy of Reinhold
Niebuhr / Henry B. Clark.
        p. cm.
    Includes bibliographical references and index.
    ISBN 0-8298-1004-8 (alk. paper)
    1. Niebuhr, Reinhold, 1892–1971. 2. Theologians—United States—
Biography. 3. Theology—History—20th century. 1. Title.
BX4827.N5C57 1994
230'.092—dc20
[B]   94-21482
                                         CIP

His influence is all around us. Many Americans who never read a word Reinhold Niebuhr wrote have been altered by his ideas and outlook, just as many who never even heard of him will recognize his famous prayer: "O God, give us serenity to accept what cannot be changed, courage to change what should be changed, and wisdom to distinguish the one from the other."

—Hans J. Morgenthau

The great virtue of biblical faith is that its sense of a divine mystery does not prevent it from affirming unambiguous moral principles. The Prophet Isaiah expressed the transcendent mystery in these words: "For the heavens are higher than the earth, so are my ways higher than your ways, and my thoughts than your thoughts." But this sense of religious mystery does not prevent a vigorous moral demand: "Cease to do evil, learn to do good. . . . Defend the fatherless, plead for the widow."

—Reinhold Niebuhr

Contents

Acknowledgments

Acknowledgments are probably of very little importance to anyone except the author, but from his or her point of view they are indispensable. It would be impossible for me to mention everyone who helped me gather research materials or sort out the meaning of all that they contained, and it would be impossible for me to express my appreciation to my most helpful colleagues as fully as I would like. Be that as it may, a partial list of those to whom I should like to express special gratitude would certainly include John C. Bennett, Ron Stone, Jack Crossley, Ronald Preston, Paul Cox, Richard Brown, and Charles C. Brown. My wife Lyn deserves a warm word of thanks for putting up with me during the period when I was totally absorbed in the project, and the University of Southern California deserves mention for providing that multitude of essential support services which faculty members usually take for granted, but without which few books would ever be written.

In that connection, I would like to pay tribute to the graduate students in the Social Ethics Program at the University of Southern California who participated in what they called—not unkindly, I hope—the "Love Thy Niebuhr" seminar. Their (sometimes resistant) attitudes toward Christian Realism convinced me that this book might be both needed and wanted by another generation of conscientious citizens, and their questions helped shape its focus. What they demanded was a clear exposition of key theological and ethical principles, with enough explanation of what Niebuhr said on the particular issues of his day to illustrate his use of the principles. Both new-comers to Niebuhr and scholars should be especially interested in chapters 6 and 7, because that is where I make a forthright attempt to respond to recent criticisms of Niebuhrianism.

Introduction

From 1935 to 1965, the name of Reinhold Niebuhr was very familiar to college students enrolled in religion, philosophy, political science, and international relations courses. Niebuhr was a minor celebrity (and for many a public hero) because of his oftentimes controversial pronouncements on topics related to theology and ethics. Hundreds of ministers who had studied his thought (or taken courses from him at Union Theological Seminary in New York City) preached sermons built upon his ideas, and a like number of professors assigned his books and communicated his ideas to thousands of students— many of whom also had the opportunity to hear Niebuhr speak at college chapels or public lectures on campus or in the cities where their universities were located.

Niebuhr was hailed as a prophet in many quarters and denounced as a menace in others. To those who admired the Christian Realism he expounded, he was a source of enlightenment and inspiration. He was a powerful influence in the thinking and the lives of countless Americans for several decades. This book has been written in the belief that Niebuhr can still speak to the condition of a new generation of American students and dedicated church people. As Robert Bellah et al. have so eloquently pointed out, the sense of moral purpose and civic obligation Americans used to get from biblical and civic republican traditions has been steadily withering away over the past two decades. Yet many who are disturbed by the culture's loss of commitment to a noble human telos[1] (and by the difficulty of even finding a language we can use to talk about ethics)[2] are eager to develop a moral worldview that will enable them to rise above amoral individualism.

What does Niebuhr have to offer today? At the very least, his seminal ideas can act as a stimulus to reflection for a very substantial number of Americans—not only students and church people, but also ethically sensitive citizens of all ages and philosophical dispositions who are worried about injustice and are searching for wisdom and inspiration. There is every reason to suppose that many readers will be stirred to commitment and action by what they learn here concerning Niebuhr's life. He was an energetic "mover and shaker," and his zest for the battle against social injustice is contagious.

I am by no means a dispassionate observer in these matters. I took several courses from Niebuhr (including a summer tutorial that involved lengthy face-to-face discussion); I heard him preach on numerous occasions; and I read all his major works when I was in graduate school. In short, my mind has been indelibly marked by Niebuhr's ideas. Moreover, I enjoyed the benefits and the pleasures of the informal contact with Niebuhr which endeared him to so many Union students over the years.[3]

And yet I am anything but an uncritical Niebuhrian who imagines that everything the Great Man said and did was right. The last part of the book will review the principal criticisms leveled against Niebuhr since the 1960s, and will ask the question: To what extent is it advantageous to look upon Niebuhr as mentor and model? The purpose of the final chapter is to raise honest questions about the ways in which his discernment is still valid and the sense in which it might be constructive to emulate his approach to the struggle for justice in the current world situation. With my answers to these questions, I hope to demonstrate that Niebuhr was fundamentally right about a great many important things, and that it behooves us to use his ideas and follow his example today as we try to live up to the *imago dei* within.

The book is divided into three mains sections. The first (chapters 1 and 2) deals with Niebuhr's life and with his development as a rising theological luminary up to 1928. The second section (chapters 3, 4, and 5) covers Niebuhr's maturity as the founder of a school of thought known as "Christian Realism" (or, as it came to be called during the period after World War II when he focused his attention on ethics and politics, "Christian Pragmatism"). The final section (chapters 6 and 7) summarizes the major criticisms leveled against Niebuhr and ventures an affirmation of the enduring legacy of his life and thought.

Chapter 1

Who Was Reinhold Niebuhr?

Reinhold Niebuhr was the son of Gustav Niebuhr, an immigrant pastor of the German Evangelical Church. Born in Webster, Missouri, in 1892, Reinhold Niebuhr lived in the Midwest until he left the ethnic enclave of his parents and enrolled as a student at Yale Divinity School in 1913. Two years later he took on the responsibilities of his denomination's Bethel Evangelical Church in Detroit, whose pulpit he occupied until 1928. From that year until his retirement in 1960, Niebuhr served as a member of the faculty of Union Theological Seminary, where he was absorbed in teaching, preaching, lecturing, and writing on subjects appropriate to his title of Professor of Applied Christianity. After retiring from Union he served as a visiting professor at several prestigious universities, and he continued to write as much as his failing health would allow until his death in 1971.

Such a summary of the most essential facts of Niebuhr's life— his family background, his education, and his occupation—hardly begins to tell the story of the most famous Protestant thinker of twentieth-century America. Whereas most seminary professors (indeed, most professors of any kind) spend their years in genteel obscurity, Niebuhr lived most of his life in the spotlight. Whereas the scholarly output of most academic scribblers is read and appreciated by only a handful of colleagues and students, Niebuhr's every comment in his prolific outpouring of books, articles, and editorials was devoured and discussed by thousands of readers, inside and outside the church and the academy. Whereas most preachers reach only their own congregations and a relatively small number of townspeople or captive audiences at denominationally sponsored gatherings, Niebuhr's sermons were heard by thousands of students, faculty, and college community residents who, forty weekends or so each year, for several decades, flocked to campus chapels and churches all over the country to hear the message of this modern-day circuit rider. Whereas the average academic almost never captures the attention of opinion-makers and policymakers at any level, Niebuhr's counsel was sought (and sometimes heeded) by government officials, political figures, labor leaders, and culture bearers at many levels.

This book is primarily a study of Reinhold Niebuhr's thought, and I am interested in him first and foremost as a mentor, a man whose ideas about God, society, and the good life can teach us a great deal. But because I believe that Niebuhr's life is also worthy of emulation in many respects, and that in this sense he can also serve contemporary Americans as a model, I will have quite a bit to say on this score. Even so, whatever the book contains on the subject of Niebuhr s life is important mainly because of its relationship to his ideas, by way of explication or illustration.

Thus most of what is presented in this chapter on the life of Reinhold Niebuhr is intended to do one of two things: (1) to give readers a set of chronological pegs on which to hang their understanding of the evolution of Niebuhr's thought on theology, ethics, and politics, and (2) to identify certain aspects of Niebuhr's experience which help to explain why and how he addressed himself to certain themes and to clarify what he probably meant in writing what he did on these themes.

Milestones and Major Motifs

The material contained in the following paragraphs is organized in accordance with these purposes, and the entire argument is summarized in the table on pages 8–9. Considered together, both diagram and text provide an overview of the historical developments and events which were milestones in Niebuhr's life and of those aspects of his experience which found significant expression in his thought.

EVENTS IN HIS PERSONAL LIFE, THE NATION, AND THE WORLD

Childhood and Youth

Reinhold Niebuhr was not the oldest of Gustav's children, but by all accounts he was the favored son, the one who was invited to share his father's intellectual life and entertain hopes of following in his father's footsteps. This favored status expressed itself in a number of ways. Upon the occasion of the elder Niebuhr's untimely death in 1913, Reinhold assumed the role of pastor in what had been his father's church in Lincoln, Illinois. He was sent to his denomination's Eden Theological Seminary with the weighty expectation (which accompanied him to Yale after his graduation from Eden) that he would become a leader in the German Evangelical Church. In addition, he was looked upon as head of the family in his generation and given the responsibility of taking care of his widowed mother.

Niebuhr emerged from childhood with a tremendous sense of duty and honor which translated into a powerful commitment to hard work. He also seems to have developed a very strong sense of confidence in his own abilities, and this fueled his budding Promethean self-concept. He grew up in a psychosocial situation which must have provided manifold reinforcement for a mighty faith in the parts to be played by both the church and America in promoting good and overcoming evil in the world. Because a German pastor is by definition something of an intellectual, the experiences of Niebuhr s childhood encouraged him to believe that any reasonably diligent and reflective person can understand God's will and his or her own place in the moral universe. Niebuhr had ample reason to assume that the will-to-meaning which burns in every human breast is not doomed to futility but can by dint of serious study and reflection succeed in discerning and/or formulating a truthful moral worldview.

Advanced Education at Yale University (1913–15)

The relatively brief time Niebuhr spent at Yale must have had an enormous impact upon him. Being allowed to read whatever he wanted in the library of one of the most highly regarded liberal theologians of that era, D. C. MacIntosh, put Niebuhr in contact with prevailing currents of thought in the American intellectual establishment, and it no doubt stimulated his decision to strive to

The Life of Reinhold Niebuhr

	1910	1920	1930
Personal	Yale Divinity School (1912–15) Detroit Pastorate (1915–28)		Union Theological Seminary (1928–71)
World Events	World War I League of Nations	Interchurch World Movement	FDR and New Deal
Intellectual and Political Themes	Liberalism, Social Gospel, Wilsonianism	Pacifism	Socialism and Socialist Party
Key Writings	Yale theses, magazine articles *Leaves from the Notebook of a Tamed Cynic*	*Does Civilization Need Religion* *The Contribution of Religion to Social Work* *Moral Man and Immoral Society*[c]	*An Interpretation of Christian Ethics* *Reflections on the End of an Era*[d]
Label		Social Gospel Idealism	Christian Realism

[a]The Fellowship of Reconciliation was a leading pacifist organization (which is still active today). Niebuhr resigned over his willingness to approve of violent tactics in the struggle of workers to unionize.

[b]Americans for Democratic Action was a group formed for the explicit purpose of providing a forum for people with left-of-center convictions who regarded socialists as naive and communists as too dangerous.

Mid- to Late 1930s	1940	1950	1960	1970
Resigns from the Fellowship of Reconciliation[a] Starts *Radical Religion* (later *Christianity and Society*)	Resigns from Socialist Party Starts *Christianity and Crisis*	Helps found Americans for Democratic Action[b]	Severe stroke (energy and travel limited)	Dies 1971
Rise of Nazism	World War II	Cold War	Civil Rights Movement Vietnam	
	Shift to Augustian Realism; acceptance of New Deal economy	Faith in Western democracies; supports war effort American responsibility in the world arena	Questions Vietnam policy	
Beyond Tragedy	*Christianity and Power Politics*	*Faith and History* *The Children of Light and the Children of Darkness* *Discerning the Signs of the Times*	*Man's Nature and His Communities* *The Structure of Nations and Empires* *A Nation So Conceived*	
	The Nature and Destiny of Man (Gifford Lectures)	*The Irony of American History* *Christian Realism and Political Problems* *The Self and the Dramas of History*		
		Christian Pragmatism		

[c] *Moral Man and Immoral Society* was a decisive milestone, marking the beginning of Christian Realism as a new school of thought in Christian ethics and heightening Niebuhr's status as a famous and highly controversial religious thinker and leader.

[d] *Reflections on the End of an Era* was considered Niebuhr's most Marxist work.

become a cosmopolitan instead of a local. Being at Yale also sparked a decision to master the English language and make it his primary vehicle of communication for the rest of his life. So Niebuhr s celebrated activity on the college and university chapel circuit was a natural expression of this vocational commitment, as were his modest early successes as a writer for prestigious national periodicals.

The Years in Detroit (1915–28)

In Detroit, Niebuhr entered the urban technological world of the twentieth century. He achieved almost instantaneous prominence in American religious circles as well as in the great industrial city of Detroit, and he soon began to accumulate a wealth of experience dealing with politicians, businessmen, labor union officials, and ecclesiastical policymakers. He traveled widely, most importantly, perhaps, in connection with the European Seminars organized and funded by a wealthy Protestant leader named Sherwood Eddy. As a result of these seminars, Niebuhr not only met influential political figures and religious spokespersons from all over the United States and Europe, he also gained Eddy as a patron, a patron whose prestige and financial help would prove to be instrumental in bringing Niebuhr to Union Theological Seminary in 1928. It was during these years that Niebuhr put himself on the map with an astonishingly prolific outpouring of articles in both religious and secular journals. Moreover, it was during these years that Niebuhr's involvement with a host of do-gooder organizations and political movements increased both his knowledge and his ability to organize and influence others. Niebuhr's tour of duty in Detroit thus resulted in a broadening of his thinking and a multiplication of his contacts with noteworthy figures of the day, and it increased his self-confidence and strengthened his sense of vocation.

The Emergence of Christian Realism

The fourteen-year period between 1928 and 1942 was probably the most important period of Niebuhr's life. [1] In Detroit, he had been widely known as an influential clergyman, but soon after his arrival in New York he began to emerge as a theologian and ethicist of international stature. The experience of living in America's most cosmopolitan city augmented all of the benefits of stimulating interaction with important thinkers and newsmakers. Indeed, when one compares Niebuhr's life in New York to his earlier experiences in New Haven and Detroit, those earlier experiences are eclipsed by the magnitude and variety of the intellectual and cultural enrichments Niebuhr encountered "in the city." New York was already the financial, artistic, and intellectual capital of the country, and the flood of refugees who began to arrive in the 1930s added something absolutely unique. Niebuhr's contact with Jewish intellectuals was especially important, but so were his contacts with old-line Ivy League professors, political activists (of all persuasions), and spokespersons of other major religious communities.

Niebuhr's encounters with working people and pacifists in America; his reaction to Stalinist Russia, Nazi Germany, and the New Deal; and his intellectual contact with Marxism, Barth, Tillich, and the leaders of the Protestant ecumenical movement motivated him to develop Christian Realism, which was to become the most influential theory of Christian ethics in the twentieth century. The publication of books such as *Moral Man and Immoral Society, An Interpretation of Christian Ethics, Reflections on the End of an Era,* and *Beyond Tragedy* gave him a permanent place in the pantheon of contemporary religious thinkers, and his renunciation of Marxism and neutralism in favor of the New Deal and rearmament in preparation for war against the Axis powers made him a public figure who was frequently called upon for help by top-echelon political leaders in the United States. Being chosen to deliver the prestigious Gifford Lectures in 1939 not only added to his fame, it also gave him a priceless opportunity to spend (relatively) uninterrupted time in study and reflection. That time resulted in the creation and publication of his magnum opus, a two-volume work on *The Nature and Destiny of Man.*

The Christian Pragmatism of the Cold War Era

The year 1944 marked for Niebuhr a shift in focus from theology and social justice to ethics and political philosophy. *The Children of Light and the Children of Darkness* (1944) represented Niebuhr's attempt to formulate a theory of democracy which could serve to chasten postwar hopes and guide postwar domestic policy. This emphasis on political thought led, just after the end of World War II, to a preoccupation with foreign policy which resulted in a new label for Niebuhrian thinking on ethics and politics—namely, Christian Pragmatism. The audience for Niebuhr's editorials, articles, books, speeches, and sermons was larger than ever before, and his influence on sophisticated theological thought became stronger than ever because of the growing number of people who took up the study of religion and ethics in American colleges and seminaries. Niebuhr's influence was especially strong after 1950, as some of his students began to assume faculty positions and direct the studies of new student cohorts.

In 1952, at the age of 59, Reinhold Niebuhr had a severe stroke. From that point on, he was partially paralyzed, had slightly slurred speech, and was, as he sometimes put it, "only half a man." His travel schedule was drastically curtailed, and his chance to learn first-hand about people and conditions in other parts of the world (including those in Asia, Africa and Latin America) thereby disappeared. Yet Niebuhr was anything but uninvolved, and even though his participation in public events and his published output were somewhat restricted (compared with his younger days), he continued to produce books and essays, and he continued to be a powerful force in religious and political circles well into the 1960s. Reinhold Niebuhr died in 1971.

TWO CRUCIAL ELEMENTS OF NIEBUHR'S CHARACTER

Since this sketch of Niebuhr's life is intended mainly to illuminate his ideas, the focus of attention must be concentrated on two or three of the most significant psychocultural variables already alluded to, and a clear connection must be established with the body of thought most commonly known as Christian Realism. The factors I propose to emphasize are Niebuhr's Americanism, his masculinism,[2] and his Prometheanism. Because all of these themes are rooted in Niebuhr's social location as the son of a midwestern pastor in a conservative German-American family in the early years of the twentieth century, the discussion of these three major themes will be introduced by a discussion of his childhood and youth.

Social Location

Reinhold Niebuhr grew up in a provincial subculture of the Midwest, so there is every reason to believe that he shared many of the assumptions about personal responsibility, family ties and obligations, neighborliness, order, and decency which seem to have been so important in the experience and the thinking of most Social Gospel preachers. His subsequent life indicates a continuing belief in the rightness and goodness of many small-town or frontier values associated with that part of America in that particular period of American history.

But Niebuhr is by no means a perfect representative of the ethos of small-town Protestant America. Some scholars speak, for example, of a "feminization of American culture" in the nineteenth century.[3] This term refers to an increasingly pervasive assumption that women represented all that was noble and refined in civilization, and that the public sphere—commerce, industry and politics in particular—was "dirty." The argument is that clergymen (especially, of course, the Protestant ministry in a predominantly Protestant culture) were associated with women by being assigned to the private realm of family and moral values.

The point, for our purposes, is this: Reinhold Niebuhr did not fit this ideal type, nor did many other leaders of the Social Gospel. It is true that theological convictions regarding the primacy of love made ministers prefer cooperation to competition, reason and moral exhortation to force, and so on. But this is not an ethos which encouraged (or even allowed) quiet withdrawal from the public sphere. On the contrary, there was a strong sense of vocation (and of honor in the performance of one's vocation) which drove Social Gospel preachers into the world to try to make it a better place. This was amplified by the so-called Puritan work ethic, which Niebuhr embodied fully. Moreover (perhaps because of his father), he had a sense of masculine vigor which drove him in the direction of being *effective*. And this meant, finally, a realistic acknowledgment of the need for power in the pursuit of noble Promethean objectives.

In sum, Niebuhr may have been a provincial Protestant "p.k." (preacher's kid), but he was anything but feminized in the sense of being meek, passive, withdrawn from the public realm, and fixated on sweetness and light. On the contrary (partly because of his ethnic subculture, which gave him a father and a whole social network which inculcated and revered hard work directed toward Promethean striving for lofty moral goals and goods), Niebuhr had much in common with the best-known leaders of the Social Gospel who were energetic movers and shakers intent upon nothing less than what Rauschenbusch touted as "Christianizing the social order."

To be sure, Niebuhr's biographers portray him as a person who had a keen sense of humor. In his youth, he was evidently something of a prankster, one who specialized in parodies of teachers and other authority figures. He was a frequent participant in community projects intended to amuse more than to edify (e.g., the faculty plays at Union Theological Seminary).[4] But the most striking thing about him was the fact that he poured out his energies in a dazzling assortment of worthy activities in the service of various causes. Accounts of his involvement in teaching, preaching, writing, and organizing inspire amazement—so much so that it is easy to believe he "never had a date" with a young woman before he was twenty. He was simply too busy.[5]

Americanism

Scholars have commented that Niebuhr's status as a German-American made him especially eager to show his patriotism in World War I, but the psychological significance of his European background may actually go far deeper than this. At a very early age Niebuhr believed that America represented "the best hope of the world,"[6] and this faith in the country to which his parents had emigrated remained a constant throughout his life. When he called upon German immigrants to give full support to their new country in World War I, when he summoned the nation to arms in defense of "the Western democracies" in the late 1930s, when he beat the drums for "American responsibility in the world arena" in the Cold War period—he was always expressing a consistent conviction that his nation was called to heroic service in the cause of humanity.

The concept of Americanism may also be invoked in the area of Niebuhr's intellectual preferences. The penchant for "practicality" so often associated with American national character owes a great deal to the Anglo-Saxon preference for empiricism and historical experience in law and political philosophy rather than abstract rationalism. In these respects Niebuhr was a quintessential exponent of Anglo-American ideals. Add to all this the very strong influence of Jamesian pragmatism on Niebuhr's thinking, and we have a formidable force in the shaping of his mind.

Masculinism

The pattern of Niebuhr's life indicates that he was raised in a very patriarchal subculture, and the importance of this part of his experience in shaping his thought must certainly be acknowledged. In particular, the charismatic energy which so impressed Niebuhr's contemporaries and placed him in so many different positions of leadership should be emphasized. Fox observes that Niebuhr's success as a leader may have been partly the function of a particular historical moment in American culture when strong patriarchal authority was both expected and respected. The concern for effectiveness—competence plus decisiveness—which manifests itself in Niebuhr's consequentialist pragmatism is energized by a special aversion to the previously mentioned feminization of American culture. One can infer from Niebuhr's writings a powerful indignation toward the notion that clergymen (as well as women) should be relegated to the private sphere as beings who do not have the strength and vitality to manage events in the real world of industry, politics, and war.

Niebuhr's rejection of this kind of thinking can be seen in the way he and his wife Ursula raised their children. For example, each member of the Niebuhr family was expected be aware of what was going on in the world, to have a reasoned opinion about events and issues, and to be ready to act on that opinion when appropriate. Elisabeth Niebuhr Sifton describes her father as a man who felt a special responsibility to change the thinking of good Christian folk who were led astray by the simple pieties of American Protestantism. In whatever setting, she says, he tried to respond vigorously and forcefully when there was an urgent need to help people, and "he did whatever he could to alleviate suffering or correct injustices." Moreover, if active involvement was impossible, "at least one could teach and talk about the conditions and policies that gave rise to the present evils, and one should, naturally, speak of the gospel as it pertained to the sufferings and joys of experience."[7] Sifton illustrates this point by citing her father's work on behalf of refugees and working people, and she claims that he considered racial issues the most serious moral problem of America after the early 1940s. "The message was clear," she recalls. "You had to be an active citizen; you had to live your commitments."[8]

I shall not place emphasis here on some presumed androcentrism (although there was certainly a measure of this), but rather on two familiar aspects of the so-called Protestant Ethic which Niebuhr must have absorbed, as it were, with his mother's milk: the concept of inner-worldly asceticism and the concept of vocation. One need not appeal to Freud to explain why an enormously bright, gifted, and gregarious young man (who had a delightful sense of humor and could very well have been the center of attention at every gathering) might choose to have virtually nothing to do with women or dances while he was at Yale. Nor does one need any conjectures about

Oedipal ties to explain the fact that Niebuhr eschewed the company of women and lived with his mother in Detroit. His mother was, after all, a tremendous help in running the parish, thus freeing Niebuhr to concentrate on speaking, writing, and a host of organizational and political projects within and beyond Detroit. Rather, one should recognize Niebuhr's extraordinary sense of potency and mission, reinforced as it was by the accolades and continually escalating demands of his admirers. It would not be surprising if Niebuhr came to believe that he could do almost anything he set his heart on doing—and that therefore he ought to do whatever he could to advance every worthy cause which entreated his support.

Prometheanism

In addition to the facts alluded to in the earlier discussion of Niebuhr's social location, additional evidence of his Prometheanism is easy to find in the early writings. Fox reports that the sermons in Bethel often alluded to the fact that "every great saint has his cross, [because] you can't be happy in an easy way." Again, "real happiness demanded suffering and struggle."[9] The cross often seems to stand for "the way of life that combined Stoic acceptance of the tragic with active striving for the ideal."[10]

Sometimes the root motive for energetic striving seems to be simply "preserving one's moral integrity" by refusing to accept such a flawed existence as ours without protest.[11] But that is clearly a fall back position. In his meditation on the death of Bishop Williams, Niebuhr says, "One ought to strive for the reformation of society rather than one's own perfection," and he asserts that Williams has not lived in vain:

> The bishop did not change Detroit industry, but if the church
> ever becomes a real agency of the kingdom of God in an indus-
> trial civilization, his voice, though he is dead, will be in its coun-
> sels.[12]

In an entry from 1927 in which Niebuhr reveals a polemical mistrust of the Roman Catholic Church (which later embarrassed him), he deplores "religious practices which reduce religion to magic." His animus was sparked less by a fastidious concern for honesty or dignity in belief than it was by his judgment that "magic is an enemy of all morality." Why? Because "it offers a short cut to all prizes of the spirit which can be won only by heroic effort."[13] This kind of rheto-

ric, of course, is a staple of hundreds of writers whose faith in progress was beginning to be shaken by the political turmoil of the late
nineteenth and early twentieth centuries. They were not about to
abandon their hopes for a Golden Age, but they were beginning to
acknowledge that striving to attain that dream might be a Sisyphean
undertaking.[14]

There is often, in fact, a tough-mindedness about Niebuhr's
Prometheanism that surprises those who associate religious belief
with an unwillingness to make hard choices. His opinions concerning the sinking of the *Titanic* (as related to June Bingham) may be
cited in this connection:

> Reinie kept commenting on the loss of the leaders in the realms
> of art and science that went down with the ship. I protested that
> all men are equally precious in the sight of God. But he insisted
> with his passion for realism that the loss of men and women
> who are making a great contribution to the welfare of their fel-
> lowmen is infinitely greater that the loss of the rank and file of
> the human family. . . . Reinie's keener insight recognized an aris-
> tocracy within the framework of democracy, namely an aristoc-
> racy of character and service to humanity.[15]

This utilitarian logic is also expressed in Niebuhr's comment on the
tactics which ought to be used in conducting a boycott designed to
exert pressure on a particular institutional target. When the Quakers
who shared Niebuhr's position as founding members of an Emer-
gency Committee for Strikers Relief persuaded the committee "not
to offer relief, if the relief were merely for the strikers," Niebuhr
pointed out that this would be a self-defeating gesture. As Bingham
comments,

> Since the nonstrikers were being more of a help to the employer
> than to their striking coworkers, an all inclusive charitableness
> that ignored the factors of power in modern society could . . .
> have results the opposite of those intended. Nor could purity of
> motive insure validity of result.[16]

It should be noted, finally, that there is an elective affinity between Niebuhr's Americanism and his Prometheanism, just as there
is between his masculinism and his devotion to a vocation that requires inner-worldly asceticism. His astounding capacity for hard
work is a crucial ingredient in the kind of frontier spirit that led

Niebuhr to forego the company of women until he was well into his twenties.

A Model Worthy of Emulation?

The lives of thinkers almost always become subjects of interest to those who are impressed by their thought. This interest is sometimes motivated by admiration, sometimes by enmity. In the first instance, respect for ideas may turn into adulation of their author; in the latter, resistance to a line of thought may lead to a destructive attack upon the character or personality of its originator. Or there is a third possibility. One's reaction may be characterized by ambivalence: one loves the product but despises the producer, or one admires the life but dislikes its intellectual or artistic output.

These debates often produce strange outcomes. Some people are so outraged by the use to which Wagner's music was put by the Nazis that they heap scorn upon the composer and refuse to listen to his music (and even try to keep it from being performed and heard by anyone). Others agree that Wagner was a rather unattractive human being, but forgive and dismiss the importance of that because they are so utterly enchanted by his divine art. Some who perceive Albert Schweitzer as a modern saint are unappreciative of his work as musician, New Testament scholar, and philosopher of culture. Others deplore the colonialist paternalism of the Doctor of Lambarene but praise the excellence of his contributions to the world of high culture.

Some scholars feel that one's estimate of a writer's thought should be kept separate from one's attitude toward his or her life. Yet even those who admire the brilliance of Tillich or the moral and political achievements of Martin Luther King and John F. Kennedy may be embarrassed by certain disclosures concerning their off-stage activities. Some may even find their assessment of those contributions they applaud being affected in a negative way.

There is nothing in Reinhold Niebuhr's personal life to invite serious moral disapproval. But his stature as a theologian and a practitioner of social ethics is lessened in the minds of some observers because of what they regard as deficiencies in the man or his point of view on some issue that is especially dear to their hearts. There are some who are so upset by what Niebuhr said on Cold War issues or by what he failed to say on issues of racial and gender justice that they resent the admiration others have for other aspects of Niebuhr's thought or for Niebuhr as a remarkable human being.

The position taken in this book is that both Niebuhr's life and his thought are worthy of study. Criticisms of his thought will be responded to later, but first I would like to confront the questions which pertain to Niebuhr's strengths and shortcomings as a man. In doing so, I am not being the least bit coy about stating my conviction that Niebuhr was a thoroughly admirable human being whose heroic features make his thought all the more intriguing. I would also like to respond to some of the issues raised by critics, particularly some of those raised by Niebuhr's best-known biographer.[17] Despite my great appreciation for Fox's *Reinhold Niebuhr: A Biography,* I also have considerable sympathy with Ronald Stone's objection to certain aspects of Fox's attempt "to probe the inner life of Reinhold Niebuhr." Stone observes:

> It is simply not possible to find that powerful, original, acute mind in the trail of short letters and remembrances of those of Niebuhr's acquaintances whom Fox could interview. Fox did not know Niebuhr, and the ambitious, scheming, frightened figure he shows us, shaped by Freudian family conflicts, is inaccurate and largely irrelevant.[18]

CUDDIHY'S AD HOMINEM POLEMIC

One of the most savage assaults ever launched against Reinhold Niebuhr is found in John Murray Cuddihy's ingenious literary tour de force, *No Offense.* Cuddihy, who scorns Niebuhr for having betrayed Christianity by proclaiming that the Church should not be concerned with proselytizing Jews, finds a derogatory way to interpret all of the facts of Niebuhr's life summarized in the foregoing pages:

> Reinhold Niebuhr was a young man from the provinces who headed for New York, stopping off in Detroit on the way. He wrote an article [in a 1916 issue of *The Atlantic Monthly*] which he followed to New York. He made a hit and became a success. Why? Well, because he fit in. The American clergy have always been afraid of irrelevance and marginalization; they've been afraid of being pushed out. They've always had to remake—in America

anyway—their role. Niebuhr had to do that. He was a preacher. Right! He was very eloquent with words and gestures. He was a spellbinder, almost a kind of Elmer Gantry. . . . In a way he was part of a new knowledge class.[19]

And:

The fact is that [after he came to New York] "Reinie" Niebuhr was becoming "civilized." His acquaintance was widening; his commitment to tolerance and the civilities of interpersonal relations was deepening; . . . the democratic need to look inoffensive was becoming more demanding; the tyranny of democratic manners was taking firmer hold; his celebrated hard-line Christianity was becoming adjectival to his ethics and his politics, a marginal differentiation making the Niebuhrian brand of liberalism different and "interesting"; he was in great demand; and, last but not least, he was quietly moving up the social ladder.[20]

The implication, according to Richard John Neuhaus, is clear: "Jack Cuddihy contends that the virtue of courage was remarkably absent in Reinhold Niebuhr, that basically he can be explained in terms of ambition and 'making it.'" He can, says Neuhaus, be interpreted as lacking in honesty and integrity as well as courage, for he can be seen "as a man intent upon making it, someone who very carefully never offended the constituencies that mattered and that defined his status and influence. When it came to the crunch, he pulled his punches."[21]

A milder form of the same sort of criticism can be found in the words of a Union Theological Seminary faculty member who once remarked that Niebuhr had been somewhat irresponsible in the fulfillment of his duties at the seminary. The complaint of this professor was that Niebuhr simply used Union as a home base from which to launch his speaking tours, his editorials, and his books, thus enjoying the adulation of a high-class celebrity while others had to bear the brunt of committee work, teaching, and thesis supervision.

Because I see Niebuhr as a noble Promethean who spent himself utterly in a praiseworthy vocation, I am not greatly troubled by ad hominem criticisms of the kind put forth by Cuddihy, Neuhaus, or others. One can besmirch the achievements of any human being by submitting him or her to psychological reductionism—i.e., contending that what he did and said was nothing but the manifestation of inner psychic need or disposition—and thus put an uncomplimentary interpretation on whatever they have done. There may even be some element of truth in charges of this kind, and great people thus assailed might even admit that such charges contain a grain of truth.

But if the overwhelming weight of the evidence favors a more charitable interpretation, and if the achievements are mighty and the failings of little moment, what is the purpose of ad hominem assaults? I believe that the rest of this book offers a more than adequate refutation to Cuddihy's outrageous polemic (and to the lesser charge of Niebuhr's faculty colleague).

NIEBUHR AS COLLEAGUE, FRIEND, AND FAMILY MAN

The most valid element of Fox's portrayal of Niebuhr is his analysis of the cultural secrets of Niebuhr's success as a charismatic leader. Reinhold Niebuhr's rise to prominence can be explained to some extent by his social location in a culture which expected and honored patriarchal dominance. Fox even speculates on the extent to which Niebuhr's magnetism was a function not only of his restless energies but also of the respect for energetic initiative which has been typical of Western civilization since the Renaissance. Allowing that there was "something overwhelming about his presence," Fox ventures the opinion that Niebuhr probably wouldn't be able to "take immediate possession of a room" nowadays because today we are no longer so "receptive to whose who embody masculine authority."[22] This line of thought leads to further speculations about the feelings which might have motivated Niebuhr's polemics against pacifists and his "rhetorical strategies as a columnist for the *Christian Century*" during the 1920s and 1930s. Fox writes:

> When Niebuhr was a young man, what annoyed him most of all
> about liberal Protestantism was its effeminate, namby-pamby
> faith in goodness and love. He felt it wasn't tough enough to
> contend with evil forces in the "real" world. [In writing for the
> *Christian Century*] he tried to masculinize Protestant rhetoric—to
> overwhelm the Victorian niceties of [*Christian Century* editor]
> Charles Clayton Morrison with hard-hitting, pointed, hammering prose.[23]

These comments are linked to two additional attempts to understand what made Reinhold Niebuhr tick—i.e., an analysis of his personal friendships and an analysis of his decision to spend so much time on the road as a speaker and college chapel preacher. On the latter point, Fox suggests that Niebuhr's allocation of time and energy to organizational pursuits and speaking engagements was a way of avoiding the (more introspective, more difficult?) tasks of intellectual endeavor. In doing so, Fox might have appealed to Niebuhr's own admission that when, in the mid-1960s, he thought back on the course of his life, he could not help being struck by the fact that "the record reveals a certain lack of a sense of proportion, and an inclination to flee from the hard tasks of serious thought to the easier responsibilities of organization."[24] On the former point, Fox contends that

> a study of [Niebuhr's] personal friendships with men such as
> Morrison, John Haynes Holmes, and Waldo Frank would show
> how difficult it was for him to maintain close personal relation-
> ships with his peers: they took too much time, they were pas-
> sive, they were decorous, they were implicitly feminizing.[25]

There are three issues here which may be worthy of consideration. In my view, people of genius are entitled to violate some of the niceties of etiquette, for they are correct in thinking that above all they must guard their privacy and marshal their energies for optimal utilization of the gifts with which they have been entrusted. They certainly have every right to set priorities which may occasionally make them unavailable (and thus appear rude) to friends and associates who try to lay claim to their time. It strikes me as stupid and unworthy for outside observers to fault them for this. For example, some of the people involved in the 1988 Rockford Institute conference "Reinhold Niebuhr Today," which provides much of the material for this chapter, are viewed as arrogant or obnoxious by many who know them and have worked with them. But surely these are nothing more than trivial shortcomings which should not be allowed to influence one's willingness to judge what they say on its own merits. Is it not reasonable, then, to expect these scholars to adopt the same charitable disposition toward Niebuhr?

In view of the fact that some people allow Niebuhr's personal style to diminish their estimate of the substance of his life and thought, something must be said in his defense. The issues at stake are these: Niebuhr's putative rudeness in meetings where he was not front-and-center, his mistreatment of friends, and his lack of humility.

Rudeness

The written account of the aforementioned conference "Reinhold Niebuhr Today" made a good deal of the fact that Niebuhr was not always completely attentive or scrupulously polite in the role of listener in meetings when someone else had the floor. Niebuhr's biographer tells the following story:

> [Roland] Bainton was sitting next to Richard Niebuhr during one of the meetings of [an East Coast group called the Younger Theologians]. Reinhold was of course sitting at the table like everybody else, but he was very agitated. He kept climbing out of his seat; he found it very hard to sit and take in what other people were saying. He wanted to be speaking even when he was listening. So Reinhold was almost mounting the table in excitement, trying to respond to something someone was saying. At this point, so the story goes, Richard Niebuhr leaned over to Bainton and said, "I don't think Jesus ever got quite that agitated."[26]

It is not easy to fathom the meaning of this little anecdote. Most of the conferees who commented on the anecdote seemed to be of the opinion that it said more about Bainton's gentle Quaker spirit and H. Richard Niebuhr's sense of humor than it did about Reinhold Niebuhr himself. Paul Ramsey reported that Niebuhr was for the most part a consistently courteous and constructive participant in discussions and committee meetings. (According to Ramsey, if Niebuhr found himself bored, he would simply slip out a sheet of paper and begin to work on the outline for the following Sunday's sermon.)

Roger Shinn also "resisted Fox's portrait of a domineering Niebuhr" by relating the story of a two-year Columbia University seminar in which "Niebuhr was simply one of the group," and at which he at different times "listened, chimed in, and commented in the way that others did." To be sure, says Shinn, "On the night [Niebuhr] presented his paper, he took off in his characteristic way. But when another person had the spotlight (as Shinn did when, as a graduate student, he read a paper before the Frontier Fellowship), Niebuhr merely "questioned [him] and offered some comments," never raising the "slightest doubt that [Shinn], a student, was the center of the group."[27]

My personal memories of Niebuhr are not compatible with the

notion that he was rude or inconsiderate. On the contrary, I remember him as a busy, dignified, but amiable old prof whose words of greeting in the hallways or the quad were among the most enjoyable moments of a typical week at Union Theological Seminary. If he knew you by face (whether he knew your name or not) his craggy features would light up, his good arm and hand would rise in an amiable salute, and a cordial Midwestern "Hi ya!" would signal his acknowledgment of your presence. If you found yourself on the elevator with him, you could count on his passing the time of day the same way small-town residents the world over do with their fellow villagers. And if you had had the cheek to invite the eminent professor to dinner in your tiny student apartment, chances are that he would come—and you could hardly ask for a more gracious dinner guest.

Modesty

My answer to the charge concerning Niebuhr's alleged rudeness has already begun to touch on another complaint that is often made against famous people—namely, that they think too highly of themselves and are not only proud but arrogant.

There are two main responses to this indictment. First, most people didn't have that impression of Niebuhr unless they had a special reason or predisposition to dislike him or his ideas. When I was a student at Union, for example, I attended a picnic at a country church in West Virginia, and there I ran into a Protestant pastor who almost foamed at the mouth as he described Niebuhr's vigor (my word, not his) as a public speaker. This pastor told me: "He [Niebuhr] would pace back and forth on the podium, waving his arms and screaming, denouncing what most of his audience believed in. He was a fascist, that's what he was, always trying to ram his ideas down other people's throats." It isn't hard to believe that Niebuhr actually frightened some people by coming on so strong, and it's clear that he alienated some of his listeners by what they perceived as an excess of oratory zeal. But very few people saw him in that light or thought of him as a dictatorial person.

Second, Niebuhr would certainly be going against his own fully considered beliefs if did think too highly of himself or his own opinions. Everything he said about the sin of pride he applied to himself, and the context of many of his admonitions on this point makes it clear that he feared 'ideological taint' in himself and his allies as well as in his adversaries. Fox emphasizes that the "living of Christian Realism" required Niebuhr to be diffident about the correctness of his views, to be willing to admit error when convinced of it, and to have "courage to change."[28] Bingham sees this, for she says that, although "Niebuhr is anything but a relativist," he also believes "we must never confuse our fragmentary apprehension of the truth with the truth itself."

> Our fragmentary apprehension must always stand under criticism, remain open to new facts, and be subject to debate. If it is not thus maintained in tension with opposing points of view and with doubt, it may slacken into untruth or harden into fanaticism.[29]

There are a number of items of circumstantial evidence which may be adduced to support the proposition that Niebuhr was by no means an arrogant man. Fox gives an instructive account of Niebuhr's belated but heartfelt apology to Emil Brunner when it was called to his attention that he had failed to credit Brunner as the source for some of the most important ideas in *The Nature and Destiny of Man*. And June Bingham stresses the fact that Niebuhr was beset with "overwhelming contrition" when he was persuaded that he had treated an opponent unjustly.

> A colleague who has engaged in controversy with Niebuhr over the years says, "It's not easy for Reinie to say he's sorry, but when he says it, he really means it." [Another] old friend emerged from Niebuhr's office clutching his brow. "My God," he said. "By the time Reinie gets through suffering over what he's done to you, you're suffering more for him than you ever did from him. Son of a gun—how can you help forgiving him?"[30]

Two other indisputable facts are relevant in this connection. Niebuhr lived with children who were not at all bashful about questioning his political judgment or his literary tastes, and with a wife who frequently "interrupt[ed] a headlong hurtling of his thought with a smiling, 'Oh darling, what utter nonsense!'"[31] And Niebuhr loved to warn his students about getting carried away with the righteousness of a cause by quoting Cromwell's famous expostulation to a foolhardy Parliament bent upon passing some ridiculous law: "I beseech you, brethren, by the bowels of Christ, bethink you that you may be mistaken!"[32]

On more than one occasion Niebuhr declared that he wasn't really a scholar who deserved to be put in the same league with those who were lauding him or subjecting his ideas to respectful scrutiny. Indeed, he went so far as to say (in his 1956 "Intellectual Biography") that he "was always something of an impostor" at Union Theological Seminary. In a sense, Niebuhr's self-appraisal on this point is true: he was not a specialist in any particular field of scholarly Grundlichkeit, and if that were the only kind of professorial excellence needed by institutions of higher education (and by the culture-bearers of a nation), he might not have belonged at Union. But he was possessed of two other intellectual-spiritual assets which are even more rare than the skills of an academic specialist: he was a brilliant generalist (with a solid sense of confidence in the significance of that particular calling), and he was the son of a German pastor who knew how important it is to read primary sources. On the first point, he understood the danger of a university setting where "each scholar must be content to master a relatively smaller and smaller area of [knowledge]," with the result that "if we are not careful, we will all develop into a society of undereducated experts who know a great deal about a small area of life and very little about life itself."[33] On the second point, Niebuhr said (speaking of his experience at Yale) that he "desired relevance rather than scholarship," yet he declares that "the constant demand for original research in the sources themselves" and the requirement to "wade through an endless number of books" gave him a "first-hand knowledge of prominent writers [which was] more educative than any of the classroom work."[34]

Some readers will probably be tempted to dismiss Niebuhr's self-deprecating remarks (about being "a mongrel among thoroughbreds" at Yale and an "impostor" at Union) as a meaningless concession to our culture's widespread disapproval of arrogance. They are entitled to that opinion, of course, and there is no compelling way to refute it. But I cannot help feeling that there was a deep and genuine modesty in the man, a modesty I witnessed one day in a conversation I had with Niebuhr in front of Hastings Hall, a student dormitory at Union. Niebuhr was out walking his dogs (a familiar sight around the seminary in those days). When I greeted him, he started asking me about my just-completed year of study abroad, a year in which I had immersed myself in the ethical mysticism of Albert Schweitzer. In the course of answering Niebuhr's questions, I remarked, "You know, Doctor Niebuhr, the two most important influences on my formation as a student and would-be teacher are you and Schweitzer." Niebuhr's reaction was startling. He straightened up rather abruptly and almost staggered backward a step. Then he said, with the utmost gravity, "Oh, Mr. Clark, you mustn't say that." I don't remember exactly what he added to that first expostulation, but the gist of it was that he did not feel he belonged in a class with Schweitzer. In the years since that conversation took place, I have thought more than once that Niebuhr's reaction didn't really make sense. He is obviously a greater moral theorist than Schweitzer and is indubitably acknowledged as such by the academy. Niebuhr must have known that this is what most knowledgeable observers would say. Why then would he have been embarrassed by the comparison? I still don't know. Nor do I know exactly what Niebuhr might have been thinking. But the impression I got was absolutely clear, and I could swear that I read him correctly in that instant: Reinhold Niebuhr felt genuinely humble when I compared him with a Nobel Peace Laureate.

Perhaps some credit should be given to Ursula Niebuhr for preventing her husband from entertaining too lofty an estimate of his own achievements. The spirit of her affectionate "Oh darling, what utter nonsense" is conveyed in a story about a meeting of the trustees at Union. Niebuhr had become noticeably agitated over a speech being given by Henry Luce, chairman of the board. This was during the Eisenhower era, and Luce was going on and on about what a wonderful country America was and how grateful all Americans should be because of the blessings showered upon them by Providence. Niebuhr eventually leaned over to his wife and whispered indignantly, "And to think he's been listening to George Buttrick preach for twenty years." Ursula replied, in a voice which could be heard several seats in either direction, "Yes, dear, and he's read every one of your books, too."

Needless to say, Niebuhr's modesty also had relevance for his thinking on ethics and policy. A typical pronouncement on this point is recorded in his remarks at a 1960s symposium in New York:

> I know of no general principle, Christian or otherwise, which
> will solve the Cold War and the nuclear dilemma. . . . A Chris-
> tian engaged in political philosophy can do no more than seek to

prevent premature solutions of essentially insoluble problems, hoping that time will make some solutions possible tomorrow that are not possible today.[35]

This counsel against presumption is nicely summarized in a *New Yorker* cartoon which Niebuhr loved to quote during the Eisenhower years. It shows Ike entreating a frenetic John Foster Dulles, "For God's sake, John, don't just do something—stand there!"

Friendship

Harvey Cox must have been deeply affected by Fox's account of Niebuhr's awkwardness with friends for he wrote an article in which he lamented what he seemed to accept as fact—that Niebuhr ruthlessly rationed the amount of time he devoted to his friends. Cox was saddened by the inference that Niebuhr was incapable of the truest and deepest kind of friendship. This interpretation of Niebuhr's unwillingness to extend himself seems to be consistent with Fox's report that Niebuhr considered one of his most eminent colleagues a fool, and did not suffer him gladly.[36]

There is certainly another way to evaluate Niebuhr's use of his time. I am in fundamental agreement with Fox in believing that Niebuhr's behavior is to his credit, not his detriment. Fox says that Niebuhr ought to be praised for his willingness to make tough decisions about the allocation of his energies, and he ought to be credited with caring more about the advancement of important causes than about mollifying the emotions of associates. Niebuhr, however, was willing to put up a good front with people he didn't like—if doing so would serve a cause. Or, put another way, Niebuhr was dutiful in carrying out his appropriate role-responsibility whether or not he enjoyed it, even if it meant reshuffling his immediate priorities. Roger Shinn reminds us that what Fox says about Niebuhr's relationship with one or two individuals should not be taken as typical. According to Shinn, before Niebuhr's stroke in 1952, he was more generous about sharing his time with Union students than any of his professorial colleagues, and a large number of students in those years would have spoken of Niebuhr as the best friend they had on the faculty.

Tough-mindedness in budgeting one's resources is a skill every serious social reformer has to develop, and it seems ridiculous for Niebuhr's detractors to cite this as a character defect. How could he possibly have accomplished all he did without having been able to make decisions concerning social change strategy and tactics with a cool eye and a firm hand? Surely C. S. Lewis was right when he said that friends do not have to be face-to-face in intimate encounter but may also stand side-by-side, absorbed in individual tasks yet aware of each other's presence and the bond of shared purpose. By this high standard, Niebuhr's capacity for meaningful friendship was great. Ronald Stone objects to some of Fox's amateur psychologizing. "For those of us who counted Niebuhr among our closest friends," Stone says, "the picture of Niebuhr as unable to sustain a friendship is laughable."[37]

What has been said here about Niebuhr's way of relating to people in general applies also to his relationships with his immediate family. We know, for example, that Niebuhr made a home for his mother and took care of her for most of her life. And regarding Niebuhr's treatment of his wife and children, several things can be said. Shinn reports that Niebuhr was more willing to support his wife in her professional life than most husbands of that era were, and he always helped out in the kitchen when he was at home. It is true that Ursula put her career on hold in order to devote herself to taking care of her husband after his stroke, but she did so because she felt certain that he would have done the same for her. Niebuhr did not accept his wife's sacrifice unthinkingly or unappreciatively, and he often commented in classroom digressions on the injustice of the typical cultural assumption that a woman's career ought to be subordinated to the needs of her family.

I have one final anecdote to add to this discussion of Niebuhr's style of relating to other people. When Pitirim Sorokin came out with *The Crisis of Our Time,* Niebuhr wrote a scathing review. Just before the review appeared, Niebuhr's good friend William Scarlett (who had read the book and admired it greatly) had sent a copy to the Niebuhrs as a Christmas present. But as soon as Scarlett got word of the review, he dashed off a telegram imploring the Niebuhrs to return the gift unopened and instead "please buy cigarettes and yellow roses [because] they're noncontroversial." Instead, the Niebuhrs kept the unopened package on their living room table as "a symbol that friendship transcends differences of opinion." Niebuhr's January thank-you note is worth quoting at some length:

> I am sorry that about the only time that I have allowed myself to be really nasty in a review should have run across, by this curious coincidence, your great kindness to us and your thoughtfulness at Christmas-time. This will teach me a lesson never again to be uncharitable in a review and to remember "by the bowels of Christ," as Cromwell said, that I may be wrong.
>
> Anyway, we haven't disagreed for so long that it is probably a good thing to have had this disagreement.[38]

How Things Look from the Sidelines

Shortly before his death, Niebuhr wrote a piece for the *Christian Century* entitled "A View of Life from the Sidelines." It offers an instructive glimpse into the mind of a man who led an extremely active life, but now must adjust to being an observer—an observer for whom the end of the road was already in sight.

The essay contained a statement regarding Niebuhr's increasing appreciation for the Roman Catholic Church, especially its liturgy, but most of what he had to say concerned his illness and his awareness that he did not have much longer to live. His gratitude to Ursula was eloquently expressed, and it was in this connection that he referred to his wife's belief that he would have cared for her in just the same way had their positions been "reversed. "But," says Niebuhr, I doubted it, because I was inclined to affirm the superior agape of woman." He also admitted (in characteristic Niebuhrian style) that his tireless commitment to his vocation as thinker, preacher, and do-gooder may not have been without its subtle ambiguities:

> The mixture of motives in all people, incidentally, refutes the doctrines both of total depravity and of saintliness. In my case, retrospection from the sidelines prompted me to remember many instances in my earlier years when my wife had protested my making an extra trip or going to yet another conference, despite my weariness; I always pleaded the importance of the cause that engaged me, and it never occurred to me that I might have been so assiduous in these engagements because the invitations flattered my vanity.[39]

He also revealed that the mythological symbolism of Christian doctrine had come to have a very important personal meaning for him,
for he offered a rather touching meditation on the significance of
Christianity's affirmation of belief in "the resurrection of the body."
Noting that "this symbolic expression of faith is currently almost
neglected," he pondered its power as a commentary on "the final
mystery of selfhood," which is "only a degree beneath the mystery
of God." He derived consolation from the fact that "in a[n] Hebraic-
biblical faith, neither history nor human selfhood is regarded as an
illness of the flux of the temporal world from which we must escape," and he identified himself with the conviction that "the individual, though mortal, is given, by self-transcendent freedom, the
key to immortality." Niebuhr concluded the piece with these words:

> Individual selfhood is not a disaster or an evil. It is subsumed in
> the counsels of God and enters the mystery of immortality by
> personal relation to the divine. I could not, in all honesty, claim
> more for myself and my dear ones, as I face the ultimacy of
> death in the dimension of history, which is grounded in nature.[40]

Chapter 2

From Social Gospel Idealism
to Christian Realism

Christian Realism is a special brand of the Social Christianity which
arose in the nineteenth century. It was expounded in the books which
Niebuhr published in the 1930s and 1940s, and its "realism" is usually seen as a correction of the excessive idealism of the Social Gospel, which flourished from about 1860 to 1940.

Key Features of the Social Gospel

The latter half of the nineteenth century was characterized by
the birth of a tremendously important new phenomenon in the history of religion in America: the emergence of Social Christianity.
This phenomenon manifested itself in three principal ways: (1) the
Gospel of Wealth, (2) Christian Socialism, and (3) the Social Gospel.

The so-called Gospel of Wealth was an extremely conservative
brand of religious thought which was inspired in considerable measure by Social Darwinism. This self-serving theodicy of good fortune
comforted the rich and powerful by assuring them that their privileges were bestowed by God, and it encouraged prosperous church
people to imagine that their relative affluence was a sign of their
goodness in the eyes of the Lord. As a dominant school of thought
the Gospel of Wealth was nothing more than a mercifully brief aber-
ration, yet its sinister presence always lurks just below the surface,

ready to assert its spurious claims whenever the prosperous indulge themselves in pretensions of superior virtue or when right-wing church people are eager to justify their callousness by claiming that poverty-stricken people are entirely to blame for their own wretchedness.

The Gospel of Wealth advocates a "new medicine for poverty" devised by English Puritanism. R. H. Tawney, in his *Religion and the Rise of Capitalism,* states that as early as 1649 England had a law requiring that vagrants be arrested and offered a choice between work and whipping. All other poor persons, including children without any means of maintenance, should be set to compulsory labor. Not long thereafter, says Tawney, it came to be universally acknowledged

> that the greatest of evils is idleness, that the poor are victims, not
> of circumstances, but of their own "idle, irregular and wicked
> courses," that the truest charity is not to enervate them by relief,
> but so to reform their characters that relief may be unnecessary.[1]

Small wonder, then, that during the labor strife of 1877 a respectable church publication urged the powers-that-be to use draconian measures to suppress a strike mounted in the name of the workers' right to form unions.

> Bring on then the troops—the armed police—in overwhelming
> multitudes. Bring out the Gatling guns. Let there be no fooling
> with blank cartridges. But let the mob know, everywhere, that
> for it to stand one moment after it has been ordered by proper
> authorities to disperse, will be to be shot down in its tracks. . . .
> A little of the vigor of the first Napoleon is the thing we need
> now.[2]

The antithesis of the Gospel of Wealth was the radical socialist wing of Social Christianity, which was never widely accepted in America. This rather pale reflection of the Christian Socialist movement in England had as its chief spokespersons men such as George D. Herron, W. D. P. Bliss, James O. S. Huntington (founder of the Church Association for the Advancement of the Interests of Labor), and Herbert Casson, who began the famous Labor Church of Lynn, Massachusetts. Drawing on the ideas of Bellamy and Henry George, this group of idealists elaborated a vaguely socialist program which attracted considerable attention but only a small following. Its most important manifestation was the Methodist Federation for Social Service (MFSS), which was established in 1907. Under the leadership of Harry Ward, the MFSS moved from "a prewar emphasis upon reform, social service, and the socialization of evangelism, to emphasis upon outright opposition to capitalism."[3] (Ward was on the faculty of Union Theological Seminary when Niebuhr went there in 1928, and he remained a colleague—and an antagonist—of Niebuhr's until 1944.)

The most well-known and rightfully acclaimed version of Social Christianity is what has come to be known as the Social Gospel. Henry F. May observes that all forms of Social Christianity "arose partly in response to collectivist currents in sociology, economics and nonacademic radical thought," but they are primarily a response to "a series of shocking crises" in American life during the last quarter of the century:

> From 1877 through the middle nineties, it became more and more difficult to believe that strikes, depressions, unemployment and bankruptcies were part of a divinely regulated and unchangeable social order.[4]

Social Darwinism and the Gospel of Wealth tried to propagate this lie, but the brevity of their vogue is testimony to the implausibility of their claims. The Social Gospel and Christian Socialism are the movements that really deserve the appellation Social Christianity, for they made a genuine effort to face the crises of industrial society in a constructive way by acknowledging its problems and recommending attitudes and actions that would help to ameliorate them.

Yet the fundamental values of Social Gospel leaders were those of small-town and rural America. Many of the best-known preachers spent some time in proletarian neighborhoods or grew up in mill towns where they came to know the workers (as Washington Gladden did) as "men with legitimate grievances against the system." But the Social Gospel preachers' notion of what was normative was usually a function of their "placid rural background," and they placed an inordinately high value on stability. "The books of Gladden breathed the cool, benign pieties of the comfortable parishes of Springfield and Columbus; he preached for protection of the parish as well as for redemption of the proles."[5]

Among the most important leaders of the Social Gospel were Gladden, Francis Peabody, Shailer Mathews, Sherwood Eddy (later to be Niebuhr's patron), Kirby Page and George Albert Coe. By far the most significant single exponent of the Social Gospel, of course, was Walter Rauschenbusch, whose *A Theology for the Social Order* and *Christianizing the Social Order* are usually regarded as the finest statements of the movement's raison d'etre.

The Social Gospel's moment of glory came just after the end of World War I:

> When Niebuhr was beginning to make his mark as a spokesman for the Social Gospel, the Protestant clergy appeared to be on the threshold of their greatest period of power. The War was doing worlds of good for the morale of the clergy. The War years were years of happy cooperation between the American community as a whole and organized Protestantism; for no segment of the community had better served the cause of rallying the community behind the war effort. . . . The whole experience had been a heady one—and had left Protestant leadership convinced that it now enjoyed the deference of the American community as a whole. Now it could undertake to stamp its ideals on the American civilization.[6]

But the moment quickly passed, for a crucial confrontation with steel magnate Judge Gary resulted in the kind of minimal achievements which amount to failure, and the utopian hopes of the Interchurch World Movement speedily came to naught. When Woodrow Wilson's idealism was thwarted, Prohibition failed, and the Great Depression struck, the social reform enthusiasm of the churches dissipated rather quickly and completely.

> The general disillusionment of the postwar decade greatly affected the Protestant churches. Very soon after the collapse of the Interchurch World Movement, in which millions of dollars to undergird a forward thrust of the churches were to have been raised, the crusading mood was over. [Church historian Winthrop S. Hudson has said that] nothing is more striking than the astonishing reversal in the position occupied by the churches and the role played by religion in American life which took place before the new century was well under way. By the 1920s, the contagious enthusiasm which had been poured into the Student Volunteer Movement, the Sunday School Movement, the Men and Religion Forward Movement, the Laymen's Missionary

Movement, the Interchurch World Movement, and other organized activities of the churches had largely evaporated.[7]

The Social Gospel did not vanish overnight, but it "lost much of
what lay support it had had." In the early 1930s, the editor of the
Christian Century said: "The Social Gospel up to date has been a
preacher's gospel. The laity have little share in it. They do not know
how central and dominant it is in the thinking of their minister." And
by the 1940s "the Social Gospel as a distinct, self-conscious movement with a clear sense of direction had largely disappeared."[8]

SALIENT BELIEFS

As church historian Robert T. Handy says, the Social Gospel is
noteworthy for three salient beliefs: the immanence of God (manifested in Christ and Christ's living Spirit), the worth of man (which
includes a limitless potential that can be tapped by education and
exhortation), and the Kingdom of God (which can be brought about
by "winning the world to Christ in this generation"). It is clear, of
course, that the primacy of love shines out in all three of these, as
does an enormous optimism about the role of the Church and its
leaders (the preachers of Christ and Christ's love).

Niebuhr came to believe that the goals of the Social Gospel were
hopelessly utopian and naive. Whether he was correct in that judgment or not, it can certainly be asserted that its goals were extraordi-
narily idealistic:

> The mainline Social Gospel scenario for social reconstruction ran
> along these lines: "[The] economic millennium must be reached,
> first of all, through the consecrated initiative of component indi-
> viduals. . . . The pillars of modern industrial life are securely set
> in the moral stability of the vast majority of business lives. Mil-
> lions of such persons, as they scrupulously discharge their busi-
> ness obligations, are meeting the demand of Jesus, 'Whosoever
> would be first among you shall be your servant' [Matt.
> 20:27]. . . . The Christian problem of the industrial world is
> to multiply lives like these. . . . If the principles of the teach-
> ing of Jesus should come to control the existing economic sys-
> tem, a revolution in the industrial order would seem to be un-
> necessary."

Thus, the judgment against capitalism could work itself out; a
more Christian social order could come to replace it—if only

sufficient well-placed capitalists would apply the ethics of Jesus
to their daily lives.[9]

This definition of goals has its logical corollary in an understanding of means which highlights the all-important (and all-
sufficient) strategy of converting people of wealth and power to the
gospel of Jesus and to the expression of Jesus' benevolent love in all
human affairs.

> For them [believers in the Social Gospel], both optimism and co-
> herence depended upon regarding power as opportunity for stra-
> tegic conversions and not merely as obstacle. To evangelize and
> convert power rather than to bring countervailing power against
> it seemed the essence of strategy. Once converted, power would
> offer itself freely to control and equalization. Evangelism would
> in fact draw out something like the "altruistic self-effacement" of
> a class.[10]

Kirby Page, for example, always maintained a sort of stubborn deontological idealism which opposed pragmatic compromises. In his
defense of pacifism he argued that "aggressive good will could have
freed the soil [of Belgium] of German invaders." How?

> By convincing the German people that they had no reason to
> fear invasion of their own land, and thereby depriving the mil-
> itarists of their support and driving them out of control of the
> government.[11]

Francis Peabody was also an apostle for the tactic of evangelical
conversion:

> Jesus' method was the conversion of the individual heart in di-
> rect, personal evangelism. Such direct conversion must remain
> the method [of the Social Gospel]; what had to be changed was
> simply its content—from the old gospel of individualistic piety
> and salvation to the Social Gospel. Once men were converted to
> the correct gospel, right social relations would emerge.[12]

A logical corollary of this line of thought was the conviction
that Christian churches had a tremendously important role to play in
bringing about societal salvation. For George Albert Coe, a disciple
of Dewey, religious education was the key. This was the burden of
his teaching as a professor at Union Theological Seminary and later

at Teachers College. Coe believed that the church was in a unique position to teach people that there was a smooth congruity between altruism and enlightened self-interest: in the great struggle between selfishness and unselfishness in the human soul, the latter was destined to win because it "promised permanent, total equilibrium." And because "group selfishness was the projection of individual selfishness," the enlightenment of individuals would result in the salvation of society. According to Coe, "the true variable of social morality was the reason and wisdom of scientific social science," and "the triumph of morality awaited its sway."[13]

WALTER RAUSCHENBUSCH

The portrait of the Social Gospel and its leaders which has been offered here is accurate—but it is curiously incomplete because of its omission of the distinctive arguments of Walter Rauschenbusch, who was not only the most prominent Social Gospel leader but also the wisest. It should be emphasized that Rauschenbusch was never guilty of the naivete of other Social Gospelers in his concept of appropriate tactics, for he realized that businessmen would never become altruistic as a class. This realization prompted Rauschenbusch to become an advocate of unions and of the right of workers to organize for collective bargaining purposes.

Yet Rauschenbusch exhibited the idealistic optimism of the Social Gospel in much of what he said about the ends Christians ought to seek. Because he believed that the goodness of a morally mature adult was just as natural as the selfishness of an infant, he thought that religious nurture could achieve a decisive transformation in the attitudes and the lives of individuals.[14] He also believed that societal structures and processes were capable of being greatly improved, and that the transformation of society was necessary in order to provide an environment in which individuals could consistently overcome their sinfulness. Thus the gospel of personal salvation and the Social Gospel were equally necessary, for each was dependent upon the reinforcing stimulus of the other. In his beliefs, and in daring to proclaim his hopes about "Christianizing the Social Order," Rauschenbusch was a typical exponent of prevailing liberal notions of evolutionary progress in human affairs.[15]

In other ways, however, Rauschenbusch was the forerunner of Niebuhr's Christian Realism, for his awareness of the deep-rooted strength of sin, especially his appraisal of the powerful network of evil in the collective life of humankind, was not typical of a Social Gospeler.[16] He was particularly acute in his perception of the need for class consciousness and class struggle (and hence the need for political power), as well as in his awareness that the economic power elite would never be reformed through moral education and moral exhortation alone:

> It is hopeless to expect the business class to espouse [economic fraternalism] as a class. Individuals in the business class will do so, but the class will not. There is no historical precedent for an altruistic self-effacement of a whole class.[17]

The vain hopes of Social Gospel leaders remained alive for a long time, partly because of wealthy men such as John D. Rockefeller.[18] However, the accuracy of Rauschenbusch's analysis is borne out by the experience of pastors such as Niebuhr and G. Glenn Atkins (who preached for many years at a Woodward Avenue church in Detroit). At the end of his career, Atkins said:

> Realistic laymen were, and have remained, more largely untouched by the whole movement than is generally supposed. I was during this period the minister of two churches whose congregations included men of status and force in highly industrialized cities. I do not think they shared the official social passion of the communion to which they belonged, knew much or cared much about it. That they knew no more was probably the fault of their minister. But as far as they did know, their response lacked warmth. The more conservative were politely hostile.[19]

ORGANIZATIONS AND MILESTONES

The vitality of the Social Gospel was expressed in a host of organizations and publications which endeavored to mobilize church people. The Federal Council of Churches (FCC), established in 1908, was the forerunner of the present-day National Council of Churches. The Fellowship of Reconciliation (1917) and the Fellowship for Social Order (1921) were two important pacifist groups which enlisted the energies of Reinhold Niebuhr until his resignation in 1931. Two of the most important journals for which Niebuhr wrote articles and editorials were *The World Tomorrow* and *The Christian Century*. The former became explicitly Marxist in 1934 and became defunct the following year. The latter was the main journal of Protestant opinion during the 1920s and 1930s, and was in large measure responsible for the fact that a high percentage of well-educated ministers remained pacifists right up until Pearl Harbor.

The single most important goal of the Social Gospel was economic justice, and the movement continued to produce ringing pronouncements on economic issues well into the 1940s. A good example of this kind of social witness was a document issued by the FCC in 1919 entitled "The Church and Industrial Reconstruction." It was strikingly calm in tone because it assumed that all the theological issues had been settled. It did not seek to persuade, but merely to put on record the givens which had already been accepted by enlightened people. Thus it was highly critical of current economic conditions, but took the position that the spirit of the system could be changed by evangelization of individuals and that the structures and processes of industrial society could be left more or less as they were.[20] It condemned "property for power" but legitimated "property for use," and it was optimistic about the ability of workers to obtain both justice and freedom within the wage system. Competition, it concluded, was not inherently evil, and even though "struggle is sometimes required . . . [it] should be carried on without violence, within the limits set by law." Asserting that "love creates love," then turning to ask what love must do when it has not created love, the report anticipated years of confusion and debate. The fact is, the report begged all kinds of questions about details, especially means. "It was still carried by enthusiasm for the ends [sought by the Social Gospel]."[21]

As has been noted, 1919 was the high-water mark of Social Gospel zeal in the United States. That zeal was short-lived, however, partly because of the collapse of the Interchurch World Movement (IWM) in 1921. One of the events which precipitated the demise of the IWM was the equivocal outcome of its clash with U.S. Steel and Judge Gary in 1919. This struggle with one of the greatest industrial entrepreneurs of the day was a partial success, for it changed the workday from two twelve-hour shifts to three eight-hour shifts. But despite Rockefeller's "hero/patron" actions, Gary remained recalcitrant, and the structure and processes of the company and the industry were not touched—and neither was the Social Gospel logic of benevolent paternalism:

> Conspicuously, the issue of unionization and collective bargaining was excluded from the highlight put on the twelve-hour day.

The enormously suggestive data on the ethnic tensions and conflicts within the body of labor . . . were obscured and neglected
by the sensational revelations of [company] labor spies. That the
AFL was inadequate . . . was blurred by the failure of public
press and public authorities to provide a fair, at least neutral, at-
mosphere for the conflict. Finally, discussion of the role of the
state was forgotten altogether.

Industry was conceived to be susceptible to the same type of
democratic constitutionalism as politics—and as the churches
themselves. . . . [With the coming of industrial democracy], the
factory was to become church.[22]

Niebuhr as Social Gospel Idealist

For many years, until about 1928, Reinhold Niebuhr could accurately be termed a Social Gospel idealist. But he never fit the mold
exactly, because there were always a number of striking dissimilar-
ities to go along with the numerous long-lasting (or sporadically
evident) parallels.

SIMILARITIES

Niebuhr was acquainted with Ibsen and Shaw, so he realized
how easily respect for "the claim of the ideal"[23] could degenerate into
cant or be used for hypocritical purposes. Nevertheless, Niebuhr
believed that one of the elemental insights of religion was its grasp on
the powerful spiritual truth that the ideal can become real if those
who are committed to its claims are sufficiently dedicated, wise and
effective. Even as late as 1927, when his first book *Does Civilization
Need Religion?* was published, Niebuhr felt able and compelled to
declare that "the religion of Jesus is an unfailing source of truth for
personal purity and for right social action. He maintains that "the
Gospel of Jesus is 'adequate' both as 'motive' and as 'method' for
social reconstruction." For one thing, "the art of forgiveness can be
learned only in the school of religion . . . [and] the creative and
redemptive force is a force which defies the real in the name of the
ideal, and subdues it."[24]

In 1919 Niebuhr still wanted to believe in the efficacy of Wilson's idealism, for he "shared Wilson's faith that 'words have certain
meanings of which it is hard to rob them, and ideas may create reality

in time.'"[25] In words which are astonishingly close to the rhetoric of the Social Gospel (which he would savagely lampoon only a few years later), Niebuhr says:

> The races and groups of mankind are obviously not living as a family; but they ought to. And as the necessity becomes more urgent the truth of the ideal becomes more real.[26]

Perhaps it was important for Niebuhr to be able, at this point in his evolving perception of what he often referred to as "Augustinian—or Pauline—realism," to convince himself that the American middle class could be trusted to practice a modicum of altruism because of the modest prosperity which gave middle-class people enough in the way of material security and possessions. In 1924 (while doing his "political apprenticeship" in LaFollette's campaign for the presidency), Niebuhr called for the formation of a Christian political party which would be "informed by the purest 'spiritual idealism' in program and in methods."[27] The best hope for such a development, and for political reform in the nation rested on the fact that the middle class is not prompted by its needs, for they are sufficiently acute, but . . . may be enlisted through its ideals, once they are awakened, to support a program of thoroughgoing political and economic reconstruction.[28] This optimism may be founded in part on a kind of realism which emerges only occasionally in the 1920s—namely, a prediction that "the alternative to a conversion in the hearts of the middle-classes, accomplished by the Protestant clergy, must be class warfare."[29]

As this line of thought suggests, Niebuhr's optimism regarding ends includes a conviction that people can become wise enough not to accept mere bourgeois contentment in lieu of the highest and truest kind of human fulfillment. The kind of affluence provided by Fordism—where the wealth of the majority "obscures social inequalities"—is the enemy of the good society as conceived by religious thinkers.[30]

MEANS

Reinhold Niebuhr was a Christian minister and the son of a pastor, and he spent his life as a pastor and a professor in a theological seminary, so there is no question that he had considerable faith in the potential significance of the Church as an agent of social regeneration. He recognized the many faults of church people, and he came to have doubts about most ordinary American Christians. Yet in the early years of his career Niebuhr was at one with his Social Gospel colleagues in viewing the Christian church and Christian citizens as having a noble vocation—to make the world better—and as being capable of successfully carrying out this vocation. In 1920 Niebuhr wrote an article for a Social Gospel organ called *Biblical World* (which is addressed to "those who believe in the kingdom mission"), exhorting his readers to take full advantage of "the great and unquestionable fact that the Protestant leaders command the attention of the possessing classes in 1920." Merkeley notes that Niebuhr's travels abroad in 1923 and 1924 (for Eddy's European Seminars) had the effect of intensifying his faith in religion as a "morally redemptive force" in world affairs. America could fulfill its role as "the best hope of mankind" only if the churches succeeded in "improving the moral tone of the nation" to ward off the kind of class antagonism and class conflict Niebuhr had seen in Europe.[31]

Niebuhr believed that the church could accomplish this by addressing itself to "the great task that lies ahead [which was] to 'sensitize' the middle-class conscience." Using language of this kind, Niebuhr comes very close to aligning himself with the typical Social Gospel strategy of pseudotransformationism.[32] This aspect of Niebuhr's thinking in the Detroit years is also reflected in the Jesus piety which is apparent in his journal and some of his published articles.

"Jesus' Piety"

The depth of Niebuhr's faith in what he would later be willing to call Christian mythology is apparent in his frequent references to Jesus and his self-flagellation for being something less than a true disciple of Christ. During the 1920s, says Merkeley, Niebuhr maintained a "sturdy commitment to the practicability of Jesus' love-command." He spoke of Jesus as "a great moral adventurer" whose insistence "that love is the ultimate rule of human conduct" should inspire us to emulate both his faith and his daring, and he quotes with approval a Sunday-school pupil who replied to a question concerning the problem of trusting people: "Maybe it would work if we tried hard enough."[33] This leads to a rumination on the familiar proposition that it is erroneous to contend that "Christianity has been tried and found wanting," because the truth is that "it has been found hard and not tried." In defending the position that Christianity is "perfectly practicable," Niebuhr opines that "all human relationships could be redeemed—'if we tried hard enough,'" and he translates Christian ethics into the sociological jargon of the day:

> Modern sociology's demand that the social motives of primary social groups shall become the motives of secondary groups is identical with the demands of the sermon on the mount. The progress of civilization depends upon the expansion of attitudes which now characterize family life. . . . Reason and experience will contribute to the attainment of the ideal of human brotherhood; but spiritual religion must make the major contribution. Every essential of that contribution is in the gospel of Jesus.[34]

Niebuhr's personal journal for the years 1915 through 1928 (published in 1929 as *Leaves from the Notebook of a Tamed Cynic*) is sprinkled with Niebuhr's exhortations to himself to be a better Christian by making an effort "to become a more trusting, loving person 'in all human relations,' [and to] experiment with the potency of trust and love much more than I have in the past."[35] At other times, Niebuhr rebukes himself by saying, "I am not really a Christian." Why not? Because he makes too many Aristotelian compromises, and because he is "too cautious to be a Christian."[36]

DISSIMILARITIES

From the very beginning, Niebuhr was not exactly typical of the Social Gospel preachers, and as time passed and his tendency to be both empirical and pragmatic asserted itself, he was increasingly inclined to define both ends and means in a significantly different way. Like Rauschenbusch, Niebuhr realized that class-consciousness was an essential ingredient in a realistic social analysis, and he knew that countervailing power would be required to secure results which preaching the love of Jesus to the bosses would never achieve.

Niebuhr's empirical bent was no doubt partly responsible for saving him from the seductive logic of pseudotransformationism. Not that he was immune to an occasional lapse into the sort of sentimentality which he usually deplored. After all, he defended Rockefeller's abandonment of the Interchurch World Movement by lauding Rockefeller's "sincerity."[37] But he was on the whole able to perceive what Atkins experienced without having to try exhortation alone and endure its failures. He was able to see, for example, both the shortcomings of Henry Ford's widely acclaimed "benevolent paternalism" and the weaknesses of the Church as a social change agent.

Moreover, Niebuhr's soon-to-be-famous awareness of the dangers of hubris in Prometheanism was already being expressed in the 1920s, especially in his indictment of the complacency or self-righteousness in the thinking and the lives of those who deemed themselves "virtuous." His own self-critical streak is evident in *Leaves,* and his ability to spot ideological taint in every school of thought comes out in his writings from the very beginning. This can be seen in his attack on Ford as well as in his criticisms of Versailles and Wilsonianism (including the League of Nations). In 1919, Niebuhr shrewdly explained what was happening in Europe by noting that "they [the majority of the diplomats assembled at Versailles] will let Wilson label the transaction if the others can determine its true import. Thus realities are exchanged for words."[38] As historians have observed, there is a supreme irony in the fact that American Protestantism's highest moment of hope was the year or so just at the end of World War I. And the evidence of its declining influence was already becoming apparent in 1919 with the collapse of the Interchurch World Movement, the founding of which only months earlier had been an occasion for extravagant expressions of confidence. The failure of Wilsonianism in general and of the League of Nations in particular followed soon thereafter, and when Prohibition was repealed a few years later, every discerning social critic knew that Protestantism's power was seriously on the wane.

There is, then, little evidence in Niebuhr's writings that he was ever caught up in the fatuous enthusiasm which buoyed many of his Social Gospel colleagues. He seems never to have believed that "Protestant pastors could speak 'to and for the whole population in the same tone of voice which they direct[ed] to their own memberships.'"[39] And he seems always to have been a part of the radical wing of Social Gospelers "which recognized the peril of the old habit of identifying the Kingdom with the Promise of American Life."[40] *Leaves* is full of Niebuhr's misgivings about the anti-prophetic drag on the Church's social witness caused by "the semi-pagans who fill its pews." Indeed, he realized, along with other Social Gospel radicals,

> that the church was deceiving itself to think it was setting the
> moral tone or the intellectual tone of the American community,

when in fact the community was using the church to sanctify materialistic values.[41]

Niebuhr's Position on Significant Issues and Themes

The generalizations put forth in this chapter can best be understood by exploring their expression in Niebuhr's position on a number of concrete issues during the period under consideration.

During the period from 1915 to 1928, Niebuhr evolved from a man who was "'trying to be an optimist without falling into sentimentality' to 'a realist trying to save myself from cynicism.'"[42] Three of the most significant topics in this connection pertain to the three previously mentioned topics of race, socialism, and pacifism. In addition, it is important to examine two extremely significant school-of-thought themes which occupied Niebuhr all his life, especially during the years before he developed his mature theological and ethical ideas in the 1930s.

RACE

Niebuhr's position on what was then called "race relations" was influenced (in a disappointing way) by two familiar Social Gospel characteristics—namely, paternalism and a focus on economic issues. The second of these caused Niebuhr to omit from his assessment of Ford any reference to the industrialist's relatively enlightened policy regarding black workers. Fox observes:

> A full discussion of Ford's "philanthropy" [would have] had to
> address the race issue, since Ford claimed to be fully egalitarian
> in his hiring practices—even to the point of making room for
> ex-convicts and the physically handicapped. . . . Niebuhr's
> avoidance of the whole subject is inexplicable, unless he was sim-
> ply determined not to let his pessimism on solving the racial is-
> sue interfere with his hope that industrial conflict could be settled
> in labor's favor.

But this pessimism may also have caused him, in the one *Christian Century* piece he wrote on the subject in the 1920s, to write a summary of the findings of the Detroit Mayor's Race Relations Committee which was so bland that it lacked his usual prophetic fervor.[43]

As for paternalism, it seems to have been present in much of Niebuhr's thinking on racial matters in Detroit. He was one of the Protestant ministers who protested the treatment of a black physician whose efforts in 1925 to buy a home in a white neighborhood provoked an ugly racial incident involving the Ku Klux Klan. By this time Niebuhr had become "a visible force in the Protestant community, [being] head of both the Detroit Pastors' Union and the Industrial Committee of the Detroit Council of Churches." He was therefore appointed chairman of the city government's Interracial Committee, and in this capacity he was the titular head of a four-month research project involving "empirical study of black community organizations and living conditions." Even though the 1927 report "put an official voice of criticism against most of the structures of Detroit,"[44] it was distressingly shallow and marred by a paternalistic strain which tended to undercut its merits.[45] Stone points out that the report "recommend[ed] a plan of education to help African Americans keep their neighborhoods in attractive condition," and approved of "a similar emphasis upon the personal appearance and demeanor of colored people and their children."[46] Fox is of the opinion that this report reveals

> [Niebuhr's] own inability to incorporate a critique of American race relations into his overall critique of modern industrial civilization. His Christian prophecy was so completely rooted in his reading of the industrial conflict between skilled white workers and their employers—in his hope that the American worker could join with enlightened professional people to form a Labor Party on the British model—that it had no place for the black struggle for equality. . . . As long as circumstances conspired, in Niebuhr's view, to keep American blacks cut off from industrial civilization itself—to keep them at "the brute level"—they could be objects of Christian charity, but not participants in the reform of that civilization.[47]

INDUSTRIAL JUSTICE

The issue Niebuhr pondered most deeply and wrote about most often during the Detroit years was pacifism, but his most dramatic involvement in the struggle for social justice was the challenge he ultimately delivered to Henry Ford in what *The Christian Century* dubbed "the battle of Detroit." Niebuhr said that the move to Detroit put him "up against an industrial city, [where] I saw that human nature was quite different than I had learned at Yale Divinity School."[48] His changing posture vis-à-vis Ford was a part of his evolving attitude toward socialism and the Socialist Party of the USA.

Ford

When the Interchurch World Movement collapsed, Niebuhr was still enough of a Social Gospeler to defend Rockefeller's paternalism by crediting him with "sincerity." Moreover, he waited some time before raising his voice in criticism of Ford. The delay was due in part to the fact that the dean of the Episcopal Cathedral in Detroit, the Reverend Samuel Marquis, was Henry Ford's personal pastor and intimate friend in addition to being the chief of Ford's "Sociological Department." Thus, "as long as Marquis was in charge of the Ford experiment in welfare capitalism, no respectable Detroit pastor would publicly second-guess the company's humanitarianism." So even though Niebuhr did raise questions about Ford's "huge profits" in 1923, this protest was to some extent canceled out by continued acceptance of the popular myth that Ford paid handsome wages. Nor was Niebuhr the first *Christian Century* editorialist to criticize Ford.[49] But by the time he did get around to launching his critique, Niebuhr was speaking from a position of considerable authority. And since daring to challenge Henry Ford at all put Niebuhr in an embattled position, he had to mount a vigorous attack. Among the particulars in his 1926 critique of "the pretensions of the world-famed Henry Ford" were Ford's meager philanthropy, his use of the stretch-out, his abandonment of older workers, and his refusal to grant an adequate annual wage to employees who were utterly dependent upon the company.[50]

Even more intriguing than these familiar Social Gospel complaints was Niebuhr's attack on Fordism—that is, the emerging vision of an industrial society in which hard work would bring good wages which could be used to buy happiness in one's leisure time. In some quarters this vision was associated with the name of America's heralded industrial pioneer. In an article written in 1926 for an international student audience, Niebuhr lamented the fact that America's response to "machine industry" had not been "sullen revolt but unimaginative compliance." In other words, most Americans were "part of a system of mutual exploitation that works fairly well." This indicated that Niebuhr was much less "impressed by the 'steward--

ship' of the pious rich," than he had been five years earlier, for he
now described the benefactions of the wealthy as "veils of decency
hiding essential indecencies." And he now stressed that "disproportionate power and privilege were themselves unethical [because they
were] destructive of real brotherhood." He now began to take the
position that "it was no longer enough for Christians to protest
against American luxury or complacency; it was time to disengage
from 'exploitation.'"[51]

Niebuhr was beginning to firm up a sociocultural analysis
which showed an intense awareness of middle-class complacency and
the kinds of sacrifice which would be required if American capitalism
were to overcome some of its persistent economic injustices. In his
first signed editorial for *The Christian Century* in 1922, Niebuhr
pointed out that middle-class citizens "enjoy[ed] the comforts which
the high productivity of modern industry secure[d] for them," but
were opposed to the industrial workers' right to strike because they
"blame not the entrenched but the attacking party for the conflict
which disturbs their comfort."[52] The fact is, said Niebuhr, "the
changes that are necessary in our economic order will require the
sacrifice of many privileges and rights on the part of the holding
classes." He predicted that "they will make such sacrifices willingly
only if their vision is broadened and their conscience sensitized by
such agencies as the church."[53]

Socialism

In later years, Reinhold Niebuhr remembered having been "a
simple-minded socialist" in the 1920s, but Paul Merkeley argues that
this recollection is misleading. "Looking over the record of his words
and deeds," says Merkeley, "one has to conclude that no good purpose
is served by calling him a socialist before the end of the decade."[54] To
be sure, Niebuhr's articles during this period bristled with condemna-
tions of various injustices and urged vague reforms leading toward
"industrial democracy" or "socialization" of one kind or another. But
it was not until 1928 (just one year before the stock market crash
signaled the Depression) that Niebuhr undertook to describe "the
fundamental flaw of the American economy" in these words:

> Industry [has arrived] at a production capacity which the wants
> of the community cannot absorb except the buying power of the
> workers is greatly increased. . . . With his present buying power
> the worker cannot absorb the products of his own toil . . . [and]
> competitive industry easily aggravates [this problem] of restricted

markets by lowering wages and cutting jobs, thus further re-
stricting the buying power of the public.

But this is the language of Keynes, and the remedy proposed by
Niebuhr is also Keynesian, for he wants "not to tear down and build
anew, but 'to modify the present system step by step.'" In Merkeley's view, "there is not a hint of Marxism in this gas-and-water
socialism."[55]

Stone is evidently of the same mind, for even though he reports
that Niebuhr's attack on Ford included a proviso recommending the
nationalization of a company that big, his description of "the rise and
fall of the socialist alternative" includes an account of recommendations not made to the Socialist Party until 1929. It was only then,
having just arrived in New York and having become a Socialist
candidate for the House of Representatives by a fluke, that Niebuhr
ventured to take the following position:

> Dismissing laissez-faire economic theory as a boon to the privi-
> leged which hindered necessary progress, he advocated the re-
> moval of major sectors of the economy from private ownership,
> heavier inheritance taxes, increased income taxes and extensive
> welfare assistance as the necessary ingredients of political re-
> form.[56]

But even this (with the possible exception of the first particular)
might pass as a list of reforms advocated by the New Deal only a few
years later. And it was not until the early 1930s that Niebuhr charged
that even radical Christians had been misled by their middle-class
presuppositions into thinking "that the just society could be obtained
gradually in an evolutionary movement," and that "the continued
failure of the West to reorganize itself radically along socialist lines
would probably lead to the system's violent end in a revolution."[57]

We may conclude, then, that Niebuhr's experience in Detroit
during the 1920s brought him to the brink of socialism, but that he
didn't cross the threshold until he moved to New York and compre-
hended the imminence (and soon the reality) of the Great Depression. The movement beyond anything ever envisioned by the Social
Gospel (which is by definition the moderate wing of Social Christianity, which stopped short of the radical posture achieved by Christian Socialists) was a part of Niebuhr's gradual shift away from idealism toward Christian Realism—a shift which is paralleled in his
stance regarding liberalism and pragmatism.

PACIFISM

Richard Fox makes an intriguing observation about the connection between Niebuhr's ambivalence toward pacifism and his efforts to come to terms with socialism while in Detroit:

> In Niebuhr's liberal pacifist circle it was not yet common [in 1926] to call oneself a Socialist; he did not join the Socialist Party until 1929. American socialism seemed too akin to Communism, which Niebuhr firmly condemned . . . as an irremediable "strategy of hate." . . . One side of him, outraged by Henry Ford's pious pretensions and by the standpat complacency of the AFL, was moving steadily toward socialism, [for] it was the only political position that did justice to his recent insight into the unethical character of power and privilege. The other side of him was applying the brakes because of his liberal Christian belief that the law of love had to be invoked across the board in all human relationships, individual and collective. . . . Since he could not imagine advocating force [yet!], much less violence, he did the next best thing: he began to attack those on the liberal Christian left who naively expected love to work. Lacking a positive alternative to pacifism, he leapt all the more energetically into the negative task of proving pacifism fatuous.[58]

Niebuhr at first vacillated between support for World War I and an apparently solid commitment to pacifism. This eventually gave way to an endorsement of violence in the struggle to achieve unionization, then (very gradually) to support for rearmament on the eve of World War II, and finally to a strong commitment to the war against the Axis powers.

Niebuhr's faith in America as "the world's best hope" dominated his reflections on German-American matters and made him a supporter of the Allied cause in World War I. Furthermore, his initial enthusiasm for Wilson's Fourteen Points reinforced his support for a war which would make the world safe for democracy.[59] But the failure of Versailles shook Niebuhr's confidence in Wilson and the "just war" logic of American policy. Niebuhr's travels to Europe in the early 1920s brought him back into the pacifist fold: an oft-quoted diary entry from 1923 proclaims that he has resolved once and for all to be "done with the war business." But the context of this remark and the passage which follows it reveal considerable indecisiveness:

Of course, I wasn't really in the last war. Would that I had been! Every soldier, fighting for his country in simplicity of heart without asking many questions, was superior to those of us who served no better purpose than to increase or perpetuate the obfuscation of nations. Of course, we really couldn't know everything we know now. But now we know. The times of man's ignorance God may wink at, but now he calls us all to repent. I am done with this business. I hope I can make that resolution stick.[60]

During the next couple of years Niebuhr was active in pacifist organizations such as the Fellowship of Reconciliation (FOR) and the Fellowship of Social Christians (FSC), and he wrote on pacifist themes for the *Christian Century,* where he was a regular editorialist. But by 1927 his misgivings about idealism and his rapidly increasing knowledge about the recalcitrance of sin, especially collective sin, led to an incipient break with pacifist persuasions. It was during this year that he wrote "A Critique of Pacifism" for *The Atlantic Monthly* in which, despite insisting that he was still a pacifist, "he came down firmly on the naivete of those who proposed reasonableness and goodwill as strategies of political action." In the past, he had often attacked excessive faith in reason in religious thinking. Now he "minimized its place in practical affairs."

> He of course valued it as a tool of analysis, but he repudiated it as a means of building a just world order. It made no more sense [he wrote] to preach reason and trust to the nations of the world than it did to preach them to Henry Ford. Pacifism was egregiously ignorant of the structures of international power.[61]

Worse than that, argued Niebuhr, the backers of the movement to outlaw war were guilty of ideological taint, for (as its European critics realized) American supporters of outlawry lived "in a paradise that is protected by the two walls of the tariff and immigration restriction." The movement was, in fact, "an ethical sublimation of an essentially selfish national position."[62]

The fact is, Niebuhr's years of close contact with Charles Clayton Morrison, editor of the *Christian Century* and leader of the movement to outlaw war, touched a tender psychological nerve. As has already been noted, Fox makes much of Niebuhr's dislike of many do-gooders' "namby-pamby faith in goodness and love" (contending, in fact, that this is "what annoyed him most of all about liberal Protestantism").[63] Thus Fox hypothesizes that Niebuhr's prejudice against liberalism was "partly the product of his long-standing distaste for the hundreds of pious, syrupy religious liberals he had run into since his Yale Divinity School days."[64] And that is why (as was asserted in chapter 1) Niebuhr "tried to masculinize Protestant rhetoric . . . with [the] hard-hitting, pointed, hammering prose" which he employed in his *Christian Century* editorials.[65] It follows, for Fox, that a rebellion in substance as well as style against "the Victorian niceties of [*Century* editor Charles Clayton] Morrison" and what he represented was an important way for Niebuhr to overcome his own disgust with himself for having become (while at Yale) "so much like [those syrupy religious liberals] in their easy assertions about the power of love to harmonize human relations."[66] Voicing his reservations about both liberalism in general and pacifism in particular helped "blot out the memory of his own sentimentality."[67]

Whatever the deep psychological springs of Niebuhr's motivation, his allegiance to pacifism was clearly beginning to dissolve well before the end of the decade. And the next few years would see an elaboration of Christian Realism which relegated this ethical viewpoint to the margins of authentic Christian discipleship.

LIBERALISM

Liberalism is such a spongy term that many observers deplore its continued use, and many students of Niebuhr are convinced that applying it to him causes more problems than it solves. Yet Niebuhr says in one of his later autobiographical writings that he was (and always had been) "a liberal at heart."[68] Stone makes an important contribution to our understanding on this point by specifying the sense in which Niebuhr can and cannot be called "a liberal." His most helpful point is that "Niebuhr's style has obscured his debt to liberalism."[69] Because his writing is given to "exaggeration and simplification,"

> the very vigor of his polemic often leaves the impression that he is rejecting a whole school of thought when his concern is to correct distortions within the school. Further, he concentrates his polemic on positions which he regards as possible alternatives to his own position . . . [which means that] he is frequently most critical of that in other men to which he is most tempted himself.[70]

Stone goes on to point out that what Niebuhr opposed in the liberal's devotion to the ideal of progress was not its optimism per se, but its oftentimes sentimental optimism, or its tendency to think that progress was something which could be counted on to occur automatically, no matter how stupidly or wickedly human beings behaved. Niebuhr's well-known identification of the six most egregious errors in the liberal creed was not published until 1936, but his objections to the blindness of liberalism had probably been impressing themselves upon his consciousness during the 1920s. These errors are the beliefs that:

1. injustice is caused by ignorance and will yield to education and greater intelligence.
2. civilization is becoming gradually more moral and that it is a sin to challenge either the inevitability or the efficacy of gradualness.
3. the character of individuals rather than social systems and arrangements is the guarantee of justice in society.
4. appeals to love, justice, good will, and brotherhood are bound to be efficacious in the end. If they have not been so to date we must have more appeals to love, justice, good will, and brotherhood.
5. goodness makes for happiness and increasing knowledge of this fact will overcome human selfishness and greed.
6. wars are stupid and can therefore only be caused by people who are more stupid than those who recognize the stupidity of war.[71]

Stone's list of the nine attributes of Niebuhr's thought which are to some extent derived from liberalism (or which are, at the very least, compatible with it) is equally instructive. Those attributes emphasize:

1. the authority of experience
2. ethics
3. the importance of social environment
4. confidence in reason (rightly understood)
5. a devaluation of appeals to the authority of Holy Scripture
6. acceptance of the historical investigation of Christian faith
7. a dynamic view of history

8.   the humanity of Jesus
9.   the importance of toleration[72]

Most of these criteria vindicate Niebuhr's later observation that he had always been "a liberal at heart."

Fox concurs with Stone in believing that Niebuhr does owe a permanent debt to liberalism. Indeed, Fox admits that one of the underlying aims in the interpretive thrust of his biography of Niebuhr is "to reclaim Niebuhr for the liberal tradition."[73] In comparing Niebuhr to Barth, Fox discerns what will strike some readers as a surprising affinity between Niebuhr and Dewey, for he writes:

> Niebuhr tried to seize the middle ground between the super-naturalist Barth and the naturalist Dewey, author of the recent [1934] *A Common Faith.* . . . What [his] analysis revealed, despite his inattention, was how close his own prophetic faith was to Dewey, how far away it was from Barth. His starting point, like Dewey's, was man's drive for meaning and his quest to realize ideals in history. . . . Niebuhr might put more stress on the pit-falls that men encountered—social structures, human pride—but Dewey was scarcely unmindful of them. Niebuhr could not have stomached the thought, [but] his faith was shot through with the very liberalism that he flailed at and caricatured. Like Dewey, he was a pragmatist, a relativist, and a pluralist at heart. . . . Had he [Niebuhr] unhardened his heart on the subject of liberalism he would have discovered that he was firmly cemented in the liberal tradition of John Stuart Mill; resistance to dogmatism, tolerance for diversity, openness to correction.[74]

But Niebuhr's contact with those sickeningly sweet religious liberals whom he disliked so much activated a powerful prejudice against the "tentativeness, hesitancy and inaction" of liberals as a group, and it may also have triggered a certain anxiety about himself:

> He was afraid of keeping still, pondering endlessly; he thought he would dry up, lose the vitality that he never ceased to acclaim as the crucial human attribute. He feared, as he put it in his weighty formulation of 1931, being consigned to impotence by the multitude of his scruples. Beating the straw man of liber-alism was a way of battling the threat of inactivity in his own being.[75]

PRAGMATISM

One of the intriguing claims made by numerous students of Niebuhr has to do with his alleged pragmatism. In view of the fact that Niebuhr did not object to having Christian Realism dubbed Christian Pragmatism after the late 1940s, the point may not seem worth debating. But Fox's articulation of this point is so strong as to occasion some resistance, for he reads *Does Civilization Need Religion?* as proof that by the mid-1920s Niebuhr was already "a thoroughgoing Jamesian pragmatist" and had already revealed himself as such "in his B.D. and M.A. theses at Yale."

In light of Niebuhr's later career as preacher, writer and social activist, the B.D. thesis is rather surprising in what Fox calls its "total neglect of the social dimension that the liberal Social Gospelers had been stressing for a generation, [and which] he had stressed . . . in his first Lincoln sermon." Rauschenbusch's *Christianizing the Social Order* (1912) had just been published (1912) and Eugene Debs's run at the presidency on the Socialist ticket in that same year had generated "tremendous enthusiasm among left-liberal Protestants." Niebuhr "saw in 'the trampling hosts of labor' a collective expression of 'the miraculous power of the human personality,'" and his excitement about the working class "went far beyond the more respectable liberalism of Dean Brown and others on the Yale faculty."

> Later Niebuhr would mine Rauschenbusch in earnest, join the party of Debs, and mock the tepid politics of men like Brown. [But] for the moment he was not inclined to go even as far as they did: he was immersed in matters of individual belief and unbelief. That was the tack his adviser encouraged, but it was also the one that conformed to his own expressed need for personal legitimation as a preacher of the Gospel.[76]

What the Yale theses do reflect is the preoccupation of Niebuhr's theologically liberal professors with personality, and Fox explains this as a corollary of pragmatism. Since "religious certainty could no longer be based upon 'superhuman revelation,' it had to be grounded in a philosophy of human needs and in the actual experience of belief." What is crucial here (as James had seen) was the will-to-believe, which could be exercised freely because of the fact that

> truth was not something to possessed once and for all . . . but something to be worked toward, approximated, in action. Men

did not have the right to believe whatever they wanted, but
whatever was not contrary to established facts and desired consequences.[77]

According to the later Ritschlians, "religious knowledge was 'theoretical knowledge' based not on 'complete verification' but on 'value
judgments.'"[78] *Does Civilization Need Religion?* is preoccupied with
these themes and it develops the following argument:

> By following the example of Immanuel Kant and William James,
> [we can] grant the primacy of reason in its proper sphere, then
> proceed to demarcate another sphere—that of "morality" and
> "personality"—within which not scientific reason but "practical
> reason" or "religious experience" operates as a standard of truth.
> Truth in the moral realm was personal, vital, a product of will as
> much as mind, confirmed not in logic but in experience. Truth
> was what "worked"—as long as it contravened no known
> facts—in the furtherance of desired ends. Christians could spark
> human brotherhood only by liberating the hidden resource con-
> tained in liberal Protestantism itself: Jesus' prophetic, paradoxical
> Gospel, a message not of propositional truths, but of poetic, dra-
> matic, "irrational" truths.[79]

It's an audacious argument, and yet it explains a great deal. We
will have occasion to return to this line of interpretation in chapter 3
when we consider Niebuhr's notion of the eufunctionality of illusions in mobilizing social reform zeal.

Chapter 3

The Moral Worldview
of Reinhold Niebuhr

If one had to pick the single theme with which Niebuhr's name is most often associated, it would be sin. Niebuhr first caught the eye of a large reading public in the guise of a somber prophet who had rediscovered (or reemphasized) the venerable Christian doctrine of original sin.

Niebuhr was one of the first religious intellectuals in this country to read the signs of the darkening times in the 1930s and disavow the prevailing optimism of Western culture. If Christians were really going to *do* anything to make the world better, they would have to start by facing up to the terrifying dimensions of the evil confronting them and the limits on what could be done. They would have to readjust their goals and priorities to focus on warding off the ominous forces of iniquity which had to be coped with. This would necessitate a more sober appraisal of those shortcomings which always keep people from living up to their best intentions. Traditional notions of sin offered greater wisdom on this point than any of the psychological, sociological, or philosophical teachings being propounded at the time.

It is not difficult for a present-day reader to appreciate the power and subtlety of Niebuhr's analysis of sin, for the intricacy of his argument and its cumulative thrust still speak for themselves. It is perhaps more difficult for us to grasp the consternation occasioned by this portrait of human beings as sinners and the accusations of irreligious cynicism which were leveled at the messenger who called attention to this elemental reality.

Niebuhr's point of departure in analyzing the complexities of sin is the assertion that it is different from—and more than—mere finitude. Sin is primarily the result of humankind's strength (its freedom and creativity), not its weakness. All classical and modern views of human nature which stress the bondage of spirit in flesh, the inevitability of death, or any other aspect of finitude are off the mark, as are the remedies associated with these diagnoses of the human condition: the triumph of reason, mysticism, or progress in scientific knowledge and technological ingenuity. Sin is a manifestation of the anxiety we experience when, as self-conscious beings, we begin to be aware of our freedom and ability to use this freedom creatively in productive activity. When we contrast this creativity with our obvious creatureliness, we are gripped by a state of uncertainty and fear: how can we know exactly which path to take and what to do? And even if we are able to discern the good, will we be able to live in accordance with it let alone live up to it? Our knowledge of good and evil and free will may be parts of the *imago dei* within, but they offer no guarantee whatsoever that we can overcome our continual "missing of the mark" (that is, in reference to *hamartia,* a familiar word for sin in the New Testament, our repeated failure to live up to the grandeur God intends for those who are created in God's image).

Anxiety can lead in one of two directions. Or, to be more precise, anxiety is likely to lead each individual into different paths of error at different times and in different life circumstances. It may drive us to mistrust the creator, which leads to disobedience and the rebellion of sloth or sensuality. (These are two slightly different manifestations of sin as escapism—i.e., escape from the spiritual stature for which we are destined by refusing even to try to make the best possible use of our freedom and creativity.) Anxiety may, on the other hand, drive us to an overcompensating will-to-power, which can then lead to pride, pretentiousness, and unjust (even cruel) oppression of those whom we succeed in dominating.

The dimension of sin Niebuhr singles out for particular emphasis is pride. One of the most diligently studied portions of Niebuhr's *Nature and Destiny of Man* is the section in Volume I (*Human Nature,* pp. 186–228) which contains his analysis of the pride of power as well as intellectual, moral, and spiritual pride. This portion of *Human Nature* is complemented by Niebuhr's commentary on "The Equality of Sin and the Inequality of Guilt" in *Human Destiny* (Vol. II, 219–228), in which he describes the evil typically exhibited by the powerful, the rich, and (those who imagine themselves to be) the righteous. One oft-quoted passage conveys the thrust of the argument as well as its polemical vigor:

> Wherever the fortunes of nature, the accidents or history or even the virtues of the possessors of power, endow an individual or a group with power, social prestige, intellectual eminence or moral approval above their fellows, there an ego is allowed to expand. It expands both vertically and horizontally. Its vertical expansion, its pride, involves it in sin against God. Its horizontal expansion involves it in an unjust effort to gain security and prestige at the expense of its fellows. . . .
>
> It is at this point that the Biblical insight into the sinfulness of all human nature actually supports rather than contradicts the prophetic strictures against the wise, the mighty, the noble and the good. For without understanding the sinfulness of the human heart in general it is not possible to penetrate through the illusions and pretensions of the successful classes of every age. If one did not know that all men are guilty in the sight of God it would not be easy to discern the particular measure of guilt with which those are covered who are able to obscure the weakness and insecurity of man by their good works.[1]

The pride of the powerful is also a source of the *irony* which Niebuhr considers to be a hallmark of the Christian view of history. (For a detailed explanation of Niebuhr's understanding and use of the concept of irony, see chapter 5.) Building on the proposition that Christianity holds to "the belief that the whole drama of human history is under the scrutiny of a divine judge who laughs at human pretensions without being hostile to human aspirations,"[2] Niebuhr contends that

> the ironic aspect of power and security being involved in weakness and insecurity by reason of stretching beyond their limits is matched by the irony of virtue turning into vice. The Pharisee is condemned and the publican preferred because the former "thanks God" that he is "not like other men."
>
> [Moreover,] there is irony in the Biblical history as well as in Biblical admonitions. Christ is crucified by the priests of the

purest religion of his day and by the minions of the justest, the Roman Law. The fanaticism of the priests is the fanaticism of all good men, who do not know that they are not as good as they esteem themselves. The complacence of Pilate represents the moral mediocrity of all communities, however just.[3]

The Human Potential for Goodness

Many twentieth-century theologians have found themselves in agreement with Niebuhr's sobering beliefs about the persistence of sin. On the basis of this first principle, they have formulated a deeply pessimistic view of the human condition. Yet that is not what Reinhold Niebuhr himself did, and this aspect of his thought poses a crucial question; namely, given Niebuhr's grim view of sin, how can we account for the fact that he did not retreat into quietism?

Many neo-orthodox theologians of the time reacted to the utopian excesses of the Social Gospel by renouncing all hope for societal salvation. Their parody of the famous Social Gospel hymn, "Rise Up, O Men of God!" illustrates this attitude:

Sit down, O Men of God;
You cannot do a thing.
Just when and where and as He wills
His Kingdom He will bring.

Prominent among American theologians attracted to a serious version of this sober emphasis was Reinhold Niebuhr's highly esteemed younger brother, H. Richard Niebuhr, who taught at Yale Divinity School. In a letter composed not long after the founding (in 1936) of Reinhold's new journal, *Radical Religion*—which was supposed to be an antidote to the Social Gospel irrelevancies of the *Christian Century,* Richard asks his brother to open his eyes to the full implications of his emerging doctrine of sin and attempts to persuade him to abandon his feverish efforts to bring about social reform. Richard Niebuhr argues that the time has come to renounce the pretense that one has to be "on the right side in the class struggle," for there is no "right side." Better to acknowledge, writes Richard, that

I am a bourgeois, I make my life by capitalism, I live like a bourgeois, I think like one, and I am in [the] wrong. . . . [But] that doesn't make the proletarian right by a long shot. And my business is not to try to change sides but to admit that I am wrong, to live in daily repentance, to know that something is happening all the time whether or not I "do anything about it. . . ."

Really Reinie, you aren't a religious radical at all. You are primarily religious, and radically so. And as religious, better, as a Christian, you know that we are all in the wrong before God, and there is no hope for us in the temporal, but only in the eternal.

The conclusion seems to be inevitable: if there is "no hope for us in the temporal," then it makes no sense to keep on preaching a gospel of societal transformation.[4]

If this letter is taken as a commentary on Niebuhr's doctrine of sin, it contains one crucial element of theological wisdom, that is, wisdom about every man or woman's vertical relationship to the universe and its creator: "We are all in the wrong before God." The two Niebuhrs were of one mind on this point. In addition, Richard's letter must have captured Reinhold's attention not just because it was from a dearly loved and greatly admired brother, but also because it tapped into something very strong in Niebuhr's evolving theological awareness—namely, the fundamentally Lutheran view of justification by faith which had been so eloquently stated by Kierkegaard. The elder Niebuhr acknowledges his appreciation of the Danish existentialist in his apparent endorsement of the Kierkegaardian notion that real repentance transforms the anxiety of the sinner into despair. In commenting on this point, he observes:

> The final truth about life [must be] apprehended in such a way that the "existing individual" . . . is shattered in his self-esteem and the very center of his being; his insecurity as a finite individual in the flux of time [must be] robbed of all securities of power or pride; his anxiety [must be] heightened until it reaches despair.[5]

What Reinhold Niebuhr refused to do, however—and what he utterly deplored and denounced in other theologians—was to deduce from this theological insight the proposition that in horizontal relationships among human beings there is no point in trying to make things better. Rather, we should always be trying to make things as tolerably just and humane as possible. To renounce this possibility, or to quit striving to realize it, is ignominious. Indeed, it is a betrayal of Christian ethics, and thus of Christian belief.

So Reinhold Niebuhr does not advocate quietism. Indeed, there is nothing he deplores (and abhors) more ferociously. We know this primarily because his entire life was a denial of the need to retreat and a testimony to a person's obligation to keep on trying. We also know it because of his writings, particularly his denunciations of certain twentieth-century European representatives of "the Lutheran Reformation" and of the most famous continental theologian of the time, Karl Barth.

CHRISTIANITY IS NOT A "RELIGION FOR THE CATACOMBS!"

I should like to reinforce my discussion of the logic of Niebuhr's robust convictions concerning the human potential for good with an account of a personal conversation with Niebuhr which speaks very eloquently to the point. My most memorable insight into Niebuhr's practical optimism regarding the struggle for social justice comes from a conversation I had with him when I was a first-year student at Union Theological Seminary in 1956. I had received my undergraduate education at Duke, where I had imbibed a large dose of Protestant liberalism from a faculty that included several Yale Ph.D.'s. Furthermore, I had arrived at UTS straight from a three-year hitch in the navy, where I had had ample time to read—and develop a fierce prejudice against—what I called "neo-orthodox theologians" (Barth, Brunner, and Niebuhr). Armed with this impressive sophistication, I lost no time in asking for an appointment with Niebuhr, so that I could accost him with a host of (loaded) questions about the negativism of neo-orthodoxy.

Niebuhr quickly spotted the chip on my shoulder and knocked it off. "Listen here, Mr. Clark," he said (not with animosity, but with the forthright impatience of a man who spends an inordinate amount of time disabusing people of their wrongheaded notions about his thought): "If you classify me with Barth and Brunner as a 'neo-orthodox' theologian, you are making a stupid mistake. Barth's theology is a religion for the catacombs; mine is a religion of political involvement and social action. I don't think there is any such thing as a 'neo-orthodox' school of theology, but if there is, I should not be considered a part of it."

WHAT THE WRITINGS SAY

I attach a more than personal significance to this exchange because I believe it can be read as a peculiarly emphatic expression of what Niebuhr wrote about the ethical imperative to work as hard as one can to realize the "indeterminate possibilities for good" in human life. The argument regarding this aspect of the Niebuhrian view of human nature is spelled out in four important arguments:

1. his concept of "the equality of sin but the inequality of guilt"
2. his analysis of the theological doctrine of "original righteousness"
3. what he says about the "wheat" of ethically praiseworthy human accomplishment "in the finite flux" of time
4. his beliefs concerning grace as a source of both forgiveness and power

The Equality of Sin and the Inequality of Guilt

We have already noted that Niebuhr is very "Lutheran" (even Barthian) in his espousal of the idea that the righteousness of humankind is as nothing in the eyes of the creator: we are all equal in sin. Niebuhr could agree with his brother that all human beings are subject to sin as a fact of life which is "not necessary but inevitable." What this means is that all humanity is the same in its sinfulness vis-à-vis the righteous God, but guilt is not apportioned equally because it is a function of the evil which free moral agents choose (consciously or subconsciously) to commit.

Thus to say that we cannot earn our forgiveness by works-righteousness does not mean—and must never be interpreted to mean—that we are absolved of the responsibility of making discriminate judgments about relative goods and evils in human affairs, and committing ourselves to diligent effort on behalf of the relative good. To see vertical lostness as a tacit recommendation for horizontal apathy and inaction was quietism, and there was nothing which alarmed or infuriated Niebuhr more. His commentaries on the "dialectical theologians" (he avoids the term "neo-orthodox") from whom he wants to dissociate himself are unequivocal and frequently vehement in their denunciation of this error. In his discussion of the legacy of the Lutheran Reformation, for example, he attacks Hans Asmussen for dismissing the significance of the struggle against social injustice, contending that Asmussen's emphasis on waiting for God's action at the end of history tends to "destroy the meaningfulness of history and to rob all historic tasks and obligations of their significance."[6] In a similar vein, Niebuhr also attacks Brunner for interpreting the doctrine of justification by faith "in such a way as to lead to a complacent acceptance of injustice." He concludes:

> The Lutheran Reformation is thus always in danger of heightening religious tension to the point where it breaks the moral tension, from which all decent action flows. The conscience is made uneasy about the taint of sin in all human enterprise; but the conviction that any alternative to a given course of action would be equally tainted and that in any case the divine forgiveness will hallow and sanctify what is really unholy, eases the uneasy conscience prematurely. Thus the saints are tempted to continue in sin that grace may abound, while the sinners toil and sweat to make human relations a little more tolerable and slightly more just.[7]

(As an illustration of this folly, Niebuhr cites an amusing little story told by Augustine about a group of rather lazy monks who resist "being taken to task for their moral sloth into which their piety had degenerated." The monks protest that "it is not we who act but God who worketh in us both to will and to do." They admonish their superiors not to reprove them "when we are at fault, since we are such as God has foreseen us to be and his grace has not been given us to do better.")[8]

Of course, the dialectical theologian most in vogue in the first half of the century was Karl Barth, and thus it is Barth whom Niebuhr lambasts with special ferocity. In the late 1920s and the early 1930s, Niebuhr welcomed certain Barthian ideas and applauded Barth's role in producing the famous Barmen Declaration denouncing German religious support for Hitler. During this period, Niebuhr was perhaps predisposed to have a favorable view of Barth because he liked the Christian socialist circles in which Barth moved and therefore assumed that the eminent Swiss theologian must be on the side of the angels. But when Niebuhr began to perceive that Barthian theology was being used by some German Christians to justify support of Nazism, he became very critical of Barthianism. Later in the 1930s he accused Barth of duplicating the errors of the Lutheran tradition by "sharpening the contrast between the human and divine" in such a way as "to 'justify' the hopeless world in its imperfections." He goes on:

> Here religious absolutism which begins by making the con-
> science sensitive to all human weakness ends in complacency to-
> ward social injustice. The selfishness of privileged groups who
> are trying to prevent the organization of a social order in which
> all men will have basic security is confusedly identified with hu-
> man selfishness in general, and the workers are told that they
> must suffer from injustice as punishment for the sins of man-
> kind.[9]

In 1948, Niebuhr inveighed against Barth's contention that "the care of the world is not our care" on the grounds that it tends to "annul the church's prophetic function to the nations."[10] Niebuhr laments the fact that "judgment so frequently leads to despair rather than repentance," and he opines that this emphasis has no "guidance or inspiration for Christians in the day-to-day decisions which are the very warp and woof of our existence."[11] He ventures to suggest that this brand of crisis theology (another name for Barthianism) "seems to have no guidance for a Christian statesman for our day":

> There is a special pathos in the fact that so many of the Christian
> leaders of Germany are inclined to follow this form of flight
> from daily responsibilities and decisions. . . . Yesterday they dis-
> covered that the church may be an ark in which to survive a
> flood. Today they seem so enamored of this special function of
> the church that they have decided to turn the ark into a home on
> Mount Ararat and live in it perpetually. . . . We seem always to
> be God rather than men in this theology, viewing the world not
> from the standpoint of the special perplexities and problems of
> given periods but sub specie aeternitatis.[12]

In 1958 Niebuhr reacted to Barth's apparent conviction that Communism was no worse than "the free world" by asserting that "the Barthian approach to the political order [constitutes] 'a church for the catacombs.'"[13] The fatal error here is that "Barth's view makes no provision for discriminating judgments, both because of its strong eschatological emphasis and because of the absence of [ratio-nal] principles and structures of value."[14]

The decisive point is this: although Niebuhr was more than ready to admit that the extent to which the finest human dreams of the good society are limited by the moral ambiguity of even the finest actualizations of the good self, he was never willing to admit that we should quit trying to approximate those "indeterminate possibilities for good" of which we are capable and toward which we ought to strive. He could maintain his hope for such possibilities because of a curiously optimistic aspect of his concept of human nature which is often overlooked.

Original Righteousness

Chapter X of Niebuhr's treatise on human nature is entitled "Justitia Originalis." It begins with a quote from Pascal to the effect that "the greatness of man is so evident that it is even proved by his wretchedness."[15] What this means, Niebuhr declares, is that every human being has an intuitive awareness of the fact that he or she is destined for a degree and kind of moral goodness which is higher than that which is "naturally" achieved: "No man, however deeply involved in sin, is able to regard the misery of sin as normal." Moreover, the parable of the Rich Young Ruler reminds us that

> what lies in the uneasy conscience of the sinner is not so much a
> knowledge that the ultimate law of life is the law of love as the
> more negative realization that obedience to the ordinary rules of
> justice and equity is not enough."[16]

What does this mean, this insistence that the darkness of sin stands side-by-side with at least the flickering light of an innate moral sentiment which keeps human beings from total depravity? At the very least, we can say with considerable assurance that it does mean this: human beings are possessed with an intuitive perception of right and wrong and of their moral duty in this regard, which provides a modicum of motivation for constructive action. Perhaps one might even hope for an occasional bit of success in one's attempts to live toward (not up to, but in the direction of) the law of love. To say that there is a higher side to one's nature is to imply that one is meant to try to live in accordance with it.

The notion of original righteousness does not mean that those who try hard to be good and who achieve occasional success can move consistently forward to sanctification. We must never forget that we are continually subject to the corruption as well as the failure of our best efforts, and to imagine that we have broken out of this limitation once and for all is the kind of spiritual pride which leads to disaster. Declares Niebuhr:

> Repentance does initiate a new life. But the experience of the Christian ages refutes those who follow this logic and without qualification. The sorry annals of Christian fanaticism, of unholy religious hatreds, of sinful ambitions hiding behind the cloak of religious sanctity, of political power impulses compounded with pretensions of devotion to God, offer the most irrefutable proof of the error in every Christian doctrine and interpretation of the Christian experience which claim that grace can remove the final contradiction between man and God. The sad experiences of Christian history show how human pride and spiritual arrogance rise to new heights precisely at the point where the claims of sanctity are made without due qualification.[17]

It might be instructive to make an analogy between Niebuhr's disclaimers regarding sanctification and his strictures against "liberalism." We have already noted that Niebuhr misled his readers by the polemical vigor with which he attacked certain aspects of liberalism—e.g., naive or sentimental optimism. These polemics tended to make Niebuhr's readers forget that he remained very much devoted to certain liberal convictions, including wise, open-eyed, qualified optimism. In the same way, his emphasis on what he often referred to as the "persistence" of sin (especially those prideful manifestations of sin which overcompensate for anxiety by cultivating too much will-to-power and allowing too much pretension) may have given the impression that the possible hazards of Promethean striving are so frightening that it would be better to play it safe and not strive for anything lofty. But the overall record of what Niebuhr wrote and the way he lived is ample proof that his fears about hubris were never so great as to negate his faith in the rightness of striving mightily.

The Permanent Importance of Relative Goodness and Grace

Niebuhr is sometimes rebuked by his critics for having what Daniel Day Williams called "a Calvinistic doctrine of meaning"; that is, an understanding of history which "finds meaning only in complete victory over evil," and which therefore implies that "history depends upon something 'beyond history' for its meaning, because there is no complete victory in history."[18] Many other observers seem to be in fundamental agreement with this point because of their view that Niebuhr's main hope was for some kind of decisive triumph of God at the end of history (that is, beyond the limits of ordinary history on this earth). Thus, they look upon Niebuhr's realism as defeatism.

This interpretation of Niebuhr's thought is both right and wrong. It contains a measure of truth because, as Ron Stone has commented, "those most eager to move beyond Niebuhr to new forms of political imagination and more hopeful attitudes toward social life [agree] that realist analysis promote[s] despair or defeatism," and this self-reinforcing agreement can easily be justified by reference to H. Richard Niebuhr's "criticism of Reinhold's view of history as tragic." It is also based, says Stone, on the fact that "Reinhold Niebuhr's view of history mellowed with time, [because] the categories of irony were substituted for the emphasis upon tragedy." Even so, says Stone, "Reinhold's hope was more inclined to be a fulfillment beyond history," for his

> hope is not in the divine creative process, or the newly emerging order, or man's involvement in shaping his destiny. The hope is in God's triumph at the end of history.

As proof, Stone cites a portion of Niebuhr's address to the Evanston Conference of the World Council of Churches in which he declares that "We are saved, not by what we can do, but by the hope that the Lord of history will bring this mysterious drama to a conclusion [in which] the suffering Christ will in the end be the triumphant Lord."[19]

On the other hand, one would be seriously in error to jump to the conclusion that Niebuhr's pessimism concerning the limitations of human striving translated into *defeatism*. It most assuredly does not—for (quoting Stone once again), "If H. Richard had greater hope for society, still Reinhold labored more realistically within the given political alternatives to improve society. Love rather than hope was the major motivation for his action."[20] Support for this argument is to be found in a well-known passage from *The Nature and Destiny of Man* where Niebuhr (despite realizing that the *ultimate* and *complete* triumph of God would not occur until the end of history) expresses his conviction that

> Life in history must be recognized as filled with indeterminate
> possibilities, [for] there is no individual or interior spiritual situa-
> tion, no cultural or scientific task, and no social or political prob-
> lem in which men do not face new possibilities of the good *and
> the obligation to realize them.*[21]

The solution to this puzzle is easy to spot. What we have here is
yet another example of the familiar "both/and" character of Reinhold Niebuhr's thought. Just as the true meaning of justice cannot be
understood apart from the fact that it must be continually pulled
upward by the love ideal, so Niebuhr's concept of hope cannot be
grasped without the realization that it includes a historical as well as a
transhistorical dimension. Just as love in its highest and purest form
can never be realized in any given human collectivity (or, for that
matter, in any *relationship* between two sinful human beings), the *full*
meaning of history cannot be attained or disclosed until its end. Yet
the struggle for justice invites our participation because of the impossible yet relevant ideal of love, and *in the light of this ideal,* and the
indeterminate possibilities which can be achieved have a great deal of
intrinsic significance (despite the imperfection of all approximations
of justice and love which are achieved). Niebuhr is absolutely clear
about the fact that God's

> ultimate mercy does not efface the distinctions between good and
> evil. . . . The very rigour with which all judgments in history
> culminate in a final judgment is thus an expression of mean-
> ingfulness of all historic conflicts between good and evil.[22]

In commenting on "the double aspect of grace," he refers to "the
obligation to fulfill the possibilities of life [as well as] the limitations
and corruptions of all historic realizations." He maintains that the
doctrine of the Atonement expresses "the wrath and judgment of
God [as] symbolic of the seriousness of history" as confirmation of
the fact that "distinctions between good and evil are important and
have ultimate significance."[23] In affirming that "the realization of the
good must be taken seriously," he likens historically achieved goodness to "the wheat, separated from the tares, which is gathered 'into
my barn.'" This means, says Niebuhr, "that the good within the
finite flux has significance beyond that flux."[24]

Why Civilization Needs Religion

We have just seen that one answer to the puzzle concerning Niebuhr's optimistic view of human potential (despite his gloomy view of the persistence of sin) is his notion of original righteousness. Another answer can be found in Niebuhr's belief in the power of religious faith—his assumptions concerning humanity's undeniable need for religion and what religion (particularly Christianity) has to offer.[25]

RELIGION IN GENERAL

In the 1920s, when Niebuhr still viewed himself primarily as a Yale liberal who wanted to translate the unpalatable particularities of Christian faith into universal philosophical truths, he often voiced the opinion that civilization needs religion because religion provides a wholesome supplement to the insights and the energizing motivation supplied by reason. In a 1929 book entitled *The Contribution of Religion to Social Work,* he observed: "If a new society is to be built, we may be sure that religion will have a hand in building it." Why? Because religion provides something unique—and uniquely necessary—to would-be social reformers.

Religion helps in at least three vital ways. First, it inspires a motive for vigorous ethical commitment: we love (and are capable of loving) because God has first loved us, and the gratitude we feel engenders a response. We do not love God because God is divine, but rather because "something of the transcendent unity, in which we are one with God, shines through."[26] The kind of love generated in us is active, aggressive, and universal.[27]

Second, religion supplies the humility and sense of proportion so desperately needed to temper the pretentiousness of humanity. Religious insights

> guarantee the ethically striving soul a measure of serenity and
> provide the spiritual relaxation without which all moral striving
> generates a stinking sweat of self-righteousness and an alternation
> of fanatic illusions and fretful disillusionments.[28]

Specifically, religion enables one to forgive those whose recalcitrance makes justice difficult to approximate,[29] it keeps one from being vindictive in administering retributive justice,[30] and it forces one to see oneself as a sinner whose egoistic limitations constantly threaten to corrupt even one's best efforts and intentions.[31] Niebuhr observes that this last feature of Christian theology is "the socially relevant counterpart of love."[32]

All of this contributes to a third benefit of religious faith, namely, a secure wisdom that manifests itself as a peace of mind that is diametrically opposed to mere apathy. This wise serenity does not lead to quietism but rather to a sense of perspective that insures moral stamina over the long haul. Faith "sees the possibilities of new beginnings in history only upon the basis of the contrite recognition of [the contradiction between human history and the divine]." And this benefit of religion is to be found with special clarity and force in Christianity.

It goes without saying that when Niebuhr voices convictions about the truth and goodness of religion, he is talking about *religion*—not about the cheap religiosity which has masqueraded as the genuine article since the time of the prophet Amos. Niebuhr had nothing but scorn for the "cheap grace" of the so-called "religious revival" of the Eisenhower era. He thought that the personal success cult proclaimed by Norman Vincent Peale and the pietistic evangelicalism of Billy Graham were a far cry from true biblical faith. The former "induced complacency rather than repentance," and the latter tended to baptize political irrelevance by its peddling of "individualistic and perfectionistic illusions" (e.g., its suggestion that "conversion to Christianity could solve the problem of the hydrogen bomb").[33] He thought that President Nixon's attempt to gain political mileage out of bringing prominent clergymen to the White House to celebrate the goodness of the nation and its chief executive was even more despicable. He cited Amos's denunciation of such hypocritical religiosity and compared clergymen who were willing to be exploited in such a way to Amaziah and the other court priests of eighth-century Samaria![34]

CHRISTIANITY IN PARTICULAR

Niebuhr is an apologist for Christian faith, not just religion in general. He argues that "the Cross" or "the Atonement" furnish the best lens available for grasping the enlightenment and empowerment which can be found in religion. The nature of God as suffering love which is revealed in the *agape* of Christ reveals the norm of a new life as well as the divine mercy. Such a point in human history (the Christ-event) can be regarded as both the beginning of a new age for all mankind and as a new beginning for every individual who is called by it. If this truth is apprehended at all, it is apprehended in such a way that "the old self, which makes itself its own end, is destroyed and a new self is born—in principle. That is why a true revelation of the divine is never merely wisdom but also power."[35]

Niebuhr's conviction concerning religious faith as a source of both insight and vigor is explained in many different ways. We have already noted that considerable emphasis is placed upon awareness of one's perpetual frailty and vulnerability to error, and surely this ought to afford some protection against the excesses of pride and will-to-power which we rightly fear. The Atonement, for example, teaches us about

> what man ought to do and what he cannot do, about [our] obligations and final incapacity to fulfill them, [and] about the importance of decisions and achievements in history and about their final insignificance."[36]

In so doing, it encourages us to work hard for worthy endeavors without being so invested in their ultimate outcome that we are unduly gratified by success or crushed by failure.

The promise of empowerment is important because it emboldens us to run risks in undertaking noble causes. Moreover, if Niebuhr is right, it delivers on its promise of power and thus enables us to do things we might otherwise be unable to do. At the very least, grace is experienced as a "release from self" which is actually "a miracle which the self could not have accomplished,"[37] and this freedom from self-preoccupation makes available a great deal of energy which might have been squandered in vanity or fretfulness.

Mythopoeic Profundity

To understand Niebuhr's apologetics on behalf of Christianity, we must understand his concept of "the truth in myths." To borrow a term from *The Intellectual Adventure of Ancient Man* (which Niebuhr greatly admired and assigned in his course on the history of ethical thought), the mythopoeic profundity contained in religious symbolism goes deeper and generates more wisdom and power than pure (mere?) rational speculation on the meaning of life. Thus Christians should not view biblical mythology as an embarrassment to be dispensed with, and they certainly should not jump to the fatuous conclusion that the secularism of urban technological society implies "the death of God."[38] On the contrary, they should appreciate the unique capacity of biblical mythology (similar to that of poetry and drama) to express the most profound answers that can be given to humankind's perennial questions about existence.

Niebuhr was sufficiently honest to know that orthodox ecclesiastical dogma was not intellectually acceptable. At the same time, however, he was wise enough to realize that the "Truth with a capital T" of Christianity could best be conveyed through myth, so he did not abandon biblical mythology in his critique of any too-literal reading of it. The origin of Christian Realism, in fact, lies in Niebuhr's experimentation with competing moral worldviews in the late 1920s and early 1930s. In a 1939 article called "Ten Years That Shook My World," he wrote: "Even while imagining myself to be preaching the Gospel, I had really experimented with many modern alternatives to Christian faith, until one by one they proved unavailing."[39]

As the other gods failed, Niebuhr came back to a newly envisioned and freshly appreciated affirmation of Christian faith, convinced that it offered a struggling humanity its best available lens for understanding and living life. In the "Intellectual Biography" of 1956, he summed up what happened:

> It is difficult to know whether the criticism of both liberal and
> Marxist views of human nature and history was prompted by a
> profounder understanding of the Biblical faith; or whether this
> understanding was prompted by the refutation of the liberal and
> Marxist faith by the tragic facts of contemporary history.[40]

In a famous essay on "Coherence, Incoherence and Christian Faith," he maintained:

> The negative proofs of the Christian faith are not lost on the
> most sophisticated moderns who have recognized the inadequacy
> of the smooth pictures of man and history in modern culture. "It
> cannot be denied," writes an historian, "that Christian analyses
> of human conduct and of human history are truer to the facts of
> experience than alternative analyses.[41]

Niebuhr admitted that "whether the truth of these analyses can be derived only from the presuppositions of the Christian faith" was a moot question, but his appreciation of Christianity as a trustworthy lens remained. And he gradually became convinced that his most important task as a theologian was to recommend this lens and grind it to exactly that sort of refraction which would enable reflective twentieth-century persons to use it for themselves:

> He could not fall back into the classic liberal argument that 'if only" men would believe, all would be well. Of course, if neo-orthodoxy were to become the faith of all men, it would be the way out . . . but so would liberalism, if all men believed. Niebuhr appreciated that there were timely obstacles to belief. Not calculated "study," but "the pressure of world events" had inspired his religious turn, along with his political turn. Not clean, logical, unbroken lines of positive argument, but the broken, often incomplete lines of "the gradual exclusion of alternative beliefs" made up the plot. Neo-orthodoxy was what was left after faith in social science, in liberalism, in Marxism (as well as in apolitical orthodoxy, conservatism, etc.) was excluded.[42]

It should be emphasized that my position on this matter is echoed and confirmed by other observers as diverse as Gustafson, Fox, and Hauerwas, each of whom puts a different evaluation on the fact that Niebuhr admired and made use of Christian mythology because of its wisdom and its ability to mobilize ethical commitment and social action on behalf of justice. Gustafson does not pass judgment; he merely advances his (rock solid) opinion that what we find in Niebuhr is "theology in the service of ethics."[43] Fox seems to applaud Niebuhr's virtuosity as a pamphleteer (propagandist) who was smart enough to see what a valuable resource was at hand in the stirring drama of the Cross, for he says:

> For Niebuhr, myth is an action-oriented, almost propagandistic instrument for generating and sparking movement, especially [in *Moral Man and Immoral Society*] in the working class. But [later] not only there. Niebuhr was always a propagandist, which I mean in a nonpejorative sense. He wanted to generate commitment and action in defense of certain ideals and certain realities . . . [And] this is also the Niebuhr of the 1950s: he wanted people to believe intensely in America. . . . We can't generate such belief simply by telling people it's reasonable to have it; we need to generate it in a much more powerful way.[44]

Hauerwas, on the other hand, joins Cuddihy in condemning Niebuhr's apologetic attempt to broaden the appeal of Christianity by stripping it of its offensive particularities. He faults Niebuhr for creating, as he argues, the most dangerous form of (merely) civil religion yet expounded. "What Niebuhr wants to do," he contends, "is make Christ a symbol, a solution to an eternal human problem . . . [thereby ignoring] the significance of Jesus as the Jewish Messiah."[45] According to Hauerwas,

> For Niebuhr, the kingdom is always an ideal that stands over against any possible realization in history. What that means is that he doesn't have any concrete manifestation of God in history. He just has the ideal standing over against historical realities. And I don't know if you need Jesus for that project.[46]

More will be said on this score at the end of this chapter, when we summarize the significance of Niebuhr's mythopoeic profundity and evaluate the merits of the critique leveled by commentators such as Hauerwas. For now, suffice it to say that I agree with both Fox and Hauerwas on one salient point: Niebuhr's Christian Realism is in a certain sense and to a certain degree a remythologization of Christian belief.[47] Much of the remainder of the chapter is devoted to an explanation of what this means.

Two Misleading Moral Worldviews

One of the earliest and most secure of Niebuhr's insights as an inquiring experimentalist with various schools of thought had to do with the inadequacy of both Christian orthodoxy (especially its sentimental pietistic versions) and philosophical rationalism. As a circuit rider to the pulpits of college chapels all over the country, Niebuhr observed that "there was, as a matter of fact, little difference between the secular and Christian versions of the optimism of the nineteenth-century culture." He continues:

> For years I commuted, as it were, between ecclesiastical and academic communities. I found each with a sense of superiority over the other either because it possessed, or had discarded, the Christian faith. But this contest was ironic because the viewpoints of the two communities were strikingly similar, and both were irrelevant to the ultimate realities.[48]

On the first point, we may cite his fondness for quoting Sidney and Beatrice Webb's famous complaint about Christianity's "ridiculous deification of a man named Jesus," and his savage polemics against the naive utopianism of those exponents of the Social Gospel who thought that "love" could solve all the world's problems, and that cooperation could easily replace competition in human affairs if everyone would follow in the steps of Jesus.[49] In a 1937 essay on "The Truth in Myths," he observes:

> Whenever orthodoxy insists upon the literal truth of . . . myths, it makes a bad historical science out of true religious insights. It fails to distinguish between what is primitive and what is permanent, what is prescientific and what is supra-scientific in great myths.[50]

He made essentially the same point in a slightly different way when he observed that excessive claims concerning one's knowledge of the nature and will of God are worse than agnosticism. In a 1930s essay on "Mystery and Meaning," he satirized the pretentiousness of dogmaticians:

> The testimonies of religious faith are confused more greatly by those who claim to know too much about the mystery of life than by those who claim to know too little. . . . Agnosticism sees no practical value in seeking to solve the mystery of life. But there are not really very many agnostics in any age or culture. A much larger number of people forget that they see through a glass darkly. . . . They define the power and knowledge of God precisely, and explain the exact extent of His control and foreknowledge of the course of events . . . They know that man is immortal and why; and just what portion and part of him is mortal and what part immortal. . . . They know the geography of heaven and of hell, and the furniture of the one and the temperature of the other.[51]

As for the rationalists, they go even further in an erroneous attempt to "destroy the penumbra of mystery" which clouds our finite existence: "The new age of science attempted an even more rigorous denial of mystery [than that carried out by classical Roman Catholic theology]." From the standpoint of the scientific-technological worldview,

> mystery was simply the darkness of ignorance which the light of knowledge dispelled. Religious faith was . . . merely the fear of the unknown which could be dissipated by further knowledge. . . . The "natural," the "temporal," and the "material" are supposedly comprehended so fully that they cease to point beyond themselves to a more ultimate mystery.[52]

Needless to say, the mistakes of both kinds of dogmatic orthodoxy are compounded by the pride of those who see themselves as custodians of the "Truth." Proud metaphysicians of this kind confirm the wisdom of the New Testament's rebuke of those who imagine themselves wise and noble, and they demonstrate the folly of Nietzsche's charge that the transvaluation of values proclaimed by Christianity constitutes a threat to human achievement.[53] Niebuhr thought that Christian faith provided an especially instructive explanation of this irony:

> The whole drama of human history is under the scrutiny of a divine judge who laughs at human pretensions without being hostile to human aspirations. The laughter at the pretensions is the divine judgment. The judgment is transmuted into mercy if it results in abating the pretensions and in prompting men to a contrite recognition of the vanity of their imagination.[54]

The Lens of Faith

The preceding quote reveals that Niebuhr thought the agnostic error was ignominious and unnecessary, for a proper comprehension of religious faith as trust (as opposed to the spurious notion that ecclesiastical dogma constitutes some kind of knowledge which is comparable to scientific truth) can lead to valuable insights. It is unnecessary to be agnostic, for even though at this time we see through a glass darkly, we can see enough to realize that all is not mysterious or hopeless. Indeed, the prophetic tradition is just as clear in its imperative regarding justice as it is in its reverence for the divine mystery.[55] And it would certainly be unworthy to feign ignorance as an excuse for not pouring oneself into the fight for a tolerable justice in humanity's collective existence.

One of the most memorable expressions of Niebuhr's understanding of belief as trust is found in his sermon on Providence and the two different attitudes about this topic held by two different parishioners in his parish in Detroit.[56]

> One old lady was too preoccupied with self, too aggrieved that Providence should not have taken account of her virtue in failing to protect her against a grievous illness, to be able to face death with any serenity. She was in a constant hysteria of fear and resentment. . . . The other old lady [had experienced many sorrows], but she was particularly grateful for her two daughters and their love; and she faced death with the utmost peace of soul.

The message is clear, and it is repeated numerous times in the Niebuhr corpus: religious faith cannot demand, and must not be thought to yield, any absolute certainties about the mysteries of existence. Above all, it must not be imagined that faith (even faith expressed in virtue) is a guarantee against bewilderment, pain, and death.

There are three specific themes to be explored in this connection. The first involves the validity of myth as a vehicle of truthful understanding. The second has to do with the content of biblical mythology and the secret of its mythopoeic profundity. And the third concerns the significance of the truths thus disclosed for one's comprehension of ethical obligation.

Trust in God—the righteous God of justice and compassion proclaimed by the prophetic tradition and revealed with ultimate power in Jesus as the Christ—can give a believer a partial (but sufficient) revelation of the meaning of life and the duties incumbent upon faithful disciples, as well as a convincing, energizing hope for an even fuller revelation (and an even more complete vindication) of the wisdom and goodness of God at the end of history. In the present, the cosmic drama of the cross constitutes a tangent toward eternity which points to—and underscores—the validity of sacrificial love as the impossible possibility which constantly serves to pull mere order toward justice and justice toward a covenant view of human interaction which is higher than the calculation of quids pro quos outlined in contracts. In the future, it offers a fulfillment of history in which (to combine Niebuhrian with Tillichian language) the contradictions and contingencies of history which express non-being are encompassed in being itself.

In Christianity, these truths are expressed in myth and symbol because there is no other way they might be expressed so richly and powerfully. Niebuhr illustrates what he means by this in a host of passages written at different times in his life, but the point is also made in a story from H. Richard Niebuhr.[57] It is the story of an Englishwoman who came to America to live and work as a writer because of a terrible falling-out with her parents. For years she had no communication whatsoever with her father, even at the time of her mother's death. Then one day she received a letter informing her that her father was coming to visit her in Seattle. By this time her father was in his late seventies and, even though the letter said nothing conciliatory, she guessed that he might be coming to patch things up before he died. So she awaited his arrival with mingled trepidation and hope.

Then he arrived. They shared a meal and took a walk in one of Seattle's many lovely parks. It was a beautiful spring day, and both father and daughter were filled with joy at seeing each another again. They remembered that once, long ago, they had had an awful fight, but that day in the park they couldn't remember why it had seemed so important at the time. Even their regrets about having been alienated from one another for so many years were swallowed up in the happiness they felt at being reunited.

In writing about the experience in her next book, the English author said "I heard a nightingale sing in the park." But a careful reader wrote in to correct her: there are no nightingales in Seattle, Washington. Maybe not, said Richard Niebuhr. Maybe she did not speak scientific truth when she said that she had heard a nightingale sing. But there was no more eloquent way for the Englishwoman to express this most significant and precise "Truth with a capital T" of her inner history. And that is the kind of Truth (as opposed to detailed historical truth) which mythology communicates.

The two most important articulations of these convictions in Reinhold Niebuhr's writings are found in the lead chapter of *Beyond Tragedy* (1937) and in "The Truth in Myths," which appears to be a slightly altered version of the same essay which appeared about the same time.[58] The latter distinguishes between permanent myth and primitive myth, conceding that "religion has no right to insist on the scientific accuracy of its mythical heritage." Having allowed that religion must and should retreat from defense of "that part of mythology which is derived from prescientific thought," Niebuhr goes on to maintain that religion has every right to continue to speak through the still tenable and abiding part of myth which "deals with aspects of reality which are supra-scientific rather than prescientific." He proposes an analogy between religion and art, both of which are "deceivers, yet true" in their presentation of that which is real:

> The problem of the [portrait] artist is to portray the inner consistency of a character which is never fully expressed in any one particular mood or facial expression. This can only be done by falsifying physiognomic details. . . . A moment of time in a personality can be made to express what transcends the moment of time only if the moment is not recorded accurately. It must be made into a symbol of something beyond itself.[59]

A parallel illustration is to be found in Niebuhr's conception of the discipline of history itself, which he regards as more closely akin to mythology than to philosophy. He criticizes three misleading historical myths—those of Progress, traditional Christianity, and Marxism—yet he nonetheless clings to the view that "because modern culture is too empirically rationalistic, it cannot do justice to the very history of which it is a contemporary spectator." Therefore, history must have "a vision of the whole which would give meaning to the specific events it seeks to comprehend . . . [which] is possible only if it is assumed that human history has a meaning." This assumption—of which "modern empiricism is afraid"—is interpreted as an indication that "meaning can be attributed to history only by a mythology."[60]

Christianity as a Source of Mythopoeic Profundity

Students of Niebuhr will forever debate the question of whether his appropriation of a reinterpreted version of biblical faith (which at various times he called Pauline realism, Augustinian realism, or simply a chastened yet passionate apprehension of the gospel) is a kiss of death which amounts to a betrayal of the church. But those who believe instead that it is the best interpretation of Christianity to appear in the twentieth century have a wealth of material to which they can appeal in the form of Niebuhr's own intentions and his own conception of what he had accomplished.[61]

Niebuhr's affirmation of traditional Christian belief was defined—or qualified—by a rather curious and somewhat puzzling concept which he referred to as the "hidden Christ," which is found buried in a footnote of *The Nature and Destiny of Man:*

> While Christians rightly believe that all truth necessary for [a properly sober yet hopeful] spiritual existence is mediated only through the revelation in Christ, they must guard against the assumption that only those who know Christ "after the flesh," that is, in the actual historical revelation, are capable of such a conversion. A "hidden Christ" operates in history. And there is always the possibility that those who do not know the historical revelation may achieve more genuine repentance and humility than those who do.[62]

It may be inaccurate or unfair to suggest that Niebuhr placed his notion of the hidden Christ in a footnote because he saw it as a potentially embarrassing contradiction to the respectably dialectical content of his magnum opus. Niebuhr was by no means a stranger to paradox; indeed, he seemed to glory in the multiplication of "both/ and" paragraphs in which the left hand seems to take away a good part of what the right hand has just delivered. In any case, he balances his ostensible acceptance of his own version of the scandalously particularistic fundamentals of orthodox Christian faith with his universalism by declaring that the truths of revelation are confirmed by (and, apparently, available in) perennial human experience. But he also maintains that these truths are best expressed through biblical mythology:

> Though human knowledge and experience always point to a source of meaning in life which transcends knowledge and experience, there are nevertheless suggestions of the character of this transcendence in experience. Great myths have actually been born out of profound experience and are constantly subject to verification by experience. It may be simplest to illustrate this point in terms of a specific religious doctrine, the Christian doctrine that God is love and that love is the highest moral ideal.
>
> The ideal of love is not a caprice of mythology. It is not true because the cross has revealed it. The cross justifies itself to human faith because it symbolizes an ideal which establishes points of relevance with the deepest experiences and insights in human life.[63]

As noted above, Niebuhr likens religious myths to the brushstrokes in a painting, where combinations of color and textures which do not represent reality accurately when viewed too closely, nevertheless create a striking impression of some view of truthful reality when viewed at the proper distance and in the right perspective.[64]

It should be reiterated, incidentally, that it is not only the Christ of faith but also the Jesus of history who is important for Niebuhr. In the mid-1950s, in a piece called "How My Mind Has Changed," Niebuhr wrote:

> The actual wisdom of the man Jesus is worth searching for, I believe, even though modern biblical criticism makes it more and more difficult to distinguish the actual sayings and attitudes of Jesus from what is attributed to him in the *kerygma*. It is yet possible to have a vivid impression of the man Jesus who condemned those "who do all their works to be seen of men." I

think this Jesus of the prophetic tradition is important, though I
believe in . . . the Christ of the faith which brought the Church
into being and which, broadly stated, rests on the idea that the
drama of Christ's life and death and resurrection is more than the
tragic death of a noble hero; it is a drama in which the human
situation and the divine mystery are ultimately and definitively
revealed.[65]

Once again, illustrations and elaborations of the general point
abound. One of the most intriguing articulations of the partic-
ularity/universality theme is incorporated into the argument of what
Niebuhr himself called his "most Marxist book," *Reflections on the
End of an Era*.[66] In the chapter entitled "Assurance of Grace," he
writes:

Essentially the experience of grace in religion is the apprehension
of the absolute from the perspective of the relative. The un-
achieved is in some sense felt to be achieved or realized. The sinner is "justified" even though his sin is not overcome. The
world, as revealed in its processes of nature, is known to be im-
perfect and yet it is recognized as a creation of God. Man is regarded as both a sinner and a child of God. In these paradoxes
true religion makes present reality bearable even while it insists
that God is denied, frustrated and defied in the immediate situation.

In Jesus' religio-poetic conceptions of life and the world, [there
is present a conception] of a God who, in spite of his transcendence, does not negate the forces of nature but reveals himself in
them . . . . The whole world process is endowed with spiritual
meaning which reveals both the judgments and the mercy of
God. In this imaginative insight the relation of the assurance of
forgiveness to the demand for perfection in high religion is revealed at its best. Nothing in conceptions of orthodox and con-
ventional religion approaches this profundity.[67]

What we find here, I submit, is a remarkably edifying and energizing
combination of realistic acceptance of the baffling imperfections of
life and a stirring impetus to co-creative activity. The same posture is
adopted in Niebuhr's famous prayer beseeching serenity as regards
those things one cannot change, courage to improve the things one
can, and wisdom to know the difference. It is a part of the essence of

wisdom to be able to resign oneself to the tragedies of historical contingency without lapsing into hopelessness or inertia. "We are perplexed, but not unto despair," states one of Niebuhr's favorite biblical texts.

> When these problems of man in nature and man in society [these problems of "the semi-conscious cruelties of conscious men" and "'the trampling march of unconscious power'"] are seen as perennial problems of the human spirit, and not merely as injustices of an era, men will have to learn once more that though evil must be resisted there are limits to the possibility of resistance and some evil must be borne. . . . Men will learn that nature can never be completely tamed to do man's will. . . . Then men will see again the importance of accommodating the vision of perfection to an imperfect world without losing the urge to perfect the world . . . [And] the inevitable imperfections of life and history will be borne with the greater serenity if the ego recognizes that the blind forces of nature which frustrate the spirit are in the self as well as outside it.[68]

We should not be surprised that (to use James's pragmatic criterion) the ultimate cash value of the mythopoeic wisdom of Christianity is couched in such a way as to emphasize the ethical vitality which ought to be the fruit of faith. The final paragraph of *Reflections* puts it this way:

> These religious insights guarantee the ethically striving soul a measure of serenity and provide the spiritual relaxation without which all moral striving generates a stinking sweat of self-righteousness and an alternation of fanatic illusions and fretful disillusionments. Naturally it is not easy to preserve a decent balance between the ethical urge to realize perfection in history and the religious need of reconciliation with imperfection. In particular periods of history one will devour the other. Sometimes the ethical urge will degenerate into an illusion-crammed ethical utopianism; at other times religious insights will betray the soul into a premature peace with and transcendence over the world's imperfections. But the human spirit will always discover in time that sanity and wholesomeness are possible only when two partially incompatible and partially supplementary attitudes toward life are both embraced and espoused. Then it will find its way back to the profound mythologies which do justice to both; and

it will disavow not only the moribund religion which solves the problem of the spirit in nature by magic but also the superficial rational moralism which dreams of gaining a quick and easy victory of the spirit over nature.[69]

This passage should be read in connection with the famous conclusion of *Moral Man and Immoral Society,* where Niebuhr bluntly asserts that the "most effective agents" of social redemption "will be men who have substituted some new illusions for [those they have] abandoned." The most important of these is the illusion "that the collective life of mankind can achieve perfect justice." Niebuhr admits that this illusion "is dangerous because it encourages terrible fanaticisms," and it "must therefore be brought under the control of reason." Nevertheless, he comments (in the very last sentence of the book) that one "can only hope that reason will not destroy it before its work is done."[70]

This rather astonishing passage is echoed in even more extravagant terms in an earlier chapter of *Moral Man in Immoral Society,* where Niebuhr contends that "without the ultrarational hopes and passions of religion no society will ever have the courage to conquer despair and attempt the impossible" (i.e., realization of "the vision of a just society," which is impossible but "can be approximated only by those who do not regard it as impossible"). He concludes:

> The truest visions of religion are illusions, which may be partially realized by being resolutely believed. For what religion believes to be true is not wholly true but ought to be true; and may become true if its truth is not doubted.[71]

What is especially striking (and important) in this comparison is that, sometime during the two years between *Moral Man in Immoral Society* and *Reflections on the End of an Era,* Niebuhr changed his mind about two things. He came to see that the dangers of fanaticism were so great as to demand debunking of the hope for a perfect society in history, and that the disarming of illusion could be better accomplished through the mythopoeic wisdom of religion than through reason alone. As Dennis McCann observes, "Experience [soon] convinced Niebuhr that the perils of fanaticism in fact were greater than the pitfalls of compromise."[72] One can see the change quite vividly by comparing the passage just quoted with certain passages in *An Interpretation of Christian Ethics* (also published in 1934) where

Niebuhr ridicules the Social Gospel preachers who cling to illusory hopes for social transformation. He pokes fun at the "love perfectionism" of sentimentalists such as Shailer Mathews, whose point of view is satirized as follows:

> Christianity, in other words, is interpreted as the preaching of a moral ideal, which men do not follow, but which they ought to. The Church must continue to hope for something that has never happened.[73]

He goes on to attack several of the Social Gospelers whom he has been savaging:

> The unvarying refrain of the liberal Church in its treatment of politics is that love and cooperation are superior to conflict and coercion, and that therefore they must and will be established. The statement of the ideal is regarded as a sufficient guarantee of its ultimate realization.[74]

We know something of the importance Niebuhr attached to the need for a level-headed assessment of any cause by virtue of the fact that in later years he admitted being embarrassed by his earlier embrace of the functional value of illusion. He then advances a concept of the "aesthetic motif in religion" which transcends illusion.[75]

An Evaluation of Niebuhr's Notion of Myth

The changes taking place in Niebuhr's thought during these years are tremendously important for understanding the nature of Christian Realism. A close reading of the passages just cited will show that his return to a more sympathetic view of traditional Christian belief is anything but a cold-blooded functionalist decision to use familiar religious symbols and ecclesiastical language in a disingenuous way to perpetrate a pious fraud. On the contrary, by 1934 Reinhold Niebuhr had decided that the most significant truths concerning human nature and destiny were best expressed in the biblical drama of Jesus as the Christ. These truths were confirmed by human experience, and to some extent they could be *discerned* by reflective persons whose moral imagination was informed by the "hidden Christ" rather than the Christian Church, but these ontologically valid truths could most readily (and most powerfully) be grasped through biblical mythology. It follows that Niebuhr had a deep intuitive understanding of the importance of feeling in religious belief:

> The human story [is] too grand and too awful to be told without
> reverence for the mystery and the majesty that transcend all hu-
> man knowledge. . . . Only humble men who recognize this
> mystery and majesty are able to face both the beauty and terror
> of life without exulting over its beauty or becoming crushed by
> its terror."[76]

A PIOUS FRAUD?

Bronislaw Malinowski regarded religion as a "necessary pragmatic figment" of the cultural imagination which was indispensable
for a healthy society.[77] In terms of the theory of the social construc-
tion of reality made popular in recent years by Peter Berger and
Thomas Luckmann, this means that religion provides certain objec-
tivations without which the legitimacy of "our way of doing things"
may not be secure in the minds and hearts of the citizenry. Can
Niebuhr, who eventually came to accept the label of "Christian pragmatism" as an accurate description of his thought, be accused of the
same sort of crass utilitarianism in using Christian ideas and images
for psychocultural purposes which he wanted people to believe in
and act in accordance with?

The concept of the pious fraud—a lie put forward in the interests of some kind of human utility, an immoral means to a morally
desirable end—has intrigued a host of writers over the years. Two of
the most celebrated examples of this theme are embedded in Un-
amuno's story, "San Miguel Bueno, Martyr," and Richard Kim's
novel, *The Martyred*. "San Miguel" is the story of a young Spanish
Communist whose older brother is a priest in a remote village. When
the older brother commits suicide, the villagers are thrown into utter
spiritual confusion. The surviving brother is so touched by the pain
of these unlettered folk that he pretends to become a believer so that
he can replace his brother as their priest, thus restoring their peace of
mind. In *The Martyred,* a community of Korean Christians is saved
from disillusionment and despair through the lies of a minister's son
who conceals the cowardly betrayal of a group of Christian prisoners
by concocting a false narrative about their heroic resistance against
their Communist captors.

Some of Niebuhr's critics accuse him of perpetrating a kind of
pious fraud by his disingenuous remythologizing of traditional belief. In addition to Hauerwas, earnest Catholics often find Niebuhr's
position unsatisfactory—Christopher Wolfe and John Murray Cud-

dihy, in particular. On the basis of what he heard at the Rockford Institute Center on Religion and Society conference (see chapter 1), Wolfe decided that it would be a waste to spend additional time studying Niebuhr's thought. Why? Because, Wolfe says, "Christians have to expect from somebody who claims to provide a Christian social ethic that he or she will be rooted in Christian orthodoxy." But the conclusion Wolfe drew from the conference was that "Niebuhr isn't—and that's why I'm going to look elsewhere for guidance in Christian social ethics and political problems."[78]

There is probably no absolutely compelling way to refute this kind of dismissal, and the same is true (even more true) of the sort of polemical caricature sketched by Cuddihy. People who have other reasons for hating Niebuhr and wanting to discredit him will be drawn to such a denunciation of the man. But there are several kinds of refutation which may be offered.

The first line of defense is to point out that an attack upon a spokesperson's putative motives is an ad hominem argument which has very little bearing on the defensibility or fruitfulness of the intellectual position in question. If Niebuhr's position holds water, it may be argued that it doesn't matter whether or not he was sincere in articulating it.

But this is a minimalist reply which is likely to satisfy neither friends nor critics. Unless the charge of insincerity is answered directly and persuasively, the very possibility that it might be true will seem to taint the position and the person who presents himself as a spokesperson for religion. So a second line of defense will doubtless strike Niebuhr's admirers as far more appropriate and far more convincing—namely, to deny that he is (consciously or unconsciously) putting forth a fraudulent functionalist argument and insist that, on the contrary, he is advocating the deepest convictions of his soul. That very few conference participants gave any credence to Cuddihy's far-fetched account is significant, and many voiced their confident judgment that Niebuhr's religious faith was absolutely genuine. Even Hauerwas agreed that Niebuhr's prayers are stirring: "He never prayed to the congregation; he prayed to God."[79]

In saying this, Hauerwas shows remarkable perspicacity, for he aligns himself with one of Ursula Niebuhr's main arguments in the volume of Niebuhr's prayers and sermons she edited under the title *Justice and Mercy.* The principal thesis of this slender volume is that Niebuhr was always and ever a Christian who believed in and cared about prayer and liturgy (partly, no doubt, because of his Anglican wife). He is portrayed as, above all, a preacher a preacher whose religious convictions were absolutely essential to whatever he said or did in the areas of ethics and politics. Ursula writes: "He confessed to theological students in 1955 that he was 'one who loves preaching more than teaching, a sort of preacher by instinct—no, I won't say by instinct, but by preference.'"

Yet Niebuhr was very much aware of the preacher's temptation to bombast and self-aggrandizement, and this was one of the reasons he believed in the importance of the "priestly function." He urged his audience of pastors to use prayer materials from all prayer-book sources, including prayers written long ago, which "it is well to read . . . for the sake of acquiring a decent style." He says:

> If style may seem an inconsequential matter to passionate
> prophets of the gospel it may be well to remind them that with-
> out it they will merely parade their own personalities and preju-
> dices in prayer. A good style is a cloak of anonymity. That cloak
> is very much needed in our Protestant churches. We preachers
> constantly border on the abyss of exhibitionism.[80]

Emphasis on prayer and liturgy also had something to do with Niebuhr's distaste for "triviality and simple moral absolutes," which he regarded as "the two besetting sins of the preacher."[81]

Anyone who reads what Niebuhr wrote and listens to his re-corded sermons cannot help but agree that his religious faith was entirely authentic. He may, of course, have been wrong in his beliefs, but he was certainly not pretending to believe in order to further some hidden agenda. His is not really a theology in the service of ethics or anything else; it is a passionately held theological world-view in which ethics has an indispensable part and plays an abso-lutely central role.

This matter may be clarified by considering it in light of an exchange which took place in the pages of *Harper's Magazine* in 1959. In a series of articles on contemporary religious faith, the essay on Protestantism was written by William Bartley III, a former editor of the *Harvard Crimson* whose adolescence had led him from Episco-palianism to skepticism and back to a kind of non-ecclesiastical spiri-tualism which was probably closer to Quakerism than anything else. Bartley complained that "neo-orthodox" theologians such as Barth, Tillich, and Niebuhr were disingenuous in their exploitation of traditional religious language. According to Bartley, they read a radically new meaning into familiar Christian concepts and symbols without announcing that they were doing so. His article prompted a response from Huston Smith, an eminent historian of religion, who rejected this charge and in turn accused Bartley of being too simple-minded in his understanding of religious terminology. Smith pointed out that every major world religion has been interpreted in different ways by different kinds of people at different levels of learning and sophistication in various cultures at various times in history. Therefore, there is nothing at all shocking or inappropriate about the fact that when a hundred churchgoers join in reciting the Apostles' Creed at the same service, each of those hundred worshipers may attribute a different meaning to the words of the creed.[82]

IS NIEBUHR'S APOLOGETIC TOO WISHY-WASHY?

The concern about Niebuhr's possible disingenuousness may be related to the question of whether his espousal of Christian mythology is too mushy to be significant. If everything is advanced as a both/and proposition in which nothing is asserted without being surrounded by qualifications, what becomes of the *thrust* of the argument? (Those who feel this way about Niebuhr's style may be reminded of Paul Van Buren's story concerning the God who was felled by "the death of a thousand qualifications."[83])

It is certainly easy for the relatively uninitiated reader to be annoyed by Niebuhr's fondness for paradox and to be occasionally puzzled by the frequency with which he resorts to a form of rhetoric which says "on the one hand this, but on the other hand that." But the more familiar one becomes with the substance of Niebuhr's thought, the more one realizes that these features of his prose are not merely a stylistic quirk. On the contrary, they are a necessary part of the explanation he is constrained to give of the complicated realities of the moral and spiritual life. It is not meaningless to describe love as "an impossible possibility"; it is a way of pointing out that no complete actualization of love can ever be attained by sinful humans. Such an actualization of the ideal in society is not the best way to conceive of the goal one ought to pursue. But the ideal is nonetheless relevant as a spur to one's best effort at approximating the ideal or moving toward the goal.

Part of Niebuhr's fondness for myth stems from his awareness of the limitations of pure logic and the futility of much scholastic hair-splitting. I believe the wisdom of Niebuhr's position can be better appreciated if we examine Albert Schweitzer's reply to a friend who questioned him about apparent inconsistencies in his thought. Oskar Kraus, a professor of philosophy at the University of Prague, rebuked Schweitzer for sounding like an orthodox Christian in many of his writings but then using an entirely different vocabulary and seeming to be a pantheist in other published works. Kraus besought Schweitzer to be honest with his readers by explaining his position once and for all: Christian or non-Christian? Theist or pantheist?

Schweitzer began his answer by accusing Kraus of the same kind of small-minded oversimplification William Bartley was to exhibit several decades later. Schweitzer said that the reality of which he spoke was so real and powerful that it didn't make any difference whether he referred to it as "God" or as "Universal Will-to-Live." So when he was addressing a Christian audience, he spoke of God and Jesus, for those were terms that audience could understand. On the other hand, when he was writing a philosophy of civilization and trying to reach philosophers, he used non-theistic terms. The ideas about the reality were important; the labels put upon that reality and the semantic vehicles employed were of little consequence.[84]

IS "MYTHOPOEIC PROFUNDITY," AFTER ALL, AN ILLUSION?

The most radical question is that posed by the cynical skeptic who doubts the truthfulness of any mythological expression of faith in Providence, no matter how sincerely held or nobly motivated. If all religious ideas are nothing but illusory wishful thinking (or fear), then proclaiming that truth may be the essence of goodness (even if the truth, by our feeble standards, is painfully ugly).

This, too, is a theme which has fascinated many a literary virtuoso. According to George Bernard Shaw, Ibsen is a ruthless opponent of "the claim of the ideal" which was so often glorified by nineteenth-century European intellectuals, and he satirizes dishonest, self-serving, and self-aggrandizing appeals to heroism which really fortify untruth and illusion in many of his plays (notably *Brand, An Enemy of the People,* and *The Wild Duck*). Eugene O'Neill takes a more compassionate view (or is it more cynical?) in *The Iceman Cometh,* where the loss of one's pipedreams about one's worth and possibilities for achievement is equated with death.

Here again it is impossible to dismiss the challenge of the skeptics with absolute certainty that their charges are totally groundless;

they probably aren't. And one of the virtues of Niebuhr's realism is the fact that he constantly warns against self-deception and urges us to admit that everyone, even the noblest among us, is often driven in this direction by pride or sloth. But the other side of the coin is that the will-to-believe may be a force for redemption as well a source of obfuscation and deceit. In his famous essay on this subject, William James pointed out that the will-to-believe may frequently be an indispensable factor in enabling us to make use of our best resources and mobilize our energies for the best performance of which we are capable. It is possible, of course, to treat religious belief as an instrumental good which one adopts in order to produce the desired consequences in performance, and this is the caricature of liberal Protestantism in twentieth-century America which is belittled in H. Richard Niebuhr's famous remark about "a God without judgment who redeems man without sin through the agency of a Christ without a Cross." But now we are back to the notion of pious fraud, and I can only reiterate my judgment that the weight of the evidence in Niebuhr's life and thought simply will not sustain such a charge.

I conclude with a comment on the relevance of Niebuhr's use of myth for some of the most widely discussed philosophical issues of the day. At a time when we are beset with a powerful yearning for lost certitude, it may be helpful to reappropriate the wisdom of Niebuhr's elegant conception of religious faith. It is all well and good to acknowledge the importance of the questions raised by writers such as Bellah, MacIntyre, Hauerwas, and Bloom, and to join in their quest for a conception of the nature and destiny of humankind with teleological substance. But we must not succumb to their insistence that we return in a too-simple way to the eternal verities as encapsulated in Aristotelian virtue, traditional notions of Christian character, or the Great Books. Niebuhr's balanced view of the combined sinfulness and creativity of a creature who is, in fact, made in the image of God and therefore destined to co-creative activity aimed at forging a tolerably just society is a splendid golden mean between the too-narrow essentialism of the right and the cynical, self-indulgent, and socially irresponsible nihilism of the left.[85]

Niebuhr, in clergy attire, around the publication of *Moral Man and Immoral Society* (1932)

Niebuhr as a Union Theological Seminary
professor in the 1930s

Professor Niebuhr with a student at Union Theological Seminary

Niebuhr and his poodles Vicky and Winnie (named after Winston Churchill) in the mid-1950s

Niebuhr ca. 1960

Niebuhr in his seventies

Niebuhr and long-time colleague John Bennett in 1966

Chapter 4

Guidelines for Ends and Means

Reinhold Niebuhr was not simply a theologian who was preoccupied with the human soul and its relationship to God. He was equally concerned with relationships among human beings. So one of the signal contributions of Christian Realism is its analysis of the proper ends to be sought and the appropriate means to be used by wise social reformers. With regard to goals, Niebuhr argues against both the soft utopianism of the Social Gospel and the hard utopianism of Communism. The key argument is that justice (defined as mutual rather than sacrificial love) is the most relevant moral ideal in social ethics, and that social reform goals should be envisioned in such terms. With regard to means, Niebuhr's celebrated realism comes to the fore: he warns "the children of light" against assuming that they possess a superior virtue which sets them apart from and above "the children of darkness" against whom they see themselves arrayed. He advises those who aspire to do the Lord's work on earth to be realistic about their need to develop and use power in struggling to promote justice in the relentless ambiguity of the human situation.

Salient Principles and Goals

One of the most significant aspects of Niebuhr's intellectual work is his analysis of the normative principles which ought to govern the quest for the optimally humane society. In contrast to more idealistic approaches, Niebuhr arrives at a less utopian definition of the goals of social reform, and a more tough-minded analysis of the means to be used in pursuing them. The Niebuhrian analysis presents itself, first of all, as an exposition of the meaning and significance of societal norms such as order, justice-love, and community.

ORDER

Like Machiavelli and Luther before him, Niebuhr was realistic in regarding order as the most fundamental prerequisite of a civilized society. His insight on this point is linked to his awareness of the realistic requirements of power and a balance of power in any viable human collectivity. Tyranny is a condition in which there is too much order (or an illegitimate kind and degree of order), and it is rather unstable: unjust order soon collapses and reverts to insufferable disorder. The extreme opposite of tyranny is anarchy, which (as the social contract theorists observed) is apt to be a "war of all against all." Although Niebuhr's main focus in social ethics after the 1930s is on politics rather than economics, it is apparent in all of his books and articles that he recognizes how indispensable it is for any civilized society to have order in its mobilization of its resources in consistent productivity. Without this ordering of collective effort, people will starve, freeze to death, succumb to natural disasters and human enemies, or live at a subhuman subsistence level.

Power does tend to corrupt, and absolute power may corrupt absolutely, but there is nothing intrinsically evil about power, and lack of power can also corrupt. The fact is, writes Niebuhr: "All social cooperation on a larger scale than the most intimate social group requires a measure of coercion." Why? Because the inability of all persons "to transcend their own interests sufficiently to envisage the interests of their fellowmen as clearly as they do their own makes force an inevitable part of the process of social cohesion."[1]

It follows, then, that no just (or even stable) order can be maintained without the presence of "two aspects of social power . . . the coercive and organizing power of government" and "the balance of vitalities and forces in any given social situation." According to Niebuhr:

> These two elements of communal life—the central organizing
> power, and the equilibrium of power—are essential and perennial
> aspects of community organization, and no moral or social ad-

vance can redeem society from its dependence upon these two principles.[2]

Yet each of these necessary ingredients in collective life is subject to abuse. The former may drift toward tyranny; the latter all too easily degenerates into anarchy. Niebuhr writes: "These twin evils, tyranny and anarchy, represent the Scylla and Charybdis between which the frail bark of justice must sail. It is almost certain to founder upon one rock if it makes the mistake of regarding the other as the only peril."[3] It is the essential task of "conscious political contrivance" to devise mechanisms for steering a middle course:

> While no society can maintain its health if the individuals who compose it do not have some sense of responsibility for their fellow men, it is also true that no society could live if it did not harness, equilibrate and deflect, as well as sublimate and suppress, self-interest. Human society is partly an artful contrivance which enables men to serve one another indirectly, even though their primary motives may be to serve themselves.[4]

And it is the statesperson who plays the role of "artful contriver" by avoiding tyranny through "balancing the vitalities, powers, interests of life into a tolerable equilibrium." To avoid anarchy, "some one, some class, some government, some nation, or some group of nations" must have more authority than others," and there is no way to obliterate entirely "the distinction between the rulers and the ruled." Yet the ruled must be given "the chance to check the rulers, [for] where there are rulers, there may also be tyrants."[5]

The relationship between a balancing of powers and justice is crucial. Any idealistic social theory which imagines that the need for power in the hands of organizing authority can be eliminated is naive and sentimental.

> All political community and justice are achieved by coercing the anarchy of collective self-interest into some kind of decent order by the most attainable balance of power. Such a balance, once achieved, can be stabilized, embellished, and even, upon occasion, perfected by more purely moral considerations. But there has never been a scheme of justice in history which did not have a balance of power at its foundation.[6]

Niebuhr also stresses that, unless order is legitimated by justice (or characterized by a sufficient degree of justice to legitimate it in the eyes of the populace), it will not endure long.

JUSTICE-LOVE

It may seem awkward to speak of "justice-love" instead of defining and discussing these enormously complicated concepts separately. But creating the compound word serves an important purpose here because Niebuhr's argument concerning the dialectical relationship between justice and love shows how misleading it can be to separate them. "Justice-love" as a term is similar to that of "equal justice," another Niebuhrian term which is intended to remind us that justice cannot really be just (i.e., benevolently respectful of particular human beings and beneficently fair to their particular needs) unless its understanding of these persons and its definition of their needs are continually being pulled upward by love. Both terms make essentially the same point, as Niebuhr's discussion of equal justice reveals:

> The perpetual recurrence of the principle of equality in social
> theory is a refutation of purely pessimistic conceptions of human
> nature, whether secular or religious. Its influence proves that
> men do not simply use social theory to rationalize their own in-
> terest. Equality as a pinnacle of the ideal of justice implicitly
> points toward love as the final norm of justice; for equal justice is
> the approximation of brotherhood under the conditions of sin. A
> higher justice always means a more equal justice.[7]

The concept of justice-love underlies the central argument of Niebuhr's chapter on "the relevance of an impossible ideal" in *An Interpretation of Christian Ethics*. Two of the relevancies assigned to love in this chapter have to do with its effect on the mood of the moral agent and on its possible effect on his or her sense of vocation. By showing us how far short of the ideal all human striving falls, love drives every sensitive spirit toward repentance and humility. Moreover, it drives some Christians away from the ambiguities of politics altogether so that they can bear witness to the truth of the gospel by seeking to exemplify love as purely as possible. This second mode of taking the impossible ideal seriously defines the vocational pacifism Niebuhr admired—that is, the kind which did not imagine that it could be successful in putting an end to war, yet stood as a constant rebuke to the inhumanity of war. The third kind of relevance of the love ideal is the most important: it pulls our aspirations upward by providing a measuring standard which, although it is in itself unattainable, nonetheless helps us decide which of the available realistic options is best.[8]

Niebuhr's view of justice is not that of a philosophical analyst or political scientist who conceptualizes justice primarily as a matter of individual rights and rules. It is, rather, a biblical notion of justice-love in which the rights and duties implicit in the concept of justice are intuited by a Christ-informed conscience. Christians who are grateful for the love and forgiveness of God are expected to want to act lovingly toward their neighbors: "We love because He first loved us." Niebuhr's lectures in Christian ethics reveal a deep admiration for the doctrine of radical stewardship in the early church fathers, whose declaration that "the cloak in your closet belongs to your neighbor" shows the uncalculating generosity of Christian love, and also for Luther's appeal for spontaneous generosity in his *Treatise on Usury*.[9]

This disinclination toward rational calculation of exact rights and obligations (as carried out, for example, in the manner of contemporary philosophy or jurisprudence) is viewed as a shortcoming by some of Niebuhr's critics, who allege that: "Niebuhr's ethics leaves the Christian caught between two worlds with two ultimate norms, 'distraught and divided in all ethical decision.'"[10] To those who believe that ethics ought to be a science, this criticism has some plausibility. But in the mind of the Christian ethicist who believes that the best kind of ethics is an art which transcends the rigidities of science, Niebuhr's analysis of justice-love will be viewed as profound rather than fuzzy, and its realism about the dialectical complementarity of justice and love will be seen as a crucial element in its profundity.

A synonym Niebuhr sometimes uses for justice is "mutual love." The purpose of the adjective is to warn against the error of assuming that perfectly disinterested love (agape, sacrificial love) can be consistently experienced or realized in human society. Niebuhr introduces one of the greatest sections of the entire corpus ("Laws and Principles of Justice," *The Destiny of Man,* pp. 247–256) with an eloquent commentary on this point:

> Mutual love (in which disinterested concern for the other elicits a
> reciprocal response) is the highest possibility of history in the

sense that only such love is justified by historical consequences but also that such love can only be initiated by a type of disinterestedness (sacrificial love) which dispenses with historical justification. Thus the pinnacle of the moral ideal stands both inside and beyond history: inside in so far as love may elicit a reciprocal response without losing its character of disinterestedness; and beyond history in so far as love cannot require a mutual response without losing its character of disinterestedness. The love commandment is therefore no simple historical possibility. The full implications of the commandment illustrate the dialectical relation between history and the eternal.[11]

This preamble sets the stage for Niebuhr's famous analysis of love as both law and transcendent ideal. It also leads to a discussion of the sense in which justice is linked to and expresses "the spirit of brotherhood" in human collectivities:

Systems and principles of justice are the servants and instruments of the spirit of brotherhood in so far as they extend the sense of obligation towards the other, (a) from an immediately felt obligation, prompted by obvious need, to a continued obligation expressed in fixed principles of mutual support; (b) from a simple relation between a self and one 'other' to the complex relations of the self and the "others"; and (c) finally from the obligations, discerned by the individual self, to the wider obligations which the community defines from its more impartial perspective.[12]

The inseparability of love and justice is further explained in a parallel passage which follows immediately in the subsequent paragraph:

Rules and laws of justice stand in a positive relation to the law of love [in the three ways alluded to above]. . . . An immediately felt obligation towards obvious need may be prompted by the emotion of pity. But a continued sense of obligation rests upon and expresses itself in rational calculations of the needs of others as compared with our own interests. A relation between the self and one other may be partly ecstatic; and in any case the calculation of relative interests may be reduced to a minimum. But as soon as a third person is introduced into the relation even the most perfect love requires a rational estimate of conflicting needs and interests. Even the love within a family avails itself of customs and usages which stereotype given adjustments between various members of the family in such a way that each action need not be oriented by a fresh calculation of competing interests.[13]

There are, in fact, two special dimensions of love which must be explained in order to clarify what Niebuhr means by justice as the most relevant ethical ideal in social and political life: self-love, and love as law.

Self-Love

For Niebuhr, ethical concern is rooted in "the law of love," an imperative which is in part natural to man and in part necessitated by the sinfulness of men. On the one hand, "[C]ommunity is an individual as well as social necessity; for the individual can realize himself only in intimate and organic relation with his fundamental requirement of his social existence."[14] In another context, Niebuhr says that the will-to-live can be spiritualized in two forms—either as the will-to-power or as the will-to-devote-oneself-to-others, the latter being the "will-to-live-truly."[15]

Auden exclaims: "We must love one another or die."[16] This is particularly true in this "age of technics," which has "confronted men with the problem of relating their lives to a larger number of fellowmen." The inescapable fact is that "the task of creating community and avoiding anarchy is constantly pitched on broader and broader levels."[17]

But if one accepts the law of love as an imperative, if one seeks to live truly by devoting oneself to others, where does one draw the line between self-devotion and self-annihilation? What is the place of self-love in the life of an ethical person?

On the one hand, of course, it certainly cannot be ignored:

> To understand the law of love as a final imperative, but not to know about the persistence of the power of self-love in all of life, but particularly in the collective relations of mankind, results in an idealistic ethic with no relevance to the hard realities of life.[18]

On the other hand, however, "to know about the power of self-love but not to know that its power does not make it normative is to dispense with ethical standards and fall into cynicism."[19]

There is no simple solution to this dilemma. It is naive to say that the power of self-love can be completely overcome and self-devotion made into a "successful" social ethic merely by saying that love "ought" to work in social and personal life. Even a religious conversion, a "decision for Christ" as the symbol of the impossible possibility of agape, cannot overcome the power of self-love utterly. When Jesus says that God makes his rain to fall upon the just and the unjust, "[N]othing is said about the possibility of transmuting their enmity to friendship through the practice of forgiveness," and liberal Christianity has no right to read such a "social and prudential possibility into the admonition of Jesus."[20] A similar error is found in the "love perfectionism" of Shailer Mathews, as seen in his declaration to the effect that "the emphasis laid by the gospel upon the giving of justice rather than upon the getting of justice is consonant with life as we know it." Mathews is also wrong in contending that violent revolutions "have seldom, if ever, won more rights than the more thoughtful among the privileged would have been ready to give."[21]

On the other hand, it is equally naive to contend, as psychologists such as Erich Fromm do, that love is "a phenomenon of abundance" which blossoms forth when a person is secure in the satisfaction of his own desires for love and fulfillment. Unfortunately, there is no such thing as simple satisfaction of human desires: a person always wants more of whatever it is he or she desires.[22]

In one of the most noteworthy passages he ever penned, Niebuhr concludes that

> [t]o know both the law of love as the final standard and the law of self-love as a persistent force is to enable the Christian to have a foundation for a pragmatic ethic in which power and self-interest are used, beguiled, harnessed and deflected for the ultimate end of establishing the highest and most inclusive community of justice and order. This is the very heart of the problem of Christian politics: the readiness to use power and interest in the service of an end dictated by love, and yet an absence of complacency about the evil inherent in them.[23]

The depth and persistence of self-love necessitates law, not only in society but also within the soul of the individual. The former is treated in the discussion of means later in this chapter. The latter can be explained as an essential component of conscience.

Law in the Conscience of Individuals

The question of law in the conscience of individuals is a question of balancing the push of duty and the pull of grace.[24] On the one hand, the push of duty is not strong enough. Kant was wrong in declaring, "I ought, therefore I can." Yet the pull of grace (i.e., a spontaneous desire to subordinate one's own interests to the interests of others) is not sufficient. Freedom from the law (duty) is an experience which comes only occasionally. "It certainly does not describe the ongoing experience of even the most consecrated Christian," writes Niebuhr.[25]

Confirmation of this insight can be found in the parable of the Rich Young Ruler. What is commanded here is "a state of heart and mind, a harmony between the soul and God, a harmony within the soul, and a harmony between the self and the neighbor which, if attained, would exclude all commandment." But the implication is clear:

> This harmony is not a reality. If it were a reality the "thou shalt" would be meaningless. If there were not some possibility of sensing the ultimate perfection in a state of sin the "thou shalt" would be irrelevant. . . .
>
> What is demanded is an action in which regard for the self is completely eliminated. . . . [But] all simple moralism, which assumes that the law of life needs only to be stated in order to be obeyed, is refuted by the response of the rich young ruler to this demand: "He went away sorrowful, for he had great possessions."[26]

It is clear, then, that law is a sine qua non in the conscience of a Christian, and that obedience to specific moral "oughts," regardless of subjective feelings is a necessary part of the Christian life. Although a sense of duty is not so powerful as moralistic preachers sometimes assume, it is by no means impotent, or downright self-defeating. Brunner is wrong when he reverses the aforementioned Kantian dictum by declaring, "If I ought, I cannot."[27] Niebuhr views the problem of love and law in the individual's heart as "the relation of love to the sum and total of all law and of love as defining indeterminate possibilities, transcending law."[28]

Transcendence is possible in a number of ways. For one thing, the freedom of humans over every historic situation means that obligation cannot be limited to partial communities of nature and history, to family, tribe, or nation.[29] Moreover, "the freedom of the self over itself as contingent object in nature and history means that there is a dimension of human existence in which preservation of the self in history becomes problematic."[30] To say this is to affirm the significance of sacrificial love, which is both the completion and the annulment of the law. It is completion because perfect love has no logical limit short of the point of complete readiness to sacrifice itself for the self of the other. It is annulment because the necessity for sacrifice cannot be formulated as an obligation, for "law in the determinate sense must stop with distributive justice and mutual love."[31] Yet sacrificial love cannot be separated too neatly from eros and philia, for

> without an element of heedless love, every form of mutual love would degenerate into a calculation of mutual advantages and every calculation of such advantages would finally generate resentment about an absence of perfect reciprocity.[32]

So Niebuhr's vision of justice-love identifies mutual love as the highest good possible for sinful humanity within history. Mutual love must always be drawn upward by the ideal of altruistic love which points to indeterminate possibilities for good, but realistic hopes for social betterment must be content with conceptualizing goals in terms of mutual love instead of sacrificial love or perfect community.

> Only in mutual love, in which the concern of one person for the interest of another prompts and elicits a reciprocal affection, are the social demands of historical existence satisfied. The highest good of history must conform to standards of coherence and consistency in the whole realm of historical vitality. All claims within the general field of interests must be proportionately satisfied and related to each other harmoniously.[33]

Niebuhr's analysis of the relationship between sacrificial and mutual love is exactly parallel to the preceding analysis of love and justice. On the one hand, mutual love is superior to sacrificial love as a social/historical principle because sacrificial love transcends history.[34] Sacrificial love "rises above history and seeks conformity to the Divine love rather than harmony with other human interests and vitalities. This harmony is a desirable end of historical striving, but it can never be a final norm."[35] Thus sacrificial love constitutes "a tangent toward 'eternity' in the field of historical ethics."[36] On the other hand, though, it should never be thought that sacrificial love, because unrealistic as a regularized norm, is irrelevant to historical events and striving within history, for it is an essential component of effective mutuality. Agape is the indispensable support of all historical ethics, for

> the self cannot achieve relations of mutual and reciprocal affection with others if the actions are dominated by the fear that they will not be reciprocated. Mutuality is not a possible achievement if it is made the intention and goal of any action. Sacrificial love is thus paradoxically related to mutual love; and this relation is an ethical counterpart of the general relation of super-history to history.[37]

In other words, mutual love "can only be initiated by a type of disinterestedness [sacrificial love] which dispenses with historical justification."[38]

Means

The reality of sin makes law concerning duties a necessity in the spiritual life of each individual, and the even more complicated and virulent sinfulness of collective life makes legal statutes a necessary means to tolerable justice in the social realm. Because the effectiveness of laws is a function of the degree to which they are enforced, any discussion of means must also include a commentary on power.

POSITIVE LAW AND COMMUNITY

The negative role of the state in preventing fraud, theft, and personal injury is too obvious to need explanation. More interesting for our purposes is the rationale Niebuhr gives for the positive role of the state in promoting justice by setting up structures and processes which enable people to be true to their own best intuitions by acknowledging their obligations to fellow citizens and by carrying them out. Understanding this ingredient of Niebuhr's thought leads to an examination of his notion of the relationship between law and the historical experience of a given people, whom shared experience has to some extent made into a community of shared assumptions, customs, and values.

Law—and effective observance of law—presupposes a certain sense of community which unites a people by promoting what

Durkheim emphasized as the "collective conscience." Law cannot create this psycho-social reality, but law is necessary for its implementation. Positive law (or social contracts of any kind) do not of themselves make a coherent society. Prior to law are the "existing and developing forces and vitalities of the community," in which what Niebuhr calls "social coalescence" is a major factor.[39] But given this base of legitimation, specific legal enactments can be (and can be perceived as being) "the instruments of the conscience of the community, seeking to subdue the potential anarchy of forces and interests into a tolerable harmony."[40] Negatively, the function of positive law is to prevent anarchy (by establishing order) and tyranny (by safeguarding freedom).[41] Positively, its function is to restrict freedom and mold order in such a way as to provide justice. It does this to a considerable extent by expressing what people themselves already acknowledge to be fair and reasonable when they are "at their best" in understanding their status as citizens of a commonwealth. As Niebuhr observes,

> The fact that various conceptions of a just solution of a common problem can be finally synthesized [by various individuals, groups and classes] into a common solution . . . refutes [thoroughgoing] pessimism, and with it the purely negative conception of the relation of government and systems of justice to the ideal of brotherhood.[42]

Consider, for example, what Niebuhr refers to as "the development of social conscience on the community's sense of obligation to the unemployed." On the one hand, financially secure people are willing to donate a certain portion of their money to the unemployed

> partly [as] an expression of the sense of obligation of the more privileged members of the community toward those who are less fortunate. They find an advantage in meeting this obligation according to fixed principles instead of relying upon their own occasional feeling of pity for this or that needy person. They know furthermore that their own knowledge of comparative needs is very inadequate and that they require the more impartial and comprehensive perspective of the total community, functioning through its proper agencies.[43]

On the other hand, "the benefits which are paid to the unemployed are almost always higher than the privileged would like to pay, even though they may be lower than the poor would like to receive." As a result, "the actual schedule of payments upon which the community finally decides represents the conclusions of the social, rather than any individual, mind, and is . . . a compromise between conflicting viewpoints and interests."[44] It certainly should not be imagined that payments of this kind, decided upon through the actual political and administrative mechanisms of a given society, constitutes "an unconditionally 'just' solution of the social problem involved." This is true, in part, because "the privileged may in fact accept [the burden of paying their share] for no better reason than that they fear the revolt of the poor."[45]

But the outcome is satisfactory in principle, for the solution arrived at through the political process "may become a generally accepted social standard; and some privileged members of the community may welcome it because it expresses their considered sense of social obligation upon which they would prefer to rely rather than upon the momentary power of pity."[46] Some poor people may in fact receive less than they would "by appealing to a given sensitive and opulent individual." However, the poor as a whole (and the overwhelming majority of all poor individuals) "will certainly receive more than if all of them were dependent upon nothing but vagrant, momentary and capricious impulses of pity, dormant unless awakened by obvious need."[47]

Niebuhr concludes:

> This positive relation between rules of justice and the law of love
> must be emphasized in opposition to sentimental versions of the
> love commandment, according to which only the most personal,
> individual and direct expressions of social obligation are mani-
> festations of Christian agape. Both sectarian and Lutheran an-
> alyses of the relation of love to justice easily fall into the error of
> excluding rules of justice from the domain of love.[48]

LOVE AS A FORCE THAT PUSHES BEYOND LAW

It is also true that "laws and systems of justice . . . have a negative as well as a positive relation to mutual love and brotherhood."[49] In the first place, justice falls short of love because of "the sinful element in all social reality." It is never possible to do more than approximate justice to the conflicting claims of individual men, and "a harmony achieved through justice is therefore only an approximation of brotherhood."[50] Furthermore, even this hope is endangered by "the contingent and finite character of rational estimates of rights and interests and by the taint of passion and self-interest upon calculations of the rights of others." And this fact forces us to acknowledge that "there is no universal reason in history."[51]

We are further forced to acknowledge the severe limitations of the concept of natural law. It is true that there are certain universal principles regarding justice which may be discerned from intuition and an examination of history, and these principles are extremely important in framing good positive law.[52] These principles can be classified under three main headings: (1) certain minimal and negative applications of the law of love, such as prohibitions on murder and the principle of monogamy; (2) applications of the law of love in particular situations, such as the injunction against lying; and (3) "transcendent principles of justice which float between love and justice," such as the concepts of liberty and equality. But these universal principles can never be seen or stated clearly enough in the law code of any particular nation at any particular time in history to justify the absolutizing of a humanly codified statement of natural law. What Roman Catholic moral theology calls natural law and positive law are both formulated in the partial perspective of a given age or group and are, therefore, finally relative.[53]

POWER

Christian Realism claims to bring about greater effectiveness in achieving ethically valuable goals by its honest (and accurate) acceptance of the inevitable role of power in determining what happens and does not happen in the life of any collectivity. It argues that the common good of various individuals and groups will be most justly served if no single individual, group, or set of groups has disproportionate power. Thus it contends that the "strategy of democracy" is the best means to establish a tolerably good society and conduct its affairs. This presupposes, of course, that there is a rough balance of power existing among persons and groups and that disagreements are worked out in compromise policies and programs reflecting some of the vital interests of all individuals and groupings.

Perhaps it would be wise to begin with a disclaimer. Niebuhr's realism about individual and collective sin did not keep him from sharing the salient conviction of the founding fathers about the importance of civic virtue in a democracy. In a monarchy, they believed, it was the authority and power of the king which kept people in line. In a healthy democracy, it is not fear of a monarch but a sense of obligation to the commonwealth which motivates responsible civic behavior.[54] So Niebuhr's rightly celebrated pessimism about the sinfulness of humankind should most emphatically not be interpreted to mean that he did not have high expectations for would-be moral man in persistently immoral society. He was always and forever a Christian moralist who believed in relative virtue and the absolutely fundamental importance of striving to be virtuous— despite one's inability to be completely virtuous all the time.

Even so, Niebuhr criticized both humanist idealists and (most) Social Gospel Protestants for ignoring the power realities of all known human collectivities. The kind of agape which is possible for individuals (moral man) is not a realistic possibility for social institutions and their leaders (immoral society). Therefore, Christians who want to be effective in social reform must be willing to participate in and work through the morally ambiguous power structures of society. Furthermore, they must understand the importance of developing countervailing power in situations where one group is being exploited and/or oppressed by a more powerful group (e.g., workers who must form strong unions to bargain collectively with their more powerful employers).

Realistic social ethics must begin by recognizing that all human relationships and all human endeavors can be analyzed in terms of the possession and use of power, for what is possible and what is likely to happen depend to a considerable degree on the perception and/or exercise of power. The fact that power need not be overt in order to be operative has led many thinkers, especially extreme rationalists or extreme idealists, to overlook its presence in all human interaction. But the fact is that "there is no legal authority which does not imply sanctions or the threat of coercive action against recalcitrance":

> Conscience may appeal to conscience and reason to reason. There are no conflicts in which these appeals are not made, even when the conflict has become physical. But in every conflict of interest the possibility of marshaling every possible resource on either side is implied. Most human conflicts are composed, or subdued, by a superior authority and power, without an overt appeal to force or without the actual use of force, either violent or nonviolent. But the calculation of available resources on each side is as determinative in settling the outcome of the struggle as more rational or moral considerations. Most citizens in a democracy

are unaware of the amount of coercion involved in the democratic process.[55]

We have already noted that the reality and the ambiguity of power in society means that there must be a substantial difference between the morality of moral man and that of immoral society. Niebuhr himself remarked in later years that he had probably exaggerated the difference between the realms of private and public morality, suggesting that the book should have been called "The Not So Moral Man in His Less Moral Society."[56] But the point remains: the children of darkness (although immoral, and therefore unworthy of emulation with regard to their fundamental normative assumptions) are truly wiser in their generation than the children of light, because the former have a more accurate comprehension of the sinful self-centeredness of human beings and a shrewd appraisal of the power realities of human existence. The intellectual and moral failings of individuals are accentuated, and their consequences more far-reaching, in society. "Any error in the appraisal of the moral resources of individuals is accentuated when it is made the basis of political theory and practice."[57] Furthermore, collective entities are not capable of the same kind or degree of unselfishness that individuals may achieve. The statement, "No one has the right to be unselfish with the interests of other people" is not "sufficiently qualified." However, the statement is more nearly true than untrue, because "the selfishness of human communities must be regarded as an inevitability."[58]

> The demand of religious moralists that nations subject themselves to "the law of Christ" is an unrealistic demand, and the hope that they will do so is a sentimental one. Even a nation composed of individuals who possessed the highest degree of religious goodwill would be less than loving in its relation to other nations. It would fail, if for no other reason, because the individuals could not possibly think themselves in the position of the individuals of another nation in a degree sufficient to insure pure benevolence. Furthermore, such good will as they did possess would be sluiced into loyalty to their own nation and tend to increase the nation's selfishness. . . . Religious idealism may qualify national policies, as much as rational idealism, but this qualification can never completely eliminate the selfish, brutal and antisocial elements, which express themselves in all inter-group life.[59]

Nations, for example, do not have the same kind of direct contact with other nations that individuals have with other individuals. Therefore, they do not have the same opportunity to have plain human sympathy warm their collective breasts. Increased mutual interdependence among nations increases the chance for conflict (partly because it increases competition). Desire for immediate objectives obscures ultimate self-interest more in nations; therefore, they act more prudently than individuals. Nations have military force (or other types of force, for that matter) which they are tempted to use whenever it seems advantageous to do so. And among capitalist nations, the production of goods far beyond demand brings about a situation where the larger nations compel weaker ones to trade with them under biased terms. In short, "the paradox of patriotism" operates to transmute individual selfishness into national egoism. "A combination of unselfishness and vicarious selfishness in the individual thus gives tremendous force to national egoism."[60] And the fact that patriotic sentiment is at least in part vicarious self-glorification suggests that the immorality of nations is compounded by hypocrisy. The "claim to universality" is one of the perennial pretensions of mighty nations.[61]

But Niebuhr's hope, as we have also noted, is for an approximation of justice-love which goes far beyond order. He never tires of reminding his readers that there are indeterminate possibilities for good all around us all the time and that rational and religious resources in society mean that real improvement can be effected. Sympathy for the needs and rights of others may be extended indefinitely. The morale and prestige of dominant privileged groups may be softened to the point that they cannot resist amelioration with a clear conscience. What one generation regards as shocking innovations may be accepted by the next as matters of elemental fact and decency.[62] Furthermore, the downtrodden may be made more conscious of their rights and more willing to struggle to obtain them, and a greater penetration of insight may be developed by ostensibly objective social analysts.[63] Niebuhr concludes: "The Christian faith cannot be defeatist. It sees men's sin and the tragedies of life . . . but it also sees men in the strength of God's rising to the need of the struggle, confident, victorious in spirit." He can even declare (in what must be evaluated as an uncharacteristically unguarded rhetorical flourish) that, "[f]reed from illusions we have every possibility of perfecting the justice of social institutions."[64]

IRONY

Many of Niebuhr's most instructive theoretical insights stem from his keen awareness of irony in human affairs. He defined irony as a discrepancy between one's attitude toward a prominent character trait and the real consequences which are brought about by that feature of one's being. It is ironic, for example, that some Christians overvalue meekness or "purity," and because of this overvaluation they shy away from the kind of Promethean action of which they are capable and which they need to exhibit in situations where justice is at stake. It is equally ironic when a sense of justifiable moral indignation leads a righteous person to make foolish assumptions about the ease with which his cause can "win" or about the tactics which will be most fruitful in the struggle.

Time and time again, Niebuhr took note of the fact that genuine virtue often involves difficulties and leads to handicaps in the implementation of good intentions—as, for example, when the leaders of a democratic nation find themselves less able to mobilize public support in a necessary struggle against a tyranny which does not have to bother with the delays occasioned by the need to consult or educate its citizenry. Niebuhr especially stressed the ironic involvement of idealists in the very mischief they seek to avoid or overcome:

> In America the moral confusion [of the years leading up to World War II] is even worse than in Britain because our religious life has become so completely divorced from the classical Christian faith, with its profound understanding of the complexities and tragedies of history, and has become so completely enmeshed in the illusions of rationalistic utopianism, that most of our religious idealists are quite ready to submit to tyranny in the name of peace, to enthrone a system of perpetual war in western civilization in the interest of avoiding war, and to deliver a civilization of partial justice into the hands of a barbarism which denies the very concept of justice because they have an uneasy conscience about the injustice from which civilization has been unable to free itself.[65]

Niebuhr's most extensive elaboration of the concept of irony occurs in *The Irony of American History,* where he comments on the fact that America as a nation (and the American "national character") tends to overvalue some traits which often turn out to be liabilities and undervalue other traits which are actually its major assets. His most complete definition of this concept is given in the preface to *Irony,* where four illustrations of its meaning are put forth:

> Irony consists of apparently fortuitous incongruities in life which are discovered, upon closer examination, to be not merely fortuitous. Incongruity as such is merely comic . . . [and] the element of comedy is never completely eliminated from irony. But irony is something more than comedy, [for] a comic situation is proved to be an ironic one if a hidden relation is discovered in the incongruity. [For example,] if virtue becomes vice through some hidden defect in the virtue; if strength becomes weakness because of the vanity to which strength may prompt the mighty man or nation; if security is transmuted into insecurity because too much reliance is placed upon it; if wisdom becomes folly because it does not know its own limits—in all such cases the situation is ironic.[66]

Irony presented itself in the history of our country when Americans, "in thinking of themselves according to their creeds of innocence and perfection . . . failed to recognize their real history, [which is] one of common sense, empiricism and pragmatism."[67] The book was doubtless written not only to enlighten, but also to call the nation to the kind of political resolve and action in the world arena which this enlightenment might evoke. One of Niebuhr's most perceptive students has said:

> Once brought into the light, this truth about American life would cancel the irony, leaving Americans to possess fully a rightful sense of national self, a national self suited to confront world tasks without falling into either messianic impatience or a new isolation.[68]

In view of the not altogether successful record of his presidency, Jimmy Carter's admiration of Niebuhrian thought, including Niebuhr's insights into the ambiguity of the moral virtue of "a people who deserve a government as good as they are," might very well be considered ironic in itself.[69]

Christian Pragmatism

The logical outcome of this line of thinking is Christian Pragmatism, a label which is sometimes used instead of Christian Realism to describe Niebuhrian thinking. The best single statement of Niebuhr's convictions on this point can be found in the celebrated essay on "Christian Faith and Social Action" in which he asserts that a realistic awareness of the power of self-love and of "the law of love as the final standard" of ethical human behavior leads to "a pragmatic ethic in which power and self-interest are used, beguiled, harnessed and deflected for the ultimate end of establishing the highest and most inclusive community of justice and order."[70]

INDIVIDUAL AND COMMUNITY

The means which can be used to pursue desirable goals are determined to some extent by the relationship between the individual and the community. The individual is both the beneficiary of and a responsible agent in society. Bourgeois civilization has tended to obscure the extent to which the individual is dependent upon his social environment, and it has fostered the extreme individualism of the modern age, which sometimes speaks of the individual as an isolated atom who owes no debt of gratitude or service to the community in which he lives and moves and has being. This is to forget that every individual is hopelessly indebted to the community for life, early care, language, socialization, and a recognized social location and status. On the other hand, collectivist creeds have overemphasized the rights of society over the individual. The individual must be free enough from social control to stand apart and criticize it, for only the individual can transcend history spiritually and see himself and his culture in perspective.[71]

The fact is, every particular statement of universal principles of justice is partial; the political principles derived therefrom are an additional step further away; and the specific applications of political principles are still less valid. Yet this descending scale of relativity never inhibits the bearers of power in a given period from claiming the sanctity of the pure principle for their power. Thus the individual must always be vigilant against these ideological abuses and must be in a position to warn against particular expressions of such abuse. In short, the individual is truly the conscience of the community.[72] Moreover, it is actually in the best long-range interests of the community and its leaders not to crush dissent, for palpable error may be conjoined with a hidden truth of greater magnitude, and authoritarian states lose this undetected truth whenever they suppress "error" too rigorously.[73]

The community, for its part, has a twofold influence for good on individuals. It provides both order and justice through law, and it may in its own way be the conscience of the individual. To reiterate an example cited earlier, it is clear that law enlivens conscience when taxation forces individuals to give more than they would otherwise be willing to give in order to provide for the essential needs of the least advantaged among their fellow citizens. Thus, through forced generosity and other similar measures, the collective has an elevating rather than a depressing effect on the morality of the individuals who comprise it.[74]

STRATEGY

Niebuhr's pragmatism is guided by several strategic assumptions which furnish rules of thumb for the "artful contriver" who endeavors to bring the leaven of ethical responsibility to the loaf of politics. All of these assumptions about strategy are based on the assumption that, no matter how strongly one believes in Providence or God's ultimate triumph at the end of history, human beings are responsible for forging their own collective destiny within history. Moreover, ideas about strategy are also based on the conviction that it is far more important in the long run to remedy the structural and procedural defects in a community's economic and political systems than it is to exercise individualistic piety within these systems as they are.

In seeking to alter systemic causes of injustice, of course, it is foolish to hope for sweeping change overnight. One must try to achieve incremental reforms by setting proximate goals that can be reached with the resources which are actually available (or can actually be accumulated). Particular social problems must be addressed by degrees, element by element.[75]

But wise pragmatism looks for trends, analogies, and principles (even "laws" of social and institutional behavior, if there are any) by which to avoid "fragmented adhocracy." Niebuhr actually criticizes Barth for the latter's "extreme pragmatism, which disavows all moral principles." Why? Because Barth goes seriously astray when he maintains that "the church must concern itself with political systems, not in terms of principles but as seen in the light of the Word of God" and that the church "must reject every effort to systematize political history and must look at every event afresh." This is what leads Barth to "the capricious conclusion that Communism

[is] not as bad as Nazism because it is not anti-Semitic." Says
Niebuhr:

A little concern for "principles" would have instructed
Barth. . . . Looking at every event afresh means that one is ignorant about the instructive, though inexact, analogies of history
which the "godless" scientists point out for our benefit.[76]

Unfortunately, however, principles are nothing more than heuris-
tic devices which help one make decisions about goals and priorities
(and about deontological limits on means). The intelligent social
reformer still has to translate principles into realistic and effective
policy recommendations, and this is where Christian Pragmatism
constitutes a helpful mind-set. It urges one toward "goal-directed
behavior" in which—with all due caution, but with as much zeal as
one finds appropriate—one uses available resources to approximate
those particular goals which seem to be most desirable and most
feasible in light of the particular conditions prevailing, and the particular needs of those who will be affected by the action one seeks to
mobilize.

Incidentally, Niebuhr's early writings on social change strategy
reveal a strikingly open-minded attitude toward alliances between
groups which are very far apart in their assumptions about problems,
goals and means, for he says that social reformers with a distinctive
ideological bent (such as Christians) should be willing to work with
and accept the help of almost any available group when struggling
for social justice.[77] In later years, he modified his thinking on this
point, because after World War II he was adamantly opposed to
admitting Communists to liberal non-Communist reform organizations and movements. For example, the Americans for Democratic
Action, in which Niebuhr was a very prominent figure, was organized for the explicit purpose of uniting non-Communist liberals,
and the organization was extremely firm in refusing to admit or
work with those who were suspected of being Communists or fellow travelers.

The overall theoretical perspective on the pragmatic use of principles can be illustrated with an important article on "Our Faith and
Concrete Political Decisions" which Niebuhr wrote for the Summer
1952 issue of *Christianity and Society*. In it he says

We should long since have known that there are no clear choices
between good and evil in the realm of politics and eco-

nomics. . . . [In these realms] we must harness and provisionally justify the forces of egoism and of power even though they may be ultimately hazardous either to freedom or to brotherhood. We cannot disavow the use of power because it is hazardous, but neither must we obscure the moral peril of power. This is why no political program can be simply equated with the highest sancties of life. . . . Nothing is clearer than that ideologically consistent political positions have on the whole been refuted by history, while healthy nations have preserved freedom and extended justice by various pragmatic policies which borrowed from various strategies.

This does not mean that we must not and cannot make clear-cut decisions on matters of principle. . . . In deciding for or against ["socialized medicine," for example] we decide for or against certain broad political strategies. But we ought not to decide for or against it on the basis that the policy is abstractly in violation of "freedom" or that abstractly it enhances state control. We ought to make our decision by asking such questions as these: Can a system of economic freedom in medicine guarantee minimal standards of health? Can a socialized scheme be subjected to professional rather than political standards? Is there protection in the scheme against inordinate and disproportionate demands upon it?[78]

The utility of "principled pragmatism" can also be illustrated by the axiom which Niebuhr constantly reiterates to the effect that the disinherited have more of a justification to fight for their (violated) rights than the privileged and powerful have to seek to extend theirs. Thus it is possible to distinguish between justified and unjustified self-interest and self-seeking.[79] This acknowledgment of the difference between the claims of the dispossessed and those of the privileged is extremely important, for it shows that Niebuhr always understood and affirmed what in recent years has come to be called an "option for the poor." To understand this absolutely fundamental Niebuhrian tenet is also to refute the complaint that Niebuhr's social theory fails to discriminate between the legitimate demands of the oppressed and the ideological pretensions of the powerful. (See chapter 6 for further discussion of this point.)

It follows that one can also distinguish between the need for countervailing power (on the part of a relatively disadvantaged and disfranchised group) and the claim typically made by the powerful that a diminution of their power and authority will lead to disaster. In situations where a serious power discrepancy is causing injustice, it is almost always wise and good to strive for the achievement of a balance of power between contending forces.

Finally, we must take note of a curiously conservative element in Niebuhr's strategic theory. Despite his general affirmation of the positive role of the state and his acceptance of discriminate violence as a means to important ends, Niebuhr subscribed to the view that law should not attempt to pull public opinion along (to a more enlightened position, and to behavior which would lessen injustice) too hard or too fast. This view seems to be based on a fear that such an attempt might create or solidify stubborn recalcitrance in regard to measures which people are "not ready for yet." He never ceased to believe that "politics is still the art of the possible."[80]

But Is "Christian Pragmatism" an Ignominious Retreat?

Some of the critics who deplore Niebuhr's alleged pessimism are equally troubled by his pragmatism, and one of the bones of contention here is Niebuhr's apparent lack of a theologically appropriate degree of Christian hope. This objection is frequently linked to his willingness to dispense with revolution as the course of action which Christians should be encouraged to espouse and by his willingness (as they see it) to abandon radical goals in favor of unworthy compromises.

HOPE

Despite all that was said in preceding chapters about Niebuhr's Prometheanism and his optimistic belief in indeterminate possibilities for good in human life, a few additional words must be said about the lingering misconception that Niebuhr was, in the final analysis, a deep pessimist, a defeatist. Those who persist in holding this view tend to discount everything Niebuhr says about one's obligation to support good causes as the grim bravado of a Sisyphus who knows that all of his labors are futile. They accuse him, ultimately, of lacking faith in God. In leveling this charge, they place considerable emphasis on the point that Niebuhr's main hope was for some kind of decisive triumph of God at the end of history beyond history.[81]

If I believed that the critics were correct on this point, it would certainly undercut some of my esteem for Niebuhr's thought. But I have argued (see chapter 3, pp. 70–71) that it is incorrect to characterize Niebuhr's realism as "defeatism." Daniel Day Williams was wrong in maintaining that Niebuhr did not have a proper understanding of the limited, but substantial, significance of cocreative activity within history; moreover, those whom Stone aptly describes as "most eager to move beyond Niebuhr to new forms of political imagination and more hopeful attitudes toward social life" are wrong if they fail to reckon with Niebuhr's sense of "indeterminate possibilities [for good,]" and to see that for him this amounts to "the obligation to realize them."[82]

One might argue that a sufficient rebuttal has already been given in the passage from chapter 3 cited in the preceding paragraph or in a passage quoted earlier in this chapter, viz., Niebuhr's assertion that "the Christian faith cannot be defeatist, [because] it sees men in the strength of God's rising to the need of the struggle, confident, victorious in spirit." Or one might endeavor to extend the argument along the lines developed by a left-wing critic of Niebuhr who professes to find a note of *ecstasy* in his doctrine of hope. According to Dale Patrick, it is not impossible to "reformulate Niebuhr's concept of self-sacrificial love to include ecstatic hope," since "Niebuhr's own treatment of love leads in this direction."[83] But the author of these words probably deplores Niebuhr's *lack* of ecstasy about what was actually achievable within history, whereas I believe that the zest one experiences in the *process* of (the never completely successful) striving to overcome evil with good can be described as a kind of ecstasy.

COMPROMISE

Niebuhr is good at reminding every zealot that "the righteous fury of a just cause represents the greatest danger to social health as well as its highest possibility" And he helps us realize that "every cause must be conscious of its own relativity and one-sidedness." The trouble is, according to Patrick, Niebuhr refuses to "leave open the possibility of condemning the entire sociopolitical order and working for its downfall." In fact, "it is this refusal to see reform as an end, but at most as a means of 'radicalizing,' that sets the new left apart from Niebuhr."[84]

This apparent unwillingness to pronounce a sweeping condemnation of any existing political order is sometimes connected with Niebuhr's willingness to compromise with unsavory elements in the search for "realistic" social policies. Likewise, his emphasis on grace is seen as permission for evil actions. In an article on Niebuhr entitled "Apologist for Power," Bill Kellerman writes:

> Niebuhr was the one who made the "lesser of two evils" a Christian commonplace in moral discernment. It is only a step further to the tragic necessity of "doing evil to achieve good" or "using evil to limit evil"—which are also standard ethical fare among the Niebuhrian circle.
>
> To sin is, in effect, justified (I choose the word carefully) by the universality of sin. Where sin abounds, presumably the best you can do is know you're sinning. . . . [This] essentially limits grace to a kind of solace. . . . Politically this means that the morally responsible are to be freed from their arrogant pretensions, but also from the squeamishness that holds them back from the exigencies of, say, military necessity.[85]

There is no denying, of course, that a pragmatic strategy of incremental social reform is subject to abuse and vulnerable to error. These dangers will be analyzed in some detail in the final chapter of this book. But I would like to end this discussion of pragmatism by saying that I view Niebuhr's emphasis on finding the best attainable compromise solutions to complex social problems as a strength rather than a weakness. One of the glories of Christian Realism is the fact that it is an ethic of responsibility, not an ethic of perfection: its chief concern is doing as much good as possible for the human beings who will be affected by a given action or a given policy, not keeping one's hands clean or preserving one's purity of motivation. So when Kellerman delivers what he evidently thinks is the coup de grace in his assault on Niebuhr—by charging that "in the perennial debate among Christians over faithfulness vs. effectiveness, Niebuhr is the advocate of effectiveness,"[86] I want to reply by saying, "Yes! You bet your life he is focused on effectiveness, because that's what really counts, delivering the half-loaf which is usually the best you can get in a complicated situation where there's a lot of formidable resistance to be grappled with." A more judicious reply, to be sure, would contend that Kellerman's way of pitting effectiveness against faithfulness is misleading, because the measure of faithfulness in serving one's neighbors is one's wholehearted commitment to getting the job done effectively and developing the savvy and skills to be consistently effective.

Chapter 5

Ethics and Politics

Religious people think of Reinhold Niebuhr as a preacher and a theologian, and secular people think of him primarily as a political philosopher and an analyst of the ethical dimensions of politics. Any student of Niebuhr's life and the evolution of his thought will be struck by the extent to which he devoted his last twenty years of professional activity to political analysis. Our discussion of the highlights of Niebuhr's contribution to these aspects of Christian thought will be organized under the two rather obvious headings of domestic political theory and international relations. The first of these two topics will focus primarily on what he called "the strategy of democracy"; the second, on a number of salient problems in ethics and foreign policy. This analysis is preceded, however, by an explanation of several theoretical assumptions which have a bearing on what Niebuhr said regarding all particular policy questions.

Fundamental Theoretical Principles

Any analysis of Niebuhr's contribution to political thought must concentrate, of course, on the primary sources. His most important single statement on democracy can be found in *The Children of Light and the Children of Darkness* (1944), which should be compared to and supplemented by a reading of two later works, *A Nation So Conceived* (1963) and *The Democratic Experience* (1969).[1] Niebuhr's thoughts on foreign policy are contained in topical essays assembled in *Christianity and Power Politics* (1940), *Christian Realism and Political Problems* (1953), and *Reinhold Niebuhr on Politics* (1960), all of which should be pondered in the light of the "Grand Theory" developed in *The Structure of Nations and Empires* and in Niebuhr's books on the philosophy of history (*Beyond Tragedy, Faith and History,* and *The Irony of American History*). But it is impossible to understand the real meaning and significance of the ideas articulated in these writings without understanding the context in which they arose—namely, the political-cultural crisis of the late 1930s and the period of what he called "America's precarious preeminence" in the Cold War era that followed World War II.[2]

The menace of Nazism, the crimes of Stalin, and the ideological inflexibility of American Communists and socialists led Niebuhr to a reexamination of the merits of "the Western democracies," and what he perceived as the Soviet threat in the late 1940s drove him to formulate an apologia for the use of American power for "American responsibility in the world arena." These new emphases in Niebuhr's thought flowered rather quickly because they fit in with his convictions about the positive side of human nature and destiny and with the penchant for pragmatism which was a constant factor in his intellectual position ever since his days at Yale.

COMPLEXITY AND IDEOLOGICAL TAINT

Niebuhr believed that Christians were called upon to voice their reasoned opinions on the ethical dimensions of policy issues, and he was not at all afraid to fulfill his responsibilities in this regard. But he was continually reminding himself and warning others of the complexity of politics and the difficulty of speaking fair-mindedly (let alone objectively) in our judgments concerning politics. He wrote in a 1952 election-year editorial:

> While it is certainly true that the Christian life and faith include political responsibility, it is nevertheless dangerous to derive political decisions too simply from our Christian faith. Every political decision requires dozens of subordinate and relative judgments which cannot be derived from, or sanctioned by, our faith.[3]

Moreover, he cautioned, "Christians must make these hazardous political decisions with full recognition that others equally devoted to the common good may arrive at contrary conclusions."

This means that intelligent Christian citizens must not be "affronted and baffled by the different conclusions [of others] if they have some humble recognition of the taint of individual and collective self-interest which colors even our purest political and moral ideals."[4]

The Strategy of Democracy

In the 1920s and 1930s, Niebuhr was extremely critical of American society. He rejected Marxism as a moral worldview, but he was an active member of the Socialist Party, and he believed that a proletarian revolution of some kind would be necessary to correct the injustices of the American economic system. He admired the political system and the cultural heritage of Britain, but he was not at all convinced that the New Deal was going to be an adequate approximation of the English heritage (and after Munich he lost faith in Britain as well). He believed that Christianity needed to be mixed with Marxist insights to provide a fresh concept of culture and society.

The rise of Nazism changed his point of view dramatically. In a manner quite analogous to the change in his theological views, Niebuhr began to have a new appreciation for the virtues of what he referred to as "the Western democracies." Just as "Augustinian realism" came to seem more profound than prevailing doctrines such as Communism, liberal humanism, or Social Gospel Christianity, the merits of Western democracy began to exhibit enormous goodness compared to Soviet communism and the fascism of the Axis powers. Niebuhr began to point out the irony of a situation which might cause the democratic nations to be conquered by morally inferior nations precisely because the greater moral sensitivity of the former made them unwilling to go to war to protect their superior values and way of life:

> History would add a cruel irony to the tragedy of the self-destruction of modern democracies if it developed that what is still left of a universal culture and an ordered civilization could not protect itself against moral nihilism and political anarchy because liberal civilization has assessed the weight of morality in politics too highly. . . . If the democratic nations fail, their failure must be attributed to the faulty strategy of idealists who have too many illusions when they face realists who have too little conscience. The false strategy will not be derived purely from

the illusions of the idealists about their foes but from their illusions about themselves.

The democracies may still have enough power to win a war in which they are involving themselves by trying to avoid it. But they will certainly make the catastrophe more inevitable by their effort to escape it.[5]

Thus the horrors of the Third Reich were the major stimulus to his new respect for democracy. Less important but also significant were two other realities of the late 1930s—the crimes of Stalin and the ideological inflexibility of American Communists and Socialists. Their insistence that capitalism was the crucial evil to be fought, and their attendant unwillingness to give their blessing to Roosevelt's reforms (which they saw as part of a capitalist conspiracy to justify a descent into fascism), convinced Niebuhr to reevaluate the New Deal and, ultimately (by the end of the 1930s), to support Roosevelt.

So the pressure of events forced Niebuhr to take a more sympathetic view toward the empirical realities of American democracy, and his pragmatism persuaded him to embrace it as a relative good. This intellectual shift was rendered less difficult by the fact that the optimistic aspects of his view of the human potential fit nicely with a positive view of what governments might be able to do to promote social justice and even the spirit of fraternity. Indeed, Merkeley contends that Niebuhr's most important single affirmation of democracy (*The Children of Light and the Children of Darkness*) is

a kind of codicil to *The Nature and Destiny of Man,* applying the thought of the main text to specific issues that have been especially pressing. . . . In other words, Niebuhr's ambivalent assessment of democracy; his endorsement of a more limited and critical assessment of Marxism's contribution to social theory; the arguments for a mixed (part capitalist, part socialist) economy; and the rest of the programmatic contents, *do* follow from the main line of Niebuhr's thought.[6]

Niebuhr's concept of democracy (and his decision to write a book on the subject) was also a function of his desire not to be content (or even associated) with the shallow adulation for democracy being mouthed by many "patriotic" writers during World War II. He wanted to develop a reasoned argument regarding democracy which did justice to its value without ignoring its liabilities and shortcomings, especially the kind of unqualified praise of democracy which made it into a sort of secular religion.[7]

Even in 1947, when the anxieties of the Cold War were tempting many American intellectuals and politicians to be idolatrous, Niebuhr warned that the people of this country are "particularly prone" to the sin of identifying "our particular brand of democracy with the ultimate values of life."[8] He thus refuses to proclaim that it is the business of this country to export its special brand of American democracy to every nation in the developing world. In this particular regard, Niebuhr was less pretentious than many of the Cold War ideologues among whom he is numbered by his critics. On the other hand, as Stone has admitted, Niebuhr's five cardinal traits of a "free government" are probably less wisely flexible than are the marks of a "responsible society" identified by the World Council of Churches literature on this subject. Niebuhr's list includes national unity, protection of individual rights, independent institutions, competitive elections, and "enough equilibrium [and prosperity] to exercise the positive function of government in the promotion of social justice." The WCC criteria are civil liberties, pluralism, resistance to foreign domination, and societal guidance of the economy.[9]

Niebuhr's rationale for democracy is best expressed (and most easily remembered) in the famous epigram which declares that "man's capacity for justice makes democracy possible; but man's inclination to injustice makes democracy necessary."[10] This adage is only slightly more famous that the observation that democracy is "a method of finding proximate solutions for insoluble problems."[11] A more formal definition asserts that democracy is a permanently valid form of social and political organization in which freedom and order are made to support, and not to contradict, each other. Democracy does justice to two dimensions of human existence: to man's spiritual stature and his social character; to the uniqueness and variety of life, as well as the common necessities of all men.[12]

The goal and the abiding significance of democracy are twofold: "to contribute to the establishment of order and community through the non-violent arbitration and accommodation of social conflict" and "to maintain freedom by making power responsible, checking the authority of government, and providing a form of social control over the leaders of society."[13] Niebuhr is emphatic in claiming that a democracy is better than even the most benevolent dictatorship or oligarchy would be, for

> history has proved the consequences in justice to be much higher in this freedom [of a democratic consensus] than is possible to attain when the "truth" about justice as defined by any one religious group or, for that matter, any interest group, remains unchallenged.[14]

It follows that there are a number of sources, vital prerequisites or essential attributes, without which a free society cannot flourish. Among these are: centers of value and initiative whose power checks and counterbalances that of other such centers; a degree of openness which allows the imperfections of the society "to be published abroad" for the sake of honest criticism and improvement; and the consent of the governed as registered in regularly scheduled elections, which are (assuming the principle of universal suffrage) "the pride of democracy."[15] In addition, it is important to be aware that a healthy democracy is typically rooted in shared cultural experience and the history of ideas. The collectivity must be characterized by a vital sense of national community, which cannot be created overnight by governmental decree, education, or anything else. In addition, it must partake of both the optimism recently provided in our civilization by bourgeois idealism and the pessimism long provided by biblical faith. The former assumes a citizenry that is reasonable enough to resolve conflicts and arrive at compromise measures for handling the tasks of its common life. The latter helps people avoid illusion, self-righteousness, and what Toynbee called "the idolization of ephemeral techniques."

Ethics and Foreign Policy

Niebuhr's role as a putative "Cold War ideologue" accounts for the strongest prejudice against him in the minds of many contemporary church people who have a passionate concern for social justice in the world community. Consequently, the exposition of exactly what he said on the ethics of foreign policy must be very carefully done: it must try to be meticulously accurate in setting forth the record of his pronouncements in this area.

KEY CONCEPTS

Most of the basic concepts of Niebuhrian thought have already been described, but their application to foreign policy issues requires special attention. The principal themes to be discussed are: (1) reliance on historical study and empirical analysis rather than abstract rational or scientific visions of collective life within and among nations; (2) the inescapability of one's need to use power and the obligation to use it responsibly; (3) humility, moderation, and caution; and (4) realistic idealism.

Emphasis on History and Empirical Study

Niebuhr's social theory places a great deal of emphasis on the importance of empirical study and historical knowledge (indeed, historical consciousness). This aspect of Niebuhr's thought is particularly important in his analysis of politics, for Niebuhr is a staunch disciple of Edmund Burke. The heritage of historical experience manifested in the customs and the collective conscience of a people is much more important than a written constitution and the rational principles on which it might be grounded. Niebuhr used an anecdote regarding the new nation of Israel to illustrate the point:

> The new state of Israel is composed of very religious and very consistently secular Zionists. There is a rumor that when it was proposed to have a constitution for the new state a wise man warned against the venture on the grounds that each party would try to secure a maximum of security in the constitution and accentuate the differences between them. It was better, he declared, for the two parties to live together as best they could. This common life would allay some of the fears and would throw up some
> *ad hoc* forms of accommodation which would serve the future as a constitution. So it has proved. Life is a better unifier than law. Law can only define and perfect what life has established.[16]

It is an illusion to imagine that semantic clarification (a time-consuming project dear to the hearts of both social scientists and academic humanists) can dissolve the difficulties of life in a democracy where differences about the meaning of the concept are rooted in the experience and interests of different groups. By the same token, an analysis of the conflict between Catholicism and Protestantism in Europe between 1500 and 1850 suggests that gradual

adjustment can take place where both war and utopian schemes of uni-
fication fail.[17] Niebuhr therefore believes that the rough muddling-
through of sensitive diplomacy holds more promise than a beautifully
conceived world government or a vastly strengthened United Nations.

Acknowledgment—and Use—of Power

In a fallen world, goodness can almost never be protected nor
promoted without the exercise of power and the ambiguities which
its use inevitably involves. Nothing is more contemptible (or hypocritical) than the denial that one has power or the unwillingness to
use it for good purposes when those purposes stand imperiled. This
was a crucial aspect of Niebuhr's rejection of pacifism and his argument concerning the urgency of rearmament just before World War
II. It was also the burden of his appeal to the nation just after the war:

> In less than a half-century our nation has emerged from a condi-
> tion of continental security to a position where its own security
> is intimately bound to the security of a whole community of free
> nations. Only yesterday we lived in a state of childlike innocence
> in which the contentions and alarms of world politics interrupted
> our youthful dreams only as a distant thunder may echo through
> the happy conversations of a garden party. Today we have be-
> come the senior partners in a vast alliance of nations, trying des-
> perately to achieve sufficient unity and health to ward off the
> threat of tyrannical unification of the world [by Communist ex-
> pansion].[18]

Humility and Caution

But we dare not think of American responsibility in the world
arena as the manifest destiny of a chosen people who can work their
imperialistic designs upon the rest of the world in the guise of special
privilege and special virtue. Niebuhr heaped scorn upon ideologues
who maintained (as did a certain Senator Beveridge of Indiana) that
God "has made us the master organizers of the world to establish
order where chaos reigns . . . that we may administer government
among savage and senile people." Denouncing the Senator's pretensions in claiming that God "has marked the American people as
[God's] chosen nation to finally lead in the regeneration of the
world," Niebuhr counseled humble contrition and moderation. We
must never meddle in affairs unless the situation requires us to; we
must never use disproportionate means (eschewing military force

where diplomatic negotiations or informal pressures will suffice); and we must never claim that we are motivated by altruism or expect gratitude. The most memorable statement of this tenet follows:

No nation or individual is ever good enough to deserve the position of leadership which some nations and individuals achieve. If the history that leads to a special mission is carefully analyzed, it is always apparent that factors other than the virtues of the leader are partly responsible for the position the individual or collective leader holds. Those who do not believe in God's providence in history will call these factors "accidents" or "fortunes" . . . The religious man perceives them as gifts of grace.

If we know that we have been chosen beyond our deserts, we must also begin to realize that we have not been chosen for our particular task in order that our own life may be aggrandized. We ought not to derive either special security or special advantages from our high historical mission. The real fact is that we are placed in a precarious moral historical position by our special mission. It can be justified only if it results in good for the whole community of mankind. . . .

If ever a nation required the spirit of genuine contrition and humility it is ours. The future of the world literally depends, not upon the display of power (though the use of it is necessary and inevitable), but upon the acquisition of virtues which can develop only in humility.[19]

Realistic Idealism

The pragmatic element in Niebuhr's thought comes very much to the fore in his writings on the ethics of politics, and this is especially true of his pronouncements on foreign policy issues. The logic of "national interest" thinking seems to relegate moral ideals to the periphery, and because Niebuhr was genuinely worried about the expansionist aims of Stalinist Russia during the Cold War period, it is hardly surprising that he sometimes seems to have left his idealism behind when writing about America's need to be strong and decisive in the decades after World War II.

But everything is always "both/and" in the thought of Reinhold Niebuhr, and by the 1960s he felt it necessary to dissociate himself from so-called political realists of every stripe (religious or secular) who seemed to have forgotten about the importance of viewing political realities and elaborating policy options in the light of ethical ideals. A decisively important source for this decisively important dimension of Niebuhr's thought is *Man's Nature and His Communities* (1963). The thrust of the argument here is to refute "the absolutism of the pre-democratic realists" by contending that

> political encounters and debates in a free society involve not only contests of interest and power, but the rational engagement and enlargement of a native sympathy, a sense of justice, a residual moral integrity, and a sense of the common good in all classes of society.[20]

Niebuhr criticizes Morgenthau for "obscuring the important residual creative factor in human rationality,"[21] and he concludes that

> the law of love is indeed the basis of all moral life, that it cannot be obeyed by a simple act of the will . . . and that forces which draw the self from its undue self-concern are usually forces of "common grace" in the sense that they represent all forms of social security or responsibility or pressure which prompt the self to bethink itself of its social essence and to realize itself by not trying too desperately for self-realization.[22]

This passage seems to extend the frequently unnoticed optimism of a passage from *The Nature and Destiny of Man* in which Niebuhr is at pains to refute an overly pessimistic reading of the typical selfishness of groups. He writes:

> The fact that various conceptions of a just solution of a common problem can be finally synthesized into a common solution disproves the idea that the approach of each individual or group is consistently egoistic. If it were, society should be an anarchy of rival interests until power from above subdued the anarchy.[23]

It also fits neatly with the famous passage from "Christian Faith and Social Action" cited above (which speaks of "harnessing and deflecting self-interest") and with another climactic statement from an essay on "Our Moral and Spiritual Resources for International Cooperation":

> A combination of idealism and realism is given in the great historic faiths. Without the insights of these faiths, realism may degenerate into cynicism and idealism into sentimentality. They may even degenerate within the context of these faiths. But ideally the presuppositions of Biblical faith insist on both the moral

imperative of the love commandment and the fact of the persistence of self-love in actual history. There is in this faith, therefore, a safeguard against both sentimentality and moral cynicism. This must be made available to the nation in the present period of critical decisions in which we cannot afford to disregard either the moral possibilities or the moral realities of our common life.[24]

EXAMPLES OF THE THEORY IN PRACTICE

So far, so good. Niebuhr's theory of morality and politics is persuasive. And Hans J. Morgenthau's tribute to the "universal applicability" of the "general political philosophy" which underlies Niebuhr's "concrete treatment of concrete political problems" seems to be for the most part valid:

> The method, the approach, of Reinhold Niebuhr as a political philosopher is not in essence different from—let us say— Edmund Burke's approach [in his] letter to the electors of Bristol explaining to them what he is supposed to do as their representative. . . . If one tried to judge Reinhold Niebuhr's contribution to political philosophy by such standards, I think one would arrive at a more positive conclusion than if one asks whether what Reinhold Niebuhr has said to us about our political problems has a direct relevance for the problems of other people.[25]

Morgenthau goes on to demonstrate the validity of his point by discussing Niebuhr's awareness of "the tragic character of the political act" and by praising his awareness of the salience of ideology as "a necessary concomitant of the political act itself [and] one of the preconditions for political success."[26]

But the proof should be in the pudding, and the phrasing of Morgenthau's compliment is a harbinger of the controversial nature (some would say the shortcomings) of some of Niebuhr's comments on specific foreign policy issues. I will attempt to illustrate this aspect of the topic by taking note of Niebuhr's posture on two main clusters of concern—namely, those pertaining to the international community and the cold war, and those pertaining to military policy.

THE INTERNATIONAL COMMUNITY AND THE COLD WAR

When World War II came to an end, religious leaders felt a special responsibility to support what the community of nations was hoping to do in order to rebuild the war-torn countries and promote "a just and durable peace." Richard Niebuhr was troubled by what he saw as the utopian flavor of such a lofty goal. He thought it would be appropriate to hope and strive for "a just endurable peace." Many leaders were enthusiastic for the United Nations (UN), and some wanted to go even further in the direction of a "federal world government." Most American politicians made speeches in which they paid lip service to the UN, but few were willing to go on record as supporting world government. The hopes of the political leadership were centered on alliances of free-world nations in various spheres of influence (NATO being, of course, the most important of these). The "Soviet threat" was an overriding concern, and even though there was a good deal of sincere interest in promoting economic progress and political maturity in what came to be called the "undeveloped countries," this interest also tended to be filtered through Cold War lenses.

The United Nations and World Government

Niebuhr's realism about the complexities of humankind's collective existence made him exceedingly skeptical about hopes for a world government and even for the effectiveness of the UN. He began by accepting

> the historical fact that the mutual respect for each other's rights
> in particular communities is older than any code of law, and that
> machinery for the enforcement of law can be efficacious only
> when a community as a whole obeys its laws implicitly, so that
> coercive enforcement may be limited to a recalcitrant minority.

He went on to conclude:

> The fallacy of world government can be stated in three simple
> propositions. The first is that governments are not created by
> fiat. . . . The second is that governments have only limited effi-
> cacy in integrating community. The third is that the integrative
> forces in the world community are still minimal.[27]

The big principles here are that government is not created by some one authoritative pronouncement out of the blue (it must be generated gradually by the growth of a consensus about the need for and legitimacy of a particular governing entity), and community cannot be created by government. Since the integrative forces in a fragmented world are so minimal, it follows that it is illusory to imagine that a body of diplomats from all over the world can create an effective world government simply by announcing that it exists. This hope is illusory because

> a too confident sense of justice always leads to injustice. Insofar as men and nations are "judges in their own case" they are bound to betray the human weakness of having a livelier sense of their own interest than of the competing interest[s]. That is why "just" men and nations may easily become involved in ironic refutations of their moral pretensions.

The fact is that "the sense of justice [operative in the minds of any particular group] must be supplemented by a sense of religious humility which recognizes that nations are even more incapable than individuals of fully understanding the rights and claims of others."

> Such humility ought also to reveal that the pretensions and the vanities of the other group, though perhaps different in intensity, are not different in kind from those of our own group. Finally, a genuine religious humility will prompt us to acknowledge the mystery and integrity of "the other," and will reveal to us that this other life represents a boundary which our expansive impulses must not transgress.[28]

Does this mean that the UN is an impotent fraud which has no viable status or role in international affairs? Not quite. For even though "the UN is not exactly the 'Parliament of Mankind and Federation of the World' which the nineteenth century fondly believed to be the 'one far-off divine event, to which the whole creation moves,' it is nevertheless a symbol of what was true in the illusions of the previous century."[29] The UN "serves the very necessary end of integrating the world as far as present realities permit."[30] As "a minimal bridge across the chasm between Russia and the West" and as "the meeting ground for the free nations" it constitutes "an assembly of peoples in which world opinion serves to check the policies of the most powerful nations."[31] In addition, says Niebuhr, the UN and its various agencies (especially UNESCO) "relate American power to a weakened world and American prosperity to an impoverished world."[32] American power is an immediate resource for the strength of the free world, but it is also a hazard, for it

> goes without saying that the American leadership has not been established by explicit consent. . . . It is also obvious that the

preponderance of American power is as valuable for the unity of the free world as it is dangerous to justice.[33]

The Atlantic Alliance and the Soviet Threat

So if Niebuhr's hopes for a tolerably just peace were not based on faith in some longed-for federation of the nations with a parliament of mankind, in what were they grounded? It should come as no surprise that the convictions which had led Niebuhr to favor rearmament for war against the Nazis carried on in his belief that the Western democracies (now spoken of primarily as the "free world" or, more narrowly, as the "Atlantic Alliance") must maintain a posture of wary strength vis-à-vis an expansionist Soviet Union under Stalin.

There is no question that Niebuhr saw Communism as a very dangerous moral worldview, and that he viewed Stalinist Russia as a menace to be contained by whatever force was required. He was therefore willing to accept the nuclear balance of terror as a necessary evil, and he believed that a posture of unremitting vigilance and military preparedness was absolutely essential.

For a long time Niebuhr was pessimistic about the prospects for flexibility or change in the Soviet Union. He felt that the all-or-nothing ideological character of Marxist-Leninist doctrine combined with the oppressive powers of a one-party bureaucracy in which total political and military power were concentrated made the admission of error almost impossible, and thus substantive innovations were unthinkable. When all this is reinforced and augmented by the power of propaganda, expressed in control of the mass media and the educational system, the prospects for a movement toward moderation are very bleak.[34] In the late 1950s, Niebuhr thought that "the possibilities of disarmament [were] very slim," because the evidence of history is that "disarmament has always been consequent upon, not requisite to, relaxed tensions."[35]

On the other hand, Niebuhr thought that the U.S. should try to become less rigid and self-righteous in its fundamental mind-set toward Communism, and we should aid and encourage those nations and leaders within the Communist world who appeared to be most flexible and most eager to escape from the iron dogmas of Marxism.[36] He also thought that the "common predicament" faced by the two superpowers could

contribute to our moral health in two ways. First, it will tend to mitigate the sharpness of the anxiety about a surprise attack, and consequently the clamor for ever greater military power. . . .
Second, such recognition will prepare us to live for decades in a continuation of responsibility, anxiety, tension and frustration, an experience which our young nation has never before faced.[37]

Furthermore, Niebuhr became increasingly sanguine about the possibilities for reduced tensions. Even in 1938 he entertained the idea that internal developments might conceivably change the face of Communism, so he did not fail to perceive the signs of such change when they began to appear.[38] Thus he welcomed the publication of Djilas' *The New Class* (1957) and Khrushchev's denunciation of Stalin in 1956 as a sign that Communism, "though oppressive, showed some signs of change for the better."[39] This interpretation of events was a continuation of the hope expressed in 1953 about the lessening of tensions brought about by the death of Stalin and the truce in Korea.[40] As early as 1955, Niebuhr applauded the fact that the Soviet leadership had ceased to refer to the United States as "capitalist warmongers," and he observed that "empirical reality is bound to dissolve the fanaticism which gave the Communist world its cohesion and its striking power."[41] It follows, then, that America "must modify our polemical attitudes toward the Russians, cease from ascribing to them all the ills from which we suffer, and come to regard them as partners in saving mankind from catastrophe."[42] In a 1958 editorial in *Christianity and Crisis,* Niebuhr wrote: "The fate of the world depends upon our capacity to leaven the lump of our own orthodox conceptions of an unchangeable Communist orthodoxy."[43]

Incidentally, it is crucial to note that Niebuhr's Cold War convictions were in no small measure related to his appreciation for and his sense of identification with the "Atlantic community." This community of nations "was anchored in the common culture and historical exigencies of western Europe and its North American offshoots," and its three "underlying unities" included a religious heritage "derived from Biblical faith," a relatively benign secularism which "does not seriously challenge the main ethical affirmations of that faith," and a lengthy shared "history of gradually achieved toleration."[44] This devotion to an organically created cultural and political community led Niebuhr to assert that all of its members had a duty to one another,

not only to protect the cherished values of their civilization
against a foe but to relate this achievement to a global community by striving to dissipate resentments so that Western countries would not be seen as desiring for themselves what they
were not ready to share with others.

It also led him to assert that the Atlantic nations are "so placed that,
by defending their own liberties, they also contribute to the liberties
of others not in their community of destiny."[45]

Third-World Nations

Since Niebuhr was by heritage, experience, and inclination a
markedly Eurocentric person, his appraisal of third-world issues was
usually centered on their relevance for Cold War concerns. As
Charles Brown puts it, when early in the 1960s

the Cold War shifted increasingly to the Third World and Kennedy inspired American efforts to help the emerging nations of
Africa and Asia as well as Latin America, Niebuhr enlarged upon
points he had made during the past decade and sought to define
opposition to Communism in terms broader than the defense of
Western democratic culture. Military concerns, he insisted,
should not obscure basic socioeconomic problems in those vast
areas.[46]

It must be admitted, however, that Niebuhr's understanding of these
problems and of the wide variety of peoples confronted by them was
greatly limited by his inability to travel. John Bennett argues that the
lack of first-hand acquaintance with third-world countries is one of
the most significant limitations imposed upon Niebuhr's life and
mind by his stroke in 1952.[47]

One of the issues Niebuhr might have seen somewhat differ-
ently had his travel schedule not been so severely curtailed was colonialism. Be that as it may, his writings reveal that Reinhold Niebuhr
was not a thoroughgoing critic of imperialism. He was empirically
and historically inclined to feel that the impact of colonialism in
many parts of the world was, on the whole, beneficial:

India could have become a nation only by the force of a common
resentment against the imperial master on the one hand, and by
the instruments of community which the master had furnished
on the other. The fact that many emancipated nations have not
been able to establish either stability or order . . . is proof of the

moral ambiguity, rather than the moral evil, of the imperial enterprise. . . .

American liberalism has tended to regard British "imperialism" as merely a system of exploitation—a judgment which not only disregards the very great democratic achievement embodied in the "Commonwealth" side of the British Empire, but also obscures some very real accomplishments in British colonial administration. . . . We ourselves are having to learn that power, once possessed, must be exercised; that its occasional misuse is no more grievous than an isolationist effort to disavow its responsibilities; that even the most responsible exercise of power is not free of imperial corruption; and that the danger of the exploitation of the weak by the strong can be overcome only by the gradual elaboration of the most careful political and moral restraints.[48]

It must immediately be added (and emphasized) that Niebuhr put the burden of proof on anyone who proposed to violate the political or cultural integrity of another nation and its people. Much of the polemic against those whose realism goes too far in the direction of amorality is a polemic against the tendency of American policymakers (and American public opinion) to put too much emphasis on military force and use it too quickly and too brutally. For example, when Formosa was a bone of contention in American political debate, Niebuhr criticized those extreme nationalists whose "undue reliance on purely military power" was accompanied by almost pathological impatience with the frustrations of forces beyond our control, which were new to a nation so suddenly vaulted into Western leadership.[49] He deplored the failure of American policymakers "to measure the breadth and depth of the anti-Yankee sentiment both in Cuba and the whole of Latin America," which he described as representing, in part, "a justified reaction to our economic imperialism." Likewise, he applauded the Alliance for Progress, and he opposed American intervention in the Dominican Republic.[50]

Furthermore, Niebuhr recognized that it would be folly to engage in cultural imperialism by attempting to impose the American model of democratic government on all third-world countries.[51] One important problem (which he referred to in 1963 as "the chief obstacle to the attainment of free government in nontechnical cultures") was "lack of minimal literacy, and the cultural competence based on this foundation."[52] Another is the fact that the mere acceptance of a democratic constitution and the holding of "free elections" do not accomplish very much in and of themselves.[53] In addition, what development theorists of the late 1950s called a "take-off into sustained growth" might go "hand in hand with political chaos."[54] Finally, Niebuhr conceded that Marxism

> still appears to be relevant to the recently emancipated nations of Africa and Asia, who have suffered or still suffer from foreign domination, and whose suffering has not ended with their throwing off the foreign yoke. . . . A free society is not as simple an alternative to the old feudal society as is the collectivism of communism which promises technical competence; promises, but does not grant, economic justice; and does *not* promise the individual freedom which the peoples of Asia and Africa have never enjoyed and which seems in any case to be beyond their reach.[55]

In sum,

> Democracy is at once a more tainted and at once a more impossible ideal than we have realized. . . . It has been tainted for the Asian and African nations because the democratic nations are also the technically most powerful nations, whose initial impact on the continents was imperialistic. It seems an impossible ideal because . . . [these nations] usually lack the religio-cultural foundation for individual freedom.
>
> [In addition,] they must still prove that individual liberty . . . can be made compatible with *both* justice and stability. [Beyond that, they must attain] a measure of moral and political wisdom which sets limits to party conflicts and the competition of conflicting interests within the community, [which] is not the simple fruit of literacy or even of intelligence. It is also a historical product, usually the fruit of generations of living together in freedom . . .
>
> The possibility rests upon the ability of men to transfer political skills and wisdom from one culture in which they matured into another culture in which they are not indigenous. This requires rare cooperation between the tutor nation and the apprentice; and resentments against the imperial tutor frequently make this cooperation extremely difficult.[56]

He recognized the good results achieved by one-party democracies in many parts of the world, and he contended that the non-Communist cause should be seen as more basic than the promotion of democracy. Our goal should be, to use Karl Popper's term, the preservation of an "open society."[57]

On the one hand, he believed that "the democratic alternative to communism" is by no means impossible in former colonial lands if a "rare cooperation between the tutor nation and the apprentice" can be achieved, and the realization of this possibility depends upon "the ability of men to transfer political skills and wisdom from one culture in which they matured into another culture in which they are not indigenous."[58] On the other hand, realizing that the assumptions just stated are decidedly paternalistic, he also admitted that the so-called developed nations must have "a long-range program . . . requiring not only ingenuity but patience."[59] They must realize that the ultimate benevolent interests of the free world "would best be served by countering overt Communist imperialism but allowing the developing nations to evolve their own answers to their needs."[60]

In 1956, the issue of enlightened support for emerging nations versus loyalty to NATO allies manifested itself in a brief but important crisis concerning Egypt and the Suez Canal. Israel, Britain, and France undertook to protect certain of their vital interests (assured access to the canal) by means of a joint invasion of Egypt. The Eisenhower administration was quick to denounce the action in the name of "peace, the UN, international law, and obedience to moral principle."[61] Niebuhr and other political realists deplored the administration's position, arguing that loyalty to our NATO allies and protection of their vital interests dictated a different posture. For Niebuhr, Secretary of State Dulles's rhetoric on this issue was a perfect illustration of the kind of empty moralism which prevented this country from responsible exercise of its role as leader of the free world. Reflecting on the Suez crisis several months later, Niebuhr wrote:

> Something has certainly gone wrong with the "moral influence" theory of diplomacy [articulated by Dulles]. . . . [For] idealism in politics is ineffective if it is not implemented in detailed policy. It is particularly dangerous when a great imperial power greater than that of Rome, namely, our own nation, is informed by such vague and fatuous idealism. . . . Marcus Aurelius was, in addition to his other virtues, an internationalist who said "as an Ant-

onine my city is Rome but as a man my city is the world," but the world did not profit by the confusion in which he left Rome.[62]

Niebuhr thought that the Eisenhower administration's behavior in the Suez crisis revealed "six great errors of U.S. foreign policy":[63]

1. failure to recognize European dependency upon Middle-East oil
2. failure to recognize that the Atlantic alliance was of overriding importance (making a "play for the sympathies of the uncommitted" nations a blind alley)
3. failure to realize that "the dynamism of the Egyptian dictatorship could only be contained by [military] power"
4. adoption of a policy of "absolute pacifism"
5. illusions about the U.S.S.R.
6. unrealistic expectations of the UN

Stone notes that all of these points are "related to Niebuhr's insistence that the imperial nations ought to recognize their power and attendant responsibilities and utilize force where necessary to secure the interests of their allies and themselves."

MILITARY POLICY

All of the aforementioned foreign policy issues were important— very important. But the most frightening and traumatic issues of the postwar period had to do with (1) long-term strategic doctrine regarding the nuclear balance of terror and (2) American military involvement in a country most U.S. citizens had never heard of: Vietnam.

The Nuclear Dilemma

Niebuhr's Cold War assumptions led him to endorse the strategic doctrine of nuclear deterrence. He opposed brinkmanship, and he believed that diplomacy rather than reliance on military might should be the cornerstone of an intelligent foreign policy. But he did not favor either nuclear disarmament or an iron-clad promise that America would never be the first to use nuclear weapons. He believed that there were a number of ways in which the animosity of the nuclear balance of terror could be mitigated, and he was very much in favor of following through on this effort as intelligently and as vigorously as possible.

Actually, says John Bennett, Niebuhr's thinking on the use of nuclear weapons must be understood in the context of his original postwar presupposition that any use of such weapons would be very limited. He never envisioned the possibility of nuclear winter, a concept which was much-discussed in the 1980s. Even so, he came to have second thoughts about the strategic doctrine of deterrence. He wondered, for example, "why our leaders are so complacent about the fact that physical survival seems now to mean our moral annihilation" because of the guilt we would shoulder if we actually made military use of nuclear bombs. Indeed, he declared that "even without the hydrogen bomb, a dozen Nagasaki bombs in Europe and Asia would mean the destruction of any moral claim for our civilization."[64] In 1961 he asked: "Could a civilization loaded with monstrous guilt have enough moral health to survive?" Bennett comments that in the 1960s Niebuhr "still believe[d] in deterrence but he ha[d] begun to [feel the USA should] avoid reacting to an attack with an attack."[65]

Vietnam

By the time Vietnam was turning American society upside-down in the mid-1960s, Reinhold Niebuhr was an old man and greatly enfeebled by debilitating illness. He was always worried about American policy in Southeast Asia, warning against hubris and unnecessary escalation in familiar ways, and thus he found it easy to criticize our excessive reliance upon military power and "the administration's pretense of virtue in the conflict."[66] He opposed the government's lack of candor concerning the war, but he "originally believed that our presence in Indochina was justified in order to resist the expansion of Communism."[67] And even "as late as January 1965, he entertained hopes that the administration was serving wise interests of the United States which it could not make public."[68]

But Niebuhr "soon became disillusioned by the succession of governments in South Vietnam [and] horrified by the cruelty of the war and the destruction that we were bringing to Vietnam," and before very long he "came to give moral support to the anti-war movement in our country."[69] By 1967 he was ready to go on record in opposition to the war, and he hoped that the admirable courage of draft card-burners would "change our fantastic course" in Southeast Asia.[70] In the foreword to a pamphlet containing speeches given at Riverside Church on April 4, 1967, Niebuhr voiced his deep concern about "our bloody, costly, and essentially futile involvement in a civil war in Vietnam" and denounced it as "an example of the 'illusion of American omnipotence.'"[71] A year later, he refused to back Hubert Humphrey in the 1968 presidential election. "Despite our long friendship," he wrote, "I could not endorse a candidate who is bound to our present futile policy in Vietnam."[72]

It is possible to interpret Niebuhr's denunciation of American policy in Vietnam as yet another counsel of prudence based on reasoning which was very much within the bounds of enlightened self-interest as defined by political realists. At times, he seems to be saying merely that the "imperial prestige, or the national prestige and imperial power" of the United States constituted its only real stake in the conflict and that such considerations were not "worth the price being paid to maintain them." Thus the war in Vietnam could be disavowed simply because it failed to meet the just war criterion of proportionality.[73] But John Bennett observes that "Niebuhr died before the full human cost of the war . . . was known." His last utterance on Vietnam went so far as to lament that "there is not much to choose between Communist and anti-Communist fanaticism," especially because "our wealth makes our religious anti-Communism particularly odious."[74]

But even so devoted a disciple as Ronald Stone is driven to conclude that Niebuhr was woefully slow in coming to appreciate certain deficiencies of American foreign policy which were apparent to many critics much sooner. He was especially tardy in acknowledging some of the errors (and wrongs) of U.S. policy in Latin America. (This could be in part because he was blinded by the charisma of John F. Kennedy, whose "Alliance for Progress" was hailed as a truly progressive policy initiative by many knowledgeable observers who might have been expected to know better.) But by the end of the decade of the 1960s he had come to realize that his earlier optimism concerning the subordination of the military to the political leadership of the country was suspect. In commenting on the influence of the Pentagon in 1969, Niebuhr said, "I think that the dominance of the military, whether in the ABM question or in Vietnam, is nearly overwhelming." Responding to a friendly observer's criticism on this point, he conceded: "You are right; in the light of Vietnam my confidence in the subjection of military to political authority is too simple."[75]

It is instructive to compare these comments on Niebuhr's assessment of the Vietnam War with Merkeley's critique of his overall stance toward the Soviet Union in the postwar era. In the 1930s, Niebuhr saw Communism as decidedly less menacing than Nazism. The former was a dangerous secular religion invalidated by numerous ideological rigidities and vulnerable to unconscionable totalitarian abuses (as Stalin was demonstrating). But at least it was cut out of the same cloth as other Western notions of progress toward greater justice and universal human fulfillment. Nazism, by contrast, was an atavistic glorification of barbarism. As late as 1943, Niebuhr was of the opinion that "although Communism uses dictatorship brutally, it does not exalt it as an end in itself. . . . Its moral cynicism is only provisional, and it is never morally nihilistic, as the Nazis are."[76] Indeed, at this point Niebuhr was still ready to "praise Russian achievements in the realm of social reform, and . . . allow that there was something unique in that record—something worth emulating."[77]

Only a few years later, however, Niebuhr decided that Communism was more evil than Nazism, and he allowed his estimate of the threat posed by the Soviet Union to push him in the direction of service as a Cold War ideologue. Writes Merkeley:

Niebuhr's commitment to the basic conceptions of the Cold War view of international realities was inflexible, a case-hardened tool of interpretation, hardly touched by the realities of spectacular discord within the Communist world; indifferent to the relatively humane accomplishments of Communist regimes. . . . At the root of this fixation was his patriotic ambition for America's success in the world—a success to be reckoned in terms of an ever-increasing effectiveness of her writ throughout the "non-technical world." . . . He could not envisage aggrandizement of America without diminishment of Russia. . . . No more than Woodrow Wilson was Niebuhr able to avoid the hazards for the soul of faith in the ultimate benignancy of America's imperialism. Niebuhr was fond of quoting John Adams' famous dictum on the subject: "Power always thinks it has a great soul and vast views beyond the comprehension of the weak, and that it is doing God's service when it is violating all His laws." Yet his own case for America's empire among "the weak" of the Third World was based on nothing else than his confidence in the vast views beyond their comprehension, which America's exceptional accomplishments in the realms of political and social democracy provided her.[78]

According to Merkeley, Niebuhr adopted a "bipolarism" in foreign policy (i.e., a consistent practice of viewing everything in terms of how it might affect the struggle between the two great powers). This stance was even more stringent and even more ardently anti-Communist than the geopolitical stance of secular political realists such as Hans Morgenthau. His bipolarism caused him to err in the following ways:

1. He invariably overestimated the Russian role in all of the "genuinely revolutionary" situations in the Third World.
2. He invariably overestimated the positive impact of the American presence "in the bailiwicks of her client governments in the Third World.
3. He consistently devalued the popular legitimacy of revolutionary forces in the Third World.
4. He grew steadily more pessimistic about "the prospect for orderly and humane government in the Third World."[79]

Summary

Our discussion of Niebuhr's attempt to comment on specific foreign policy issues is bound to include a frank acknowledgment of his shortcomings in this area of ethical analysis. To end this chapter on that note would be a neat segue into the next chapter, which summarizes the most important recent criticisms of Niebuhr's thought. But it would hardly be fair to bring the chapter to an end without reminding ourselves of the solid contributions to be found in his writings on these subjects. In Stone's view, Niebuhr deserves appreciation for a "moderate realism" which has the wisdom to disavow "single-factor approaches or any inclination to regard politics as a game which follows certain rules." Niebuhr was right in emphasizing

> the need for understanding material factors, the character of the political actors, the role of illusion and myth in foreign policies, the history of international politics, the tools of foreign policy, the nature of the societies under consideration and the character of international competition and cooperation.[80]

Lefever's praise parallels that of Stone on several points, but he is even more emphatic on one or two particulars. He admires Niebuhr's willingness to challenge the mistrust of the state which has often prevented sentimental moralists from acknowledging the realities of power and involved them in "the arrogance of weakness."[81] He stresses the importance of Niebuhr's healthy suspicion of both reckless intervention and counter-productive isolationism and asserts that all intelligent people who desire stability and peace should be grateful to Niebuhr as the prophet of "idealism without illusion and realism without despair." Lefever expresses his approval of Niebuhr's attack on "false prophets" in these not altogether gentle words:

> He directs his frank and powerful polemics against men with noble intentions who, instead of being as wise as serpents are as harmless as doves and as stupid as chickens. The political irrelevance and moral irresponsibility of the "children of light," he says, is a result of their [preoccupation with] virtue, their desire to be pure and right.[82]

Chapter 6

Major Criticisms of Niebuhrianism

Chapter 5 introduced a discussion of the most important criticisms of Reinhold Niebuhr's thought, particularly the allegation that he allowed himself to be exploited by the power elites of the nation during the Cold War era. The present chapter will provide a survey of other major challenges to Christian Realism during the past fifty years. But the survey of recent criticisms cannot proceed without an understanding of Niebuhrianism during the period between 1945 and 1966.

The Reign of Niebuhrianism

During the 1940s Niebuhr was the darling of sophisticated Protestant thought in the USA. Students at America's most highly regarded theological seminaries found themselves immersed in a faculty ethos dominated by Niebuhrian ideas. Many of their professors opposed various aspects of Niebuhr's Christian Realism, but even the adversaries felt called upon to proclaim their opposition, and many faculty members were zealous disciples. In any case, Niebuhr's writings were required reading (and the focus of intense interest) in academically respected institutions of religious instruction. The graduates of these seminaries, who went on to occupy the pulpits of the most "up-to-date" churches in the country, were imbued with Niebuhrian ideas and so made them the focus of many a sermon. This trend intensified during the postwar period when a sizable number of veterans took up the study of theology and went on to positions of influence in parishes, denominations, and universities across the nation.

The same was even more true of what Paul Ramsey has called the "social action curia" of the mainline Protestant denominations and the National Council of Churches (which was headquartered right across the street from Union Theological Seminary (UTS) in New York City). Shortly after the World Council of Churches (WCC) was established in the late 1940s, its Office of Church and Society was entrusted to a UTS graduate named Paul Abrecht, who spent the next thirty years organizing ecumenical study groups which brought a pronounced Niebuhrian outlook to their exploration of various worldwide social problems. Because many of the leaders of the "younger" churches in countries that had once been colonies were men and women who had studied at UTS (and other mainline Protestant seminaries where Niebuhrianism was in vogue), many of those appointed to WCC study groups from all over the world were admirers of Niebuhr's thought. So his influence on European Protestantism and on the WCC was very powerful.

This was particularly true of British theological opinion. Partly because of Niebuhr's admiration for English political leaders (such as Cripps and Churchill) and the Tawney-Temple stream of thought in Anglican social philosophy, and partly because of Niebuhr's participation in the crucial ecumenical conferences leading to the establishment of the WCC in 1948, his imprint is evident in the writings of leading British theologians and ethicists such as Denys Munby, E. R. Wickham (the founder of Industrial Mission in Britain), R. H. Preston, and John Atherton. His influence is also evident in the work of the bishops and the Board for Social Responsibility of the Church of England and in the scholarly output of the Center for Christianity and Social Policy in Edinburgh.[1]

Winds of Change in the Sixties

The winds of change were already blowing, however, not only among people in what we now refer to as the Third World, but also among women outraged by gender inequality and among African-Americans fed up with racial injustice. Several brands of liberation theology were germinating, and the WCC's 1966 Geneva Conference was a milestone in the articulation of third-world grievances which have since become familiar to anyone who reads the newspaper. These theologies of liberation frequently cited Reinhold Niebuhr as an enemy: they saw him as the epitome of the hierarchical patriarchal thinking which had been used to justify European and North American imperialism and which had for so long been a source of various kinds of oppression. Not surprisingly, liberation theology was one of the new developments which provoked the rise of a reactionary social philosophy called neoconservatism (in Britain, the "New Right"), and certain exponents of this school of thought tried to claim Niebuhr as the progenitor of their movement.

A Catalog of Criticisms

It seems to me that any student of Reinhold Niebuhr ought to feel obliged to come to terms with the most valid and important of these reactions to Niebuhrianism. If it can be shown that allegiance to Niebuhr is problematic, or that the motives of his supporters are unworthy, Niebuhrians ought to be grateful for being shown the error of their ways. What could be worse than a nagging doubt that you are invested in a particular theory or methodology simply because you once put a lot of effort into mastering its content or because you are too stubborn to acknowledge the counterproductive impact of these ideas in the current setting? So I hope the reader will credit me with being absolutely sincere and earnest in wanting to offer a fair-minded examination of the inadequacies of Christian Realism.

How best to proceed? The first task is to clear away the underbrush by listing a number of relatively indefensible criticisms which can be dispensed with in very short order. More important, an absolutely clear statement must be advanced to explain exactly what kind of evaluation is being carried out, and what its purposes are.

Several criticisms have already been dealt with in the first five chapters of the book. Christian Realism was correct in its assessment of the utopian illusions of the Social Gospel, pacifism, Marxism, and liberal humanism's faith in the inevitability of progress through education. Furthermore, Niebuhr was right in asserting that realistic social reformers must know how to generate and use power in pursuit of their worthy objectives.

But there are three other criticisms which merit brief rejoinders. They pertain to Niebuhr's status as a spokesman for orthodox Christianity, his presumed emphasis upon empiricism and history, and his role as an apologist for the "free world" in the Cold War era.

"Niebuhr Wasn't Really an Orthodox Christian"

Various theologians have taken Niebuhr to task for being insufficiently Christocentric and—in a related complaint—for paying too much attention to justification by faith and not enough to the possibilities of sanctification in the redeemed life. All of this is sometimes associated with a rebuke of Niebuhr's failure to understand Christian pacifism.

Staunch exponents of orthodoxy are understandably offended by Niebuhr's evident agreement with what Beatrice and Sidney Webb used to speak of as Christianity's "ridiculous deification of a man named Jesus." Calvinists and Methodists alike are annoyed by his skepticism concerning the ability of the forgiven sinner to "to move perfectly on toward perfection" and by his refusal to speak of this as an essential obligation for those who have been saved by grace. Many Christian pacifists are indignant over what they see as Niebuhr's culpable misinterpretation of the teachings of the New Testament and the historic peace churches on this matter. (Some pacifists are especially puzzled and angry about the fact that so many church people—especially Christian academics—seem to regard Niebuhr's refutation of pacifism as conclusive.[2]

There is probably a certain amount of truth in all of these criticisms, and those who see Niebuhr's deficiencies in these areas as damning are entitled to their opinion. Nevertheless, I think that Niebuhr is more right than wrong on all of these questions. Because the quest for mythopoeic profundity leads to an appreciation of the greatest insights of biblical faith and avoids the errors of fundamentalism or unyielding orthodoxy, one ought not to be disturbed by Niebuhr's lack of Christocentrism or his reservations about sanctification. And even though the distinctively new type of pragmatic pacifism which has arisen in recent years is of considerable interest (and is something which Niebuhr's analysis did not envision),[3] pacifists, despite their courage and idealism, are ethically irresponsible in refusing to do what must be done to protect potential victims from the savagery of evildoers. Niebuhr was fundamentally correct in his rejection of pacifism as a strategy of effective defense against state-sponsored military aggression or terrorism.

Insufficient Empiricism?

A more fundamental and far-ranging criticism has been brought forward by Beverly Harrison, who speaks from the twin perspectives of feminism and Marxism. Some of the points made by Harrison are sufficiently important to be dealt with in the following section, but some are less telling.

In charging that Niebuhr tended to romanticize the family and the extent to which intrafamily relationships could be a haven of caring, nurture, and love, Harrison is also attacking the famous thesis developed in *Moral Man and Immoral Society* concerning the qualitative differences between the private and public realms. In "predicating his entire social ethical approach on a presumed discontinuity between the dynamics of power existing in social, economic, and political life and the dynamics of power in interpersonal transactions,"[4] Niebuhr obscured the moral outrage of injustice in both areas:

> He never questioned the dualism embedded in liberal political
> ideology between the "private" sphere, that is, the arena of those
> interpersonal, humane relations of the family, and the "public"
> sphere, those "impersonal relations" of institutions and collec-
> tivities. He did not notice that this private/public split legit-
> imized both a capitalist mode of political-economic organization
> and female subjugation in personal or domestic life.[5]

Moreover, "political realism's ahistorical treatment of power remains an insurmountable limitation":

> When "power" is conceived, as Niebuhr and other realists con-
> ceived it, as an inevitable dynamic of individual and group self-
> assertion endlessly repeating itself, the particularity of historical
> process and shifting history of institutions largely drops out of
> the picture.[6]

The result, says Harrison, is "a great irony—one which Niebuhr might appreciate":

> Political realism . . . has threatened a genuinely historical sensi-
> bility in our social ethics. Realists assume that all political
> struggle is reducible to the same core dynamic, that all agents in-
> exorably are drawn to patterns of power seeking and self-
> aggrandizement mirrored at the macro-social level by the dy-

namics of nation–states. As a result, realists find little or no
moral ground for choosing between sides in such struggles for
power. [How ironic] that the empirically oriented Niebuhr actually opened religious ethics to an anti–empirical, and probably
the most anti–historical, social theory available in his time or
ours. When this paradigm is embellished with a passionate endorsement of capitalism that Niebuhr did not fully share, the historical awareness for which he pled has disappeared entirely.[7]

Harrison's assault is a startling tour de force of the critical imagination, but her conclusions do not follow from her (debatable)
premises. It is absurd to contend that anyone who wrote as much as
Reinhold Niebuhr did on particular social issues has lost touch with
"particular historical processes" or "the shifting history of institutions." And Harrison cannot legitimately interpret Niebuhr's ultimate rejection of the Marxist framework as a sign that he is ignorant
of underlying political forces and economic realities. His analysis of
the love–justice dialectic shows, for example, that even though he
seldom addressed family-related issues, he was very much aware of
the fact that all human relationships entail power dynamics, and that
(as feminists rightly remind us) the personal is (also) political. And
one cannot but be astonished by Harrison's claim that Niebuhrian
realists find "little or no moral ground for choosing sides in . . .
struggles for power," for Niebuhr's entire career was devoted to
choosing sides and formulating a theological-social analysis which
was intended to enlist ethically sensitive people in various struggles
on the side of relative good.

COLD WAR IDEOLOGY "IN TOTO"?

Critics of European and American imperialism, including the
economic imperialism of capitalist multinational corporations, often
dismiss Christian Realism as "in toto an ideology of the [Western]
establishment."[8] The best statement of this position has been composed by Cornel West; nevertheless, the sweeping implications of
West's polemic remain problematic.[9] This interpretation of Niebuhr's
postwar thought even receives a rather curious reinforcement from
the spurious attempt on the part of some self-professed Niebuhrians
to embrace their hero as the intellectual and moral progenitor of
contemporary American neoconservatism.[10]

One of the most judicious refutations of this claim has been penned by William Lee Miller:

> He did indeed turn much of his fire on the foolishness, as well as the evil, that came from the left, but he did it not as a conservative or neoconservative but as one who wanted social reform to be more effective. He did say many of the things neoconservatives now say, about the limits of what deliberate social policy can do, about the organic, nonrational bonds of society, about the unintended side effects of social action, and about the necessity of balances of power. But he said all that not to baptize the status quo and American nationalism, but to encourage a wiser and more persistent pursuit of justice.[11]

I believe that this critique of Christian Realism as pure establishment ideology is further refuted by the account of Niebuhr's pronouncements on ethics and foreign policy in chapter 5. Moreover, it is thoroughly discredited by Charles Brown and John C. Bennett's account of what Niebuhr wrote on particular foreign-policy issues in the 1950s and 1960s.[12] Given the particularities of the period—the unpalatable realities of Stalinism, and the relatively humane vitalities of the Western democracies and capitalism, it is difficult to deny the wisdom of Niebuhr's position on many specific issues.[13]

THE PURPOSE OF EVALUATION

There are three main points to be made in connection with the proper focus of analytical concern in assessing the criticisms addressed to Niebuhr's thought:

1.   The issue is not primarily Reinhold Niebuhr *l'homme*. This book argues that Niebuhr has much to offer as both model and mentor, but our argument is not centered upon the contention that Niebuhr himself was a saint any more than it is on the contention that he was correct in every word that he penned on every topic he addressed. If Niebuhr is to be pointed to as a model of Christian discipleship in the modern world, insights into his character are relevant, of course—but arguments based upon his psychological idiosyncrasies and his personality characteristics are not especially germane, and ad hominem criticisms of Niebuhr which are based on speculations of this kind carry little weight.

2. The issue is not, moreover, Reinhold Niebuhr's "batting average" on specific items of ethics and social policy. The point is neither praise nor blame of Niebuhr, but rather an appraisal of the fruitfulness of Christian Realism as a guide to effective social witness and social reform. What we want to know is: on what points, and in what specific ways, is Niebuhr a help or a hindrance in addressing the moral and political problems of our day?[14]

3. This means that, although Niebuhr himself is not the issue, we must nonetheless take stock of Niebuhr's record as a theological ethicist, a policy analyst, and a political strategist. It is imperative that we should not be misled: we have to know how much, and how, we can rely on his guidance in all three of these areas: theological insight, policy specification, and strategic savvy. We admire the theory in part because we think he was right about applied ethics on a host of problems where many other thinkers and do-gooders were wrong. But that means we should be doubly eager to check the record and figure out whether his failures of perception or action may have been caused by flaws in the theory. And that is the focus of our concern for the remainder of this chapter.

Significant Criticisms

The most formidable objections to Christian Realism can be grouped under the three major categories of psychocultural, economic, and political shortcomings. Under these headings we shall examine (1) Niebuhr's (presumably) inadequate understanding of the plight of the dispossessed, (2) his (supposedly) truncated view of the proper goals of economic life, and (3) his (allegedly) excessive optimism regarding American democracy.

THE PLIGHT OF THE EXCLUDED, THE DISPOSSESSED, AND THE OPPRESSED

Liberation theologies of all kinds have rebuked Niebuhr for having an ethnocentric, class-defined anthropology which does not fit the life-experience and the spiritual or political needs of the majority of the world's population. In *Christian Realism and Liberation Theology,* Dennis McCann puts it this way:

> [Niebuhr's] "Christian interpretation of human nature" was and
> is a promising way to establish the reference of his paradoxical
> vision of a Hidden God, since without a correspondingly para-

doxical understanding of human selfhood, this religious vision
cannot be translated into theology. Nevertheless, a difficulty
emerges as Niebuhr attempted to elaborate his anthropology into
a theology of history. Through a metaphorical extension, the
concepts defining human "selfhood" and "society" were made
virtually interchangeable. But while the metaphors of selfhood
are psychologically illuminating, they may be less adequate as a
framework of social theory.[15]

The "problem of ideological drift created by the use of Christian
Realism's anthropology as a mode of political analysis" manifests
itself in a concept of the self which has much greater relevance for
"the aggressive personality" with "a high level of vitality" than it
does for the dispossessed and the powerless. Niebuhr assumes that
"man" has "an almost spontaneous tendency to think and act in one's
own interests," and his conception of "human nature" is that of

> an active, dynamic "self," driven by anxiety, but also capable of
> a high level of personal integration—perhaps a model of the suc-
> cessful urban American of his day. For the most part, Niebuhr's
> counsels seek to channel constructively the force of this type of
> personality, by challenging him or her to adopt a measure of
> self-restraint and an attitude of self-criticism. "Humility" and
> "sacrificial love" thus are commended as the resources of Chris-
> tian faith for social action.
>
> No doubt, Niebuhr's diagnosis has the ring of truth for most
> of his North American readers. But his "self" is not the only
> personality type, and for today's social activists [who lean toward
> a special "option for the poor"] perhaps not the most imme-
> diately relevant. Recent psychological studies suggest that per-
> sons suffering the effects of oppression tend to react submissively
> to their situation. Typically, their aggression is directed not
> against their oppressors but against themselves. It is as if they
> must become "selves" in Niebuhr's sense before they can begin
> to change their situation. Thus the oppressed may have to over-
> come moral paralysis more often than the self-righteousness em-
> phasized by Niebuhr.[16]

McCann's critique, which is set forth primarily from the standpoint of Latin American liberation theology, is paralleled by the
feminist critique of Niebuhr's emphasis on "pride as *the* primary

human sin."[17] Writers such as Judith Plaskow and Valerie Saiving complain that the focus on pride is more appropriate for men than it is for women, because whereas men are socialized to be self-assertive and actively competitive, women are encouraged to be self-effacing. It is *men* who are therefore tempted to generate too much will-to-power and to become excessively proud of themselves when they succeed and pretentious in what they attempt. But women, who have been told over and over again that they ought to be submissive and deferential, and ought to renounce power for the superior virtue of sacrificial service to their families, are damaged by an over-emphasis on pride. Because women need more—not less—confidence and assertiveness, it is a genuine disservice to tell women that pride is the deadliest of sins. What they more typically need to feel guilty about, says Plaskow, is failing to develop their potential fully and instead living vicariously through their husbands and children. She uses Doris Lessing's novels to point out that the greatest danger for many women is precisely the loss of self caused by absorption in the petty flux of domestic life, not undue self-assertion, pride, or will-to-power.[18]

In addition, says Plaskow, Niebuhr's notion of grace as a greater capacity for life in accordance with agape is misleading and hurtful to women.

> Insofar as Niebuhr sees self-sacrifice as the universal norm of human existence—a response to the universal sin of pride—his account of grace is distorted in a way similar to his doctrine of sin.[19]

Again, a character from a Lessing novel is adduced to illustrate the point: "Lessing's Martha . . . is inactive; she drifts; she looks to others for self-definition; she fails to take responsibility for her own life."[20] Echoing McCann's description of the plight of poor people in Latin America, Plaskow notes that "these faults require a very different sort of grace from the shattering of the self and self-reconstitution along principles very different from those Niebuhr envisages," for "she has no self to sacrifice."

Aurelia Takacs Fule develops a more discriminating version of this argument in a very perceptive essay on "Being Human Before God: Reinhold Niebuhr in Feminist Mirrors." Contending that any anthropology which presumes to speak of humankind in general must not fail to take the specialness of women's experience seriously, she observes that one crucial deficiency in Niebuhrian thought is its inadequate appreciation of the elusiveness of selfhood in women's experience. According to Fule, Niebuhr's assumptions about the paradoxical relationship between self-negation and self-realization downplay the ability of the self to exercise "rational control of all unconscious stirrings of selfhood" and even declares that "the self [which] lacks the faith and trust to subject itself to God" ends by asserting a "self" that is "less than the true self."[21] This warning against the wrong kind of self-assertion ties in with Niebuhr's emphasis upon the highest kind of love as selflessness/self-sacrifice to produce a high degree of ambivalence about self-realization, and in our culture this translates into a reinforcement of the patriarchal notion that the best way for women to realize themselves in accordance with their true natures is to be submissive and to invest their lives in unselfish subordination to the family. If all of this is tied in with a romanticized view of the family (which, according to Beverly Harrison, Niebuhr holds and recommends), we end up with a doctrine of "man" which constitutes a formidable detriment to the right of women to determine their own personhoods and destinies in the same way that men are allowed to do (and rewarded for doing).

Fule agrees with Plaskow that the hurtful impact on women is intensified by Niebuhr's failure to understand the most important implication of sin as sensuality—i.e., the temptation to forfeit one's highest possibilities for self-development in renunciation via absorption into the life (and even the personalities) of husband and children.[22]

The dissatisfaction of feminist and third-world liberation theologians has much in common with that of African-American critics. Just as Niebuhr's failure to appreciate the distinctiveness of women's experience created a blind spot in his view of the plight of women in a patriarchal culture (or of colonial people in a world shaped by imperialism), his Eurocentrism kept him from fully appreciating the anguish of African-American people in a racist society. Herbert Edwards argues that Niebuhr (partly because of his strenuous efforts to discard his German-American heritage so that he could be "100 percent American")[23] was in many unfortunate ways "very much a white man of his times." So we should not be surprised that "civil rights had never been one of Niebuhr's preoccupations, [for] after all, it had never been the preoccupation of any of the major white, American Protestant Christian theologians and ethicists."[24] Even though he deserves some credit for "speaking out against 'racial pride' more often and more critically than any other theologian of that time," he still exhibited certain aspects of the Anglo-Saxon sense of superiority which made him something of a British colonialist in his gut feelings (and, therefore, his policy recommendations) on matters pertaining to race. This (perhaps unconscious) attribute of Niebuhr's thinking led him to "respond to the increasing restiveness among blacks and to the civil rights movement by overemphasizing their disruptive impact on the white Southern social structure and by cautioning blacks against demanding too much too soon."[25]

All of these criticisms of substance are associated with a criticism of Niebuhr's methodology—indeed a criticism of the theologizing of all academics whose social analysis is carried out in an ivory tower apart from vital contact (and solidarity) with the people in the lower strata of society. The crux of this argument has to do with its presuppositions concerning the relationship between ends and means and with the further contention that process is as important as product and must be subject to similar ethical criteria.

This point was articulated in an especially interesting way in one of the papers presented at the Reinhold Niebuhr Centenary Symposium in Montreal in 1992. In a Christian Socialist appraisal of Niebuhrian thought, Oscar Arnal attributed many of its shortcomings to the fact that—like most academicians—Niebuhr was an "armchair ethicist" whose inability (or unwillingness) to speak for the downtrodden was a function of his lack of vital contact with them. Arnal contrasted Niebuhr with a number of "worker priest" Catholics whose work was to be admired. This emphasis on solidarity with the poor or excluded is often combined in liberation thought with an insistence on interactive processes which allow genuine participation by the poor in the formulation of policies affecting them. This insistence often yields some very specific guidelines for proper methodology in "doing ethics." These are the words of a recent World Council of Churches' study group which wrestled with the implications of the idea that "the end of the action must be visible in the means used" to achieve it:

> Participation means that each person's contribution is valued, and everyone is encouraged to take an active part. The organization is non-hierarchical. . . . [and] leadership is present, but as a shared function. [This requires] (1) "protecting speaking time" by, for

example, going round the circle and allowing each person to speak for a specific time. . . . that (2) knowledge and skills should be shared and responsibilities rotated in the group. . . . [and that] (3) feelings are valued and expressed.[26]

COMPLACENCY ABOUT CAPITALISM

Criticism of Niebuhr's supposed pessimism is also linked to his position on economic issues, especially his abandonment of Socialism. Exponents of this view accuse Niebuhr of giving too little attention to economic issues after 1940 and being somewhat ignorant and astonishingly wrongheaded in many of the ideas and particular judgments he did advance in the area of the ethics of economic life. It is alleged that he retreated too far from his original interest in Marx, that his thinking was marred by a surprisingly shallow comprehension of Keynes, and that what he says about economic affairs after World War II shows scant appreciation of the importance of equality as a norm in the Christian understanding of economic justice. These theoretical errors resulted in an altogether too sanguine view of post-New Deal capitalism in America.

Beverly Harrison faults Niebuhr for having a "bias toward politics" which unduly minimizes the independent importance of economic variables and of economics as a scholarly discipline. In placing so much reliance on political philosophy and political science as the most instructive fields of academic study, Niebuhr did a terrible disservice to social theory in Christian ethics, for the "imaging of human social relations" in political realism as a social theory "simply leaves economic life out of account." This flaw is the result of "an overriding focus on political power as either self-assertion or national interest," which unfortunately "correlates with an assumption that such power invariably keeps economic power in check." Thus,

Niebuhr himself seemed never to notice that political realism arose historically to reflect and justify aristocratic class interest. . . . He pressed realism into the service of a different ideology—one at the middle of the political spectrum—and made it serve as an analytic tool for reformist welfare liberalism.[27]

One of the most deplorable consequences of this bias toward political realism is "his ongoing polemic, even diatribe, against Marx and Marxist social theory." Harrison finds this ill-informed dismissal of Marxist thought especially distressing because of the fact that it has "left us a legacy of all but impenetrable closed-mindedness about any and all social theory influenced by this architect of dissenting, radical political economy [i.e., Marx]."[28]

L. Katherine Harrington agrees with Harrison's point concerning Niebuhr's penchant for subsuming the study of economics under the study of politics. She is not disturbed by Niebuhr's retreat from Marx, but she does believe that his minimal understanding of Keynes led him to put too much emphasis on balance-of-power as a remedy for economic injustice. Because "there is an apparent ignorance on Niebuhr's part of the extent to which his own natural sympathies regarding social life aligned with Keynes'[s] views," Niebuhr never "had more than a passing understanding of Keynes' economic philosophy." Therefore, argues Harrington, Niebuhr

> . . . may have too narrowly interpreted Keynesian economic policy as "minimal function" to stabilize economic operations. Likewise, Niebuhr seems to ignore, or be ignorant of, the extent to which Keynesian thought supports government intervention through fiscal policy to increase employment and improve economic output.[29]

M. M. Thomas, a highly regarded leader of Protestant theological education in India, is as direct and judgmental as any of Niebuhr's critics in asserting that "radical changes, even sudden turn-abouts, took place in his concept of the norm and form of the 'quest for justice.'" Thomas is willing to overlook particular lapses (even "the almost unscrupulous fluctuations of his concept of justice") because he admires Niebuhr's basic achievement in "weld[ing] together the tragic sense of life and the quest for justice," especially his "exposition of the relation between eschatology and history, justifying a realistic as opposed to a utopian historical involvement in struggles for justice." Thomas goes so far as to agree with Brazilian theologian Rubem Alves that "even in Niebuhr" Christian Realism became "in toto an ideology of the establishment," but he undercuts the force of this surprisingly reductionistic judgment by maintaining that Christian Realism "also had its social revolutionary applications, depending upon an egalitarian social concern and a revolutionary reading of the dynamics of a social situation."[30]

Nevertheless, writes Thomas, Niebuhr is guilty of going through a number of somewhat bewildering "fluctuations" in his position on economic ethics. In the late 1930s, Niebuhr was a tremendous help to members of the Youth Christian Council of Action in Kerala (to which Thomas belonged), because at that time "Niebuhr's definition of justice had equality as a regulating principle, and as a criterion for evaluating societies." Thus, in his 1937 essay for the Oxford Conference (a major milestone on the road to the World Council of Churches), Niebuhr wrote: "Justice without the regulating principle of equality merely becomes a sanctification for whatever relations and uneven justice may have been achieved in a given period of history."[31]

By 1947 Niebuhr had become "'the political democrat infatuated with Burkean traditionalism' . . . with 'justice through adjustment' as its social content." By this time Niebuhr had begun to proclaim that Communism was more demonic than fascism and that, Thomas declares, was "different from his earlier stand, [and] I felt personally betrayed." After venturing the speculation that it was "Niebuhr's ignorance, willful or otherwise, of the political and moral dynamics of the non-Western world that blinded him to those implications and misled him into concentrating on democracy versus Communism as the only issue in American foreign policy," Thomas observes, "Out of touch with reality, realism can go wrong."[32]

Thomas also takes Niebuhr to task for his relative indifference to the injustices of imperialism and his excessive faith in technological modernization. In the first place, Niebuhr never "considered the Asia-African situation as an issue of social justice for their peoples. The nearest he came was when he wrote that . . . [the United States should] help the impoverished world to gain greater technical efficiency." Second, he seemed oblivious to the ambiguities of technological development as it would actually be put into effect by corporations of technologically advanced nations.

> When he emphasized "technical efficiency," did he forget that increased technical efficiency in Detroit brought increased oppression and that it might do the same in the Third World if it was not coupled with social transformation for justice? Or by this time [1952] did he accept the ideology of the American free enterprise system that technological modernization under America's leadership was for the ultimate good of all?[33]

Third, he did seem to believe this gospel of salvation through technology regarding Palestine, for he believed that the new nation of Israel

> . . . besides doing justice to Jews as a people . . . would also liberate Jewish energy and skill to turn the Middle East into a "technical and dynamic civilization." Even if the Arabs would lose their homeland and suffer injustice in the immediate round, the technical transformation of their "pathetic pastoral economy" into a modern one would do them good "in the long run."[34]

Thomas's criticism has much in common with that of Cornel West, who uses Niebuhr's pronouncements on Israel as a key example of the fact that his Europeanist bias and Amerocentric prejudice caused him to "overlook the claims of self-determination of peoples of color and colonized peoples."[35]

EXCESSIVE OPTIMISM ABOUT AMERICAN DEMOCRACY

To entertain the thought that Reinhold Niebuhr may have been a bit too timid in his definition of an optimally just and humane economic system is to raise questions about the heart and soul of Christian Realism—i.e., does its desire to be realistic lead to a consistent pattern of pusillanimity which settles for a half-loaf when the full loaf might actually be attainable and ought to be striven for?

Niebuhr vs. "The Feminist Ethic of Risk"

This excessive timidity in goal-setting is, as it happens, the (potential) defect of Christian Realism which is highlighted in Sharon Welch's *Niebuhr vs. the Feminine Ethic of Risk*. Since Christian Realism presents itself as a theory which is superior to more idealistic versions of social ethics in its emphasis on effectiveness, Niebuhrians are fond of claiming that they are less interested in being right (or appearing to be right) than they are in actually accomplishing a modicum of good in this wicked world. They are proud that their understanding of politics as the art of the possible enables them to obtain the partial good of incremental improvement instead of obtaining *nothing* while they maintain their nobility by stating and restating their demands for the ideal good of social *transformation*.

Thus it comes as a genuine shock to be confronted with a critic who asserts that the Niebuhrian approach is a hindrance to commitment and active involvement. Yet that is precisely the claim of

Sharon Welch, who views the consequentialist emphasis on being successful in one's social reform efforts as an excuse for inaction. Preoccupation with "being effective," Welch warns, can be used as a convenient rationalization of "the cultured despair" of the sophisticated spectator-citizen who will not risk involvement in any political endeavor which does not involve the prospect of winning in the next session of Congress or the next summit conference.

Welch's chief example of this disconcerting state of affairs is nuclear deterrence. She argues that it is finally ignominious to "go along with" an obviously demonic strategic doctrine when a willingness to risk aggressive support for nuclear disarmament might actually result in a change of policy on the part of both superpowers. Whether or not she is right on this particular issue, the theoretical indictment is clear: the Christian realist's fixation on achieving a certain payoff (i.e., being successful in whatever you go all out to achieve) is a counterproductive hindrance to optimal prophetic witness.

Edwards's Attack on Niebuhr's Establishmentarianism

Welch's complaint is paralleled by Herbert Edwards's assault on Niebuhr's lack of imagination (or lack of courage) in assessing racial injustice and determining the best way to overcome it. Edwards's assessment of the record on this set of issues offers a kind of case study of the excessive practicality challenged by Welch.

Edwards gives six illustrations of Niebuhr's tendency to warn blacks not to demand too much too soon. He discerns a four-step pattern which consistently "placed the black movement on the defensive," and which always follows the same logic:

First, agreement with the noble aims and ideals of the black movement, with the *moral* ideal. Second, the "realistic" analysis of the *political* situation, [which] explains why failure is all but inevitable given the nature of [the power realities of the white power structure]. Third, the attempt to locate a course of action that will not rock the boat too much, to locate an "uneasy conscience" among the enemies of "racial justice." This conscience can be appealed to by not demanding too much too soon, by demanding not what the established powers will not give but what they might be willing to cede. Finally comes the advice to the victims of racism and their supporters: Be patient.[36]

This pattern of analysis caused Niebuhr to declare that 1950 was too early to seek a Fair Employment Practices Amendment (FEPA), because "even if the FEPA had passed, it could not have been enforced since it was in conflict with the conscience of the Southern community (i.e., the white Southern community)." Better to have begun by seeking "anti-lynching and anti-poll tax legislation" since these were issues which troubled many white Southerners.[37] Niebuhr's approach even raised doubts about the NAACP's legal offensive and about its milestone victory in *Brown vs. Board of Education*. In 1956 Niebuhr was still using what Edwards characterizes as vintage Christian Realist rhetoric to counsel patience:

> Real statesmanship will be required to uphold the majesty of the law and at the same time win over a custom-bound community to fuller conformity to the law. Prudence is as necessary as courage. . . . And a genuine charity is the father of prudence. For genuine love does not propose abstract schemes of justice which leave the human factor out of account.[38]

And although Niebuhr generally approved of Martin Luther King's nonviolent tactics of "passive insistence," he argued as late as 1964 that: "Perhaps the only policy that white people concerned with the racial crisis and the perils of revolution can now follow is to keep the channels open between the Negro minority and the white majority."[39]

Edwards observes: "Many analysts would view this [type of] argument as illustrative of Niebuhr's 'realism' at its best: his ability to focus on the politically feasible route to justice, his ability to foresee the ambiguities and unintended consequences of any human action." But, says Edwards, these commentaries on the struggle against racism reveal "Niebuhr at his most establishment-oriented."[40]

A Niebuhrian Response to Critics

I believe that the major criticisms of Niebuhr can be grouped under two main headings: (1) deficiencies in vision and (2) timidity in defining policies and selecting tactics.

By deficient vision I mean a lack of sophistication regarding the extent to which the experience of one person or group is genuinely different from the experience of another person or group whose social location is dissimilar. In this connection, of course, it will be necessary to assess feminist and third-world criticisms of Niebuhr's emphasis on sin as pride (or his incomplete understanding of sin as sensuality or sloth). It will also be necessary to address the charge that Niebuhr's pessimism about human nature keeps him from being as hopeful about human destiny as a Christian ought to be. And finally, it will be necessary to comment on the "armchair theology" complaint, which attributes Niebuhr's insensitivity to dispossessed persons to his lack of actual contact with them and an elitist preference for social analysis which is performed without adequate participation by members of non-Establishment groups.

The reference to timidity in setting goals and the choice of means leads us to several criticisms of Niebuhr's policy recommendations in economic and political affairs. Was it a failure of nerve which caused Niebuhr to abandon the dream of a Socialist society and settle for the "rough justice" of capitalism? Is there a consistent tendency to shy away from disruptive tactics such as those employed in the civil rights struggle? And are both kinds of timidity a function of a class-related false consciousness which tends to make Christian Realism a support for existing inequalities?

In theory, the accusation of timidity is relatively easy to counter. Just as realism about human nature helps the Niebuhrian to avoid sentimental notions of virtue or its ability to prevail against the recalcitrance of those who have vested interests to protect, realism about inertia and power in collective life protect against utopian illusions concerning what can be achieved in the economic and political realms. One can admire the moral idealism of democratic Socialists or pacifists without agreeing with them about the most effective strategies to adopt in the pursuit of justice and peace. One can contend, as Christian Realism does, that pragmatic incremental reform is a strategy which somebody had better be carrying out at all times—for it will not only be able to attain certain half loaves which blue-sky idealism cannot, it will also enlarge the scope of what the next generation of managers and governors will look upon as possible and desirable.

What one can and should learn from the criticism is this: the self-conscious role-differentiation which calls for some social reform agents to go after idealistic goals while others seek more modest incremental improvements must also stipulate that agents of both kinds be constantly in touch with each other, sharing information and engaging in mutual instruction, encouragement, and rebuke of one another.

My response will be developed along the following lines. My fundamental posture is based on several commonsense propositions concerning salient aspects of Niebuhr's thought. After conceding the fact that Niebuhr did neglect certain significant aspects in the psycho-sociological situation of women, African-Americans, and third-world people because of apparent failure to appreciate the sense in which their experience is different from that of middle-class males with strong egos, I will try to assess the significance of this criticism and of the related complaint that "armchair theologizing" is bound to come up short in its comprehension of how relatively powerless people feel and what they want or need. Special emphasis will be placed on estimating the extent to which this lack of comprehension really does lead to specific assumptions that obscure the downtrodden's awareness of how they stand and what they can or ought to do to improve their standing.

I will argue, first of all, that it doesn't make much sense to reproach a man who stressed power and Prometheanism as much as Niebuhr did with being a foe of appropriate self-assertiveness. Second, it doesn't make much sense to bemoan his alleged pessimism and accuse him of having too little faith in the prospects for a just and humane society. The resources for developing a vigorous ethic of striving for human betterment are clearly present in Niebuhr's thought (and exemplified in his life). And third, what Niebuhr said about pride as a corrupting element in the life of all kinds of people— no matter their gender or class position—was true. His realistic optimism deserves to be understood and cultivated by all sorts and conditions of humankind.

A USEFUL SET OF ANALYTICAL CATEGORIES

Commenting on the feminist criticism of Niebuhr's emphasis on sin as pride, Ronald Stone makes the following observation:

> Niebuhr's emphasis upon the sin of the anxious, powerful male decision maker obscured other human experiences which also reinforced the unjust social situation. Niebuhr's category of sin as sensuality has possibilities for meeting the need, [for] it reveals he knew of the surrender of freedom as well as its prideful assertion. But even the development of this category could not fulfill

the need for a theology which would help people understand their apathy, self-abnegation, conformity and passivity. Black power and conscientization [along with feminist theology] have attempted to awaken people to throw off this denial of self which reinforces their oppression.[41]

I believe that reflection on the insights contained in this passage offers considerable guidance to anyone trying to cull the wheat from the chaff in Niebuhr's contribution to the study of ethics and social policy today. The passage suggests three possibilities:

1. Niebuhrian analysis can *neglect* (or ignore) something vital of which sensitive observers have become very much aware in the past twenty or thirty years.
2. It can not only neglect, but may actually *obscure,* crucial elements of a social problem.
3. It may at the same time *provide insights* or principles which can be used as resources to generate wisdom regarding the very variables which may have been neglected or obscured.

For example, Stone admits that Niebuhr failed to show adequate realization of the fact that the decisive peril for some people is not pride, pretentiousness, or will-to-power, but rather excessive diffidence or passivity. Indeed, Stone goes further by speculating that this disproportionate emphasis on the three deadly p-words may actually have made it more difficult for those mired in the mind-set of low status to acknowledge the roles they may have been playing in prolonging their own victimization. On the other hand, Stone declares that Niebuhr's understanding of sin as sensuality (and sloth) can be interpreted as a warning against undue passivity and as an admonition to develop an appropriately increased amount and type of assertiveness.

I cite this interesting commentary from one of Niebuhr's foremost interpreters because I believe that it can be extremely instructive for our evaluative efforts. It alerts one to the possibility that certain elements of Niebuhrian theory may hinder accurate perception of realities which are given inadequate attention—that is, they may obscure as well as neglect key variables. At the same time, Stone urges one to look for basic Niebuhrian insights which actually ought to serve as a safeguard against these very inadequacies.

A FAULTY VISION OF "HUMANITY"?

A response to the charges regarding Niebuhr's doctrine of "the [sinful] nature and destiny of man" must begin by acknowledging that it has a certain amount of validity. Thinkers who try to make significant contributions to the society in which they live are going to devote most of their attention to the problems the opinion-makers of that society consider most important, and this means that they are going to neglect other problems which later generations may consider significant. Plato and Aristotle were not as troubled by slavery as we think they should have been, so there's no getting around their vulnerability to moral disapprobation on this point. Virtually all Western philosophers and moralists have ignored "the rights of Nature" (especially those of "sub-human" animals) in their discussion of ethical obligation, and "New Age" thinkers, given their normative assumptions, have ample reason to condemn them for this anthropocentrism. And so admirers of Niebuhr have to admit, I believe, that Niebuhr erred in failing to analyze the special problems which Western cultural norms and the socialization process associated with them posed for women and people of color.[42]

Yet it is important to be clear about the fact that Niebuhr should not be criticized too severely because of the fact that he failed to give a high priority to the struggle for racial justice before the 1950s. He was actually ahead of his time in seeing the importance of the issue and giving time and money in an effort to mitigate the evils of segregation and prejudice. In a review of Gunnar Myrdal's *An American Dilemma* in 1944, Niebuhr referred to racial injustice as "the most vexing problem in our democratic life," one which "can be effectively [attacked] and must be attacked from every angle, educational and political, economic and religious."[43] In a 1948 article entitled "The Sin of Racial Prejudice," Niebuhr took note of a shift in student interest from a focus on economic justice to racial injustice. In 1963 he reiterated the language of two decades earlier in speaking of "the gravest social issue and evil our nation has confronted since slavery."[44] And in 1968—several years after the momentum of the civil rights struggle had already peaked—he responded to the Walker Commission Report by calling for a comprehensive assault by the entire nation, acting decisively through the next session of Congress, on the economic as well as the psychocultural aspects of discrimination. In addition, he charged the churches with special responsibilities in this campaign, "for it is the business of the church to remind the national community of its responsibilities and to remind it of its sins."[45]

In addition, conceding that Niebuhr to some extent neglected issues of gender and racial justice should not be viewed as acceptance of the charge that his emphasis on sin as pride is a fatal weakness of Christian Realism. Furthermore, we must not overlook the fact that there are ample resources in Niebuhr's view of sin as sensuality, and his social theory in general, which have clear application to the plight of the downtrodden. He may have been somewhat unaware of the special problems that women in our culture have in finding the courage to assert their individuality, but he was not mistaken in declaring that pride and pretentiousness are a universal danger to all human beings, and Niebuhr was well aware of the fact that the family is not exempt from the injustices caused by egocentric abuse of power.[46] Niebuhr neglected certain important psychological realities, but he was right about the moral and spiritual perils of self-centeredness, and what he said about the nature and destiny of humankind is accurate, pertinent, and decisively important for both women and men in every society. The poor and the powerless are no more immune to pride or misuse of power than anyone else. Power often does corrupt, but so does powerlessness, and some of the cruelest and most destructive people in the world are those whose lack of some kinds of power has embittered them and led them to the discovery and misuse of other forms of power to compensate for their frustrations. And when rebels win, as Camus has shown, they very often become murderers.[47]

One of the best illustrations of this point is to be found in what Niebuhr wrote about racial pride:

> The sins of pride are probably more stubborn in human affairs than the sins of power. The sense of racial superiority [makes one] forget the conditioned character of his life and culture and pretend that his color, creed or culture represents some kind of final and absolute criterion of the good. He proceeds thereupon to judge other people severely who do not conform to his particular standard.[48]

Many feminist writings are guilty of a parallel gender-centrism, thus tending to prove that sin as pride is a universal problem.

Niebuhr's warnings about the perils of the wrong kind of self-esteem and self-assertion pertain to "asserting ourselves vis-à-vis

God, claiming the center for ourselves or claiming universal significance for our limited values." He is *not* warning against the vital
necessities for which feminists contend in the self-consciousness of
women—namely, "standing up for ourselves, standing our ground,
not giving in, [and] making our intentions known to others."[49] It is,
quite frankly, absurd to accuse Niebuhr of recommending humility
and self-sacrifice as the essence of Christian virtue, for he knew
perfectly well that those who are incapable of anything *but* self-
effacement and self-giving love soon find themselves involved in
causing (or, at the very least, cooperating with) the perpetration of
injustice, against themselves or others or both. In *Moral Man and
Immoral Society,* Niebuhr wrote:

> The dangers of religion's inner restraint upon self-assertion, and
> of its effort to achieve complete disinterestedness, are such that
> such a policy easily becomes morbid, and that it make for injus-
> tice by encouraging and permitting undue self-assertion in
> others.[50]

To insist that Niebuhr's concept of love encourages women or
anyone else to submit graciously to unfair treatment (or to forego
development of their own unique potential in favor of vicarious living through others) is to confuse psychology with theology.
Niebuhr's appreciation of what Tillich would call "power of being"
suggests that he would be in full agreement about the importance of
"standing up for ourselves, standing our ground," and so on, in the
rough-and-tumble of political life (including the politics of interpersonal relationships). What he would oppose is the kind of exaltation
of the self and one's own desires which constitutes spiritual rebellion
against the sovereignty of God.

As for the feminist critique of Niebuhr's notion of sin as sensuality, he would probably have accepted it as a wholesome corrective
to his neglect of the specialness of women's experience. But he
would have defended himself by pointing out that his discussion of
sin as sensuality does speak to the condition of those whose primary
temptation is abdication of responsibility. Plaskow acknowledges
that Niebuhr recognizes "sensuality" as having at least two meanings, and she gives no evidence that Niebuhr would have disagreed
with her emphasis on the second. The argument is that sensuality is
especially "women's sin," not because "women are more likely than
men to 'lose themselves in some aspect of the world's vitalities'" (as

medieval monks portrayed the threat represented by female sexuality), but rather because women are more likely to "become lost in the detailed processes, activities and interests of existence."[51]

I would argue that the feminist critique of Niebuhr's concept of sin as sensuality is somewhat trivial. When Dunfee rebukes Niebuhr for failing to realize that "the forms of finitude into which one can escape need not be only aspects of one's own physical cravings, but may also be loss of one's self in other finite persons, institutions, and causes," and that "the sin of hiding can take the form of devotion to another,"[52] she makes a valid point in principle. But the criticism hardly holds up in view of the fact that Niebuhr put so much emphasis on human creativity, human possibilities for significant achievement, and power as an indispensable element of effective social reform activities. Plaskow is just plain wrong when she alleges that Niebuhr's analysis of the possible misuse of freedom identifies sin only with exaltation, not abdication: he stresses both as significant pitfalls in the exercise of free choice in the quest for the meaning of selfhood and destiny.

This discussion of the presumed defects in Niebuhr's vision of the human condition should be related to the Pauline concept of being "perplexed, but not unto despair." (A commentary on this theme, which Niebuhr often referred to in sermons, is presented at the conclusion of chapter 7.) This is a fitting motto for the sober yet resilient Prometheanism of his life as well as his teachings.

AN EXCESS OF TIMIDITY?

To those who are accustomed to thinking of Niebuhr as a veritable Amos, it comes as a bit of a shock to be confronted with the charge that he was excessively cautious in setting goals for social reform and in choosing appropriate tactics for their attainment. Yet the critics certainly have some sobering circumstantial evidence to present.

The Ambiguous Blessings of a Mixed Economy

Criticisms of what I have dared to call Niebuhr's timidity in defining the goals of reform in economic and political life centers on his disillusionment with Socialism (and with the norm of equality) and his somewhat unexpected endorsement of a welfare-state based on mixed-economy capitalism. Is this a culpable failure of nerve or a realistic expression of Niebuhr's chastened optimism?

One of the most important particulars to be addressed in this connection is Thomas's attack upon Niebuhr's dramatic shift away from equality. Do his attacks upon Marxism and Soviet Communism, and his abandonment of the Socialist Party in the USA, constitute a betrayal of his previous commitment to a prophetic understanding of social justice in economic affairs?

There are not many American observers who would say this. Since much of what Niebuhr had to say about economic justice after 1940 was written in a climate of opinion which favored a "responsible" society with a mixed economy, he was articulating the views of the vast majority of business and government leaders in Europe and North America. In Britain, especially, the Beveridge Plan expressed a tremendous amount of idealism about the possibilities for social justice in a moderate welfare state, and both Labour and Conservative governments proceeded to implement this idealism for more than two decades. Niebuhr's acceptance of these assumptions is reflected in his well-known statement to the effect that the "organization of unorganized workers changed the social and moral climate of American industry more than the nationalization of the means of production could ever have done."[53] And the reliance on balance-of-power politics to produce economic justice is even more explicitly revealed in a 1959 *Christian Century* article:

> The problem of economic justice in a highly industrialized community offers a quite different problem precisely because it has been tolerably solved by mechanisms of social equilibrium. . . .
> We were actually delivered, not by the wisdom or virtue of any group but by the providential workings of a free society, which reluctantly gave equal political power to all classes (universal suffrage) and could not prevent the gradual equalization of economic power through the organization of labor. The universal standards of justice in the "welfare state" are the fruit of this development.[54]

In addition, Niebuhr may have been tempted to lapse into a highly uncharacteristic complacency because of his familiarity with the postwar American economists who by 1959 were beginning to wax ecstatic about the benefits of economic growth. Prosperity in the private sector, it was proclaimed, would result in public sector revenues which for all practical purposes would eliminate poverty and bring about a kind of educational and cultural vitality that Americans had never dreamed of before 1950. Niebuhr's optimism regarding the economy may also have been related to his aforementioned belief in the power of technology to create "productive justice" by making a pie so big that even its smallest slices would provide a decent standard of living.[55] It must be noted, however, that Niebuhr never ceased to be wary of the spiritual impact of economic abundance. He warned that the new flood of consumer goods, which creates "a preoccupation of American culture with the comforts of this life, with ever higher standards of living . . . is a real peril to our soul." Indeed, Niebuhr said that "fatness, ease, and complacency are greater perils to our faith than lean years."[56] And despite his appreciation of what technological advance can do to promote economic sufficiency, he also—like most intellectuals who worried about "mass society" in the 1950s[57]—expressed anxiety vis-à-vis its cheapening effect on cultural standards:

> Our culture is also threatened from within by the preoccupation of our nation with technology. The resulting crudities are much more serious than those of which our fathers were ashamed.
> Our problem is not merely the synthetic and sentimentalized art of Hollywood or the even lower depths to which TV has reduced this art. It is also the problem of cheap technocratic approaches to the tragic historical drama in which we are all involved.[58]

Still, I do not believe that Thomas is correct in asserting that Niebuhr abandoned his earlier use of equality as a corrective for unimaginative concepts of justice; nor can I concur with Harrison's sweeping indictment or Michael Novak's sly attempt to claim that Niebuhr was a founding father of contemporary neoconservatism.[59] As Paul Cox comments in an unpublished dissertation on Niebuhr and the Neoconservatives: "There was never any doubt about whom Niebuhr regarded as his adversaries on the issues of political economy [after 1945]." In a 1946 essay on "Ideology in the Social Struggle," Niebuhr said:

> The owners of industry appropriated the abundance created by the modern miracle of production, and . . . they were so greedy about it that they ran us headlong into a depression. . . .
> The propaganda of our industrial overlords is in other words

not only stupid but in such flagrant contradiction to our experience that it must be regarded as dishonest as well.[60]

A year later, commenting on a National Association of Manufac-
turers (NAM) advertising campaign, he said:

> No one could be quite as ignorant to the facts of life as NAM
> pretends to be. . . . [It] is consciously or semi-consciously select-
> ing and interpreting facts in order to make them appear to justify
> an indefensible theory of *laissez faire*. The indefensible theory is
> defended because it is a facade for the interests of the business
> class.[61]

On the other hand, Niebuhr certainly was sanguine about the
success of what he saw as the reforms of capitalism instigated in
Britain and the United States since the early 1930s. He summed up
his thoughts on this matter in a remarkable passage which appeared
in an article on Norman Thomas in 1953:

> The Marxist orthodoxies proved irrelevant because meanwhile a
> democratic-capitalist society, about which most of us were so de-
> featist two decades ago, proved that there were greater resources
> in its democratic balances than we had imagined. The economic
> realm which seemed to be heading for ever increasing centraliza-
> tion of power, developed balances of justice through the forma-
> tion of what Professor Galbraith has described as
> "countervailing" power. The intervention of the state, not in or-
> thodox Marxist programs of "socialization," but in the pragmatic
> terms of the New Deal, guided explicitly by Keynesian princi-
> ples, provided the necessary balances which the economic realm
> lacked.[62]

This passage has much in common with Niebuhr's approval of a
mixed economy in his celebrated 1953 essay on "Christian Faith and
Social Action." There he described such a policy as the best expression of Christian ethics one could have in politics. What we need, he
said, is "an empirical and pragmatic approach [which] will not assume that government interference in economic process is either
good or bad; but will study the effect of each type of interference."[63]
It was in this connection during the 1950s that he clarified his stance
vis-à-vis liberalism and conservatism. He affirmed his loyalty to the
former, especially in regard to a political strategy "which sought to

bring economic enterprise under political control for the sake of establishing minimum standards of security and welfare." And he acknowledged affinities with the latter only in regard to "wanting to recognize the 'organic' aspects of community and the elements of interest and power."[64]

So it is important to explain what I have referred to as an "uncharacteristic complacency" in Niebuhr's apparent belief that balance-of-power politics had solved in principle the problems of economic justice in the United States. One explanation is contained in John Bennett's remark to the effect that Niebuhr, after becoming disillusioned with Socialism, settled for a mixed economy and lost interest in the details of the mixture."[65] Another is to be found in Ronald Stone's summary observation concerning Niebuhr's relative silence on issues of economic justice after about 1950:

> The failure of religious Socialism and political Socialism in the United States left [Niebuhr] without a developed alternative policy, [and] he never returned to the analysis of economic reality with the same energy that he had exhibited as a Socialist.[66]

We may conclude that Niebuhr to some extent lost interest in the details of a mixed economy, but he certainly did not become oblivious to the persistence of poverty in this country, and he continued to "favor New Deal type policies in the Kennedy and Johnson administrations, [because he] regarded the old laissez-faire capitalism as dead. He still regarded a policy of government activism as necessary to correct . . . inequities."[67] As noted above, Niebuhr was always "a man of the democratic left" whose retreat from socialism did not lead to any sort of conservatism whatever, but moderated to a pragmatic left liberalism.[68]

Contemporary Christian ethicists have followed Niebuhr's lead in protesting strenuously against the conservative capitalism of the Thatcher-Reagan era, and they have echoed him in denouncing the glorification of unbridled acquisitiveness which took place during those years. But they have also accepted Niebuhr's willingness to look upon a mixed economy welfare state as a passably responsible society. In doing so, they have adopted the position Reinhold Niebuhr took during the first two postwar decades.

But not many Niebuhrians have been willing (for understandable reasons) to associate themselves with Socialism. I would be willing to argue that contemporary exponents of democratic Socialism are very close (forget the label) to Niebuhr's overall position on economic ethics, and Niebuhr himself might have agreed with much of the program they advocate had he lived to see the astounding disproportions of wealth and poverty in the world today. I would argue that it is quite consistent with Niebuhr's fundamental posture, as articulated during the years when he was at least as interested in economic justice as he was in politics, for Christian ethicists to renew the struggle for a new international economic order of the kind envisioned by World Council of Churches documents. Judgments about when and where the truth may be spoken with optimal effectiveness are complicated, so it is always problematic to assume a doctrinaire position on such questions. But if the truth of the matter is that humankind needs an economic system which is significantly different from world capitalism in its present form, then this is a conviction which must—in some form, sooner or later—be proclaimed. Furthermore, it is important to take a long-range point of view. Rosemary Ruether writes:

> What we [should] seek is not only a society that dismantles class hierarchies, founded on decentralized cooperative counterinstitutions, that dismantles racist and sexist hierarchies and promotes mutually supportive relationships between human and nonhuman ecological systems. Because this project is so complex and daunting, especially at a time when even the word "liberal" has become an epithet, it is crucial at all times to maintain a sense of historical perspective. . . . [As Michael Harrington said,] "To struggle for economic democracy [in North America today] is to commit yourself to a cause you will never see fulfilled in your own country."

But, affirms Ruether, that's no reason why ethically sensitive Christians shouldn't keep trying to advance this project.[69]

Politics and Tactics

Can it be that there is a consistent tendency in Christian Realism to retreat from battles that could be won and to shy away from the use of "ungentlemanly" tactics which might be victorious?

This, for me, is the most disturbing of all the criticisms leveled at Christian Realism. Consider, for example, the discrepancy between what Niebuhr said about the importance of the issue of racial injustice (following Edwards) and what he recommended in the way of policy and tactics for dealing with it. As I have argued, Niebuhr can hardly be accused of ignoring the evils of racial injustice in America. But any admirer of his cannot help being perplexed by three aspects of his stand on this issue:

1. Why was a social problem of such dimensions given so little attention for such a long time? After all, in 1944 Niebuhr himself described it as "the most vexing problem in our democratic life," and in 1963 he referred to it as "the gravest social issue and evil our nation has confronted since slavery."

2. Why was Niebuhr apparently content to make his witness on this overwhelmingly important matter by individual or small-scale action in behalf of groups such as the Southern Tenant Farmers Union and the Delta Cooperative Farm during the period from 1935 to 1965? (In other words, why did he wait so long to urge a full-scale reform program at an appropriate scale of magnitude through the powerful political and economic institutions of the nation, and through the churches?)

3. And why was he so cautious in his judgments about the tactics being used in the struggle by those who gave it the highest priority?

There are, of course, a number of plausible explanations which can be adduced. It can truthfully be pointed out that every individual is called to enlist him- or herself in only one or two overwhelmingly significant causes and that one's credibility and clout may be seriously impaired if one tries to spread oneself too thin. J. William Fulbright could not have retained his seat in the Senate, and therefore his ability to play a decisively important role as Chairman of the Senate Foreign Relations Committee, without signing the infamous (yet totally irrelevant and ineffective) "Southern Manifesto" denouncing integration. Niebuhr may have faced similar difficulties. It can be pointed out that it is all to the good for some social ethicists to hold out for and pursue ideal solutions—while others pursue a more immediately achievable (and implementable) path. It can even be contended that pragmatic, incremental reform is by definition an "art of the possible," and Herbert Edwards may actually have been right on the money in referring to Niebuhr's posture on the struggle for racial justice as "Christian Realism at its best"—given the conditions that prevailed at the time.

Chapter 7

Can We Still Believe
in Christian Realism?

The point of this book is not to exalt Reinhold Niebuhr, but merely to recognize him as a worthy mentor and model. Thus, we must end by asking if Christian Realism as practiced today is seriously infected with establishment bias or if circumstances have changed so much that an approach which was valid fifty years ago is useless (or worse) in our day and time.

HOW BAD IS THE IDEOLOGICAL TAINT?

The problem of establishment bias which ought to concern us most is not a problem with the thought of Reinhold Niebuhr. Rather, it is the question about the possibility that those who assign his books and who study Christian Realism in universities and churches today (especially in Europe and North America) are infected with a class-related false consciousness which distorts their thinking to a serious degree. The validity of Niebuhr's insights may be affected very little by the social location in which he flourished, but if the socialization process which shapes today's practitioners of Christian Realism is corrupted, what they see through Niebuhrian lenses may be shot through with self-serving illusion. And if this is the case, then their social analysis and their policy recommendations may be subject to defects even more pervasive than those identified by Niebuhr's critics.

179

Who among us can claim to be completely free of false consciousness or the ideological taint against which Niebuhr himself so frequently warned? It is not a sufficient defense to acknowledge the ubiquity of the threat, for it is relatively easy to grasp and accept the danger of distortion as a psychological and moral reality. The hard part is to be able to discern exactly when and how the taint manifests itself and causes us to draw mistaken inferences regarding policy and implementation strategies. To put it more bluntly: how can you be sure that your ability to see what is going on in the world and decide how to improve things is not skewed by factors of which you are hardly aware? Or, to be more devastatingly precise: how can you possibly be sure that your perceptions are not skewed by factors of which you are aware in theory (since you are familiar with the concepts of ideological taint and false consciousness), but which you may have trouble recognizing when they exert themselves in specific situations where your own vital interests may be at stake?[1]

These disturbing questions help to explain one reason why the pattern of tactical timidity discerned by Edwards and the "cultured despair" seen by Welch are so sobering in their implications. For Christian Realism as practiced by Niebuhr (and his spiritual descendants who specialize in medical or business ethics nowadays) is really an elitist operation, and its elitism is very closely related to its consequentialism. The point is well illustrated by a cautionary tale related to me by one of my Yale professors whose enthusiasm for Niebuhr had led to a period of study in Washington, where he worked with Paul Nitze, a leading light of the national security establishment. When my professor asked Nitze how he found it possible to make so many wrenching decisions in situations where somebody's interests were going to be damaged no matter what he recommended, Nitze reportedly said: "Well, I certainly don't waste a lot of time flagellating myself because I can't be absolutely sure I'm making the right choice, or because there is no action option which won't cause grief to someone. If I allowed that to happen, I couldn't function in my job. So I gather as much relevant information as I can get hold of, I consider all the angles as best I can, and then I pick the best course of action available—which is often no better than the least of an assortment of possible evils. There's little time for wondering or blaming, because as soon as you finish making one of these hard choices, two or three other dilemmas present themselves and start clamoring for attention. But it's my responsibility to keep on making those decisions."

Cornel West would say that the elitism of Christian Realism is one of its most insidious flaws. After pointing out that its praise of the "wise statesman as vigilant civil servant" leads to a theory of the balance of power which always "assumes some form of U.S. dominance" and all too easily "justifies quick and often brutal U.S. military intervention," West attacks George Kennan's belief that a foreign service school patterned after West Point could "infuse wisdom into U.S. foreign policy by means of the Paideia of elite civil servants." In his view,

> the notions of balance of power and national interest and the stress on strategic and tactical thinking by historically informed statesmen-like diplomats constitute the pillars of an emergent ideology among liberal political and intellectual elites in post-World War II America.[2]

And elitism is linked to the pragmatic consequentialism which I have consistently treated as a strength. Now, in one sense, or from one point of view, it is perfectly true that consequentialism as a methodology of ethical decision-making delivers one from the errors of legalism by making it possible to ask whether or not the application of a familiar principle or obedience to a traditional rule will actually contribute to the well-being of those who are going to be affected by a given decision.[3] But calculating consequences takes a great deal of knowledge and judgment. It is an approach which requires expertise as well as the highest intentions, so it is in a certain sense a methodology for the elite (or for those who imagine themselves to be smart enough and good enough to base their actions on consequentialist calculations). It is a methodology of moral choice which flatters its users by encouraging them to believe that they need not be bound by the laws and rules which apply to ordinary folks who are not quite so well-educated nor benevolent as they. So consequentialism tends to reinforce the very pride and pretentiousness which Niebuhr so vociferously denounced.

To make the same point in a slightly different way, it may be both necessary and wise to admit that Niebuhrians are vulnerable to an ominous spiritual peril—that is, the temptation to thank God that they are not like other (more simple-minded, naive, or utopian) souls whose idealistic dreams of the good society are unrealistic. Perhaps

Niebuhrians are prone to self-congratulation because they fancy themselves to be more Machiavellian than Machiavelli himself. As a result, they may go overboard in their commitment to realism by refusing to invest their energies in supporting anything not guaranteed to be a winner.

It is a thought-provoking critique. How ironic it would be if the pragmatic consequentialism of those who see themselves as disciples of Niebuhr should serve the latent dysfunction of paralyzing them, or at least making them so cautious about going out on a limb in an attempt to attain major reforms or structural reform that they refuse to throw their weight into political activities which really deserve their support and might succeed if their support were forthcoming![4]

The theory has ample safeguards against abuse, but both consequentialism and pragmatism encourage a mind-set which easily veers toward opportunism, self-indulgence, or (at its worst) a kind of ruthlessness about means and a tunnel vision about ends that can destroy ethical effectiveness and even moral integrity. This theory may be especially dangerous when coupled with a Burkean political philosophy which says that the elected and appointed officials in a representative democracy are supposed to make the plans and decisions and go ahead and run things until the next election (when the citizens can replace them if they want to).

HOW DIFFERENT IS AMERICA TODAY?

On the whole, however, I still believe in the efficacy of the kind of pragmatic incremental reform activity advocated and carried out by Reinhold Niebuhr. I still believe that it is possible for men and women of good will to be reasonably free of the worst effects of ideological taint most of the time and to use their elite capabilities to serve the common good. And I still believe that in large collectivities (anything larger than a very small town meeting in a very homogeneous community) representative democracy is more practical—and better—than any form of so-called participatory democracy or consensus-based decision processes yet devised. Furthermore, I believe that Niebuhr was right about the futility of organizing human life, or even conceptualizing it, without reliance on power and without constantly struggling to achieve viable balances of power (which never seem to be stable for very long and must always be adjusted and readjusted). This means that I am not nearly so disturbed by the existence of hierarchies, chains of command, and decision-making prerogatives as are some of Niebuhr's critics.

But that's where the second big question comes in. How different are things today from what they were in Niebuhr's time?

Niebuhr's sanguine view of democracy was shaped by the events of the 1930s and 1940s. A Christian observer during those years had many reasons to believe that the Western democracies did in fact offer humankind's greatest hope for just societies in a tolerably just world order. They were certainly better than fascism or Stalinist Communism in the political realm. And as both Europe and North America moved toward mixed economy welfare states which could use Keynesian fiscal and monetary tools to overcome boom-and-bust cyclical fluctuations in inflation and unemployment, they seemed to offer something considerably better than a Socialist "command economy" had ever been able to deliver. Despite myriad dislocations and inequities, postwar economic and technological dynamism did seem to offer realistic prospects for overcoming famine, disease, and economic hardship.

But Niebuhr did not live to see the political and cultural decline of Anglo-American democracy which took place in the 1970s and 1980s. He did not experience the "betrayal of American democracy" brought about by television, by a culture which glorify unrestrained self-interest and unrestrained acquisitiveness, and by campaign spending practices which deliver the political apparatus into the hands of those with enough money to purchase and package candidates who further their own interests at the expense of the public interest.[5]

To what extent is it still possible to believe in the Jeffersonian ideal of a democracy whose people can be trusted to select wise rulers or in the Aristotelian ideal of intelligent political discourse concerning the common good? Many analysts are convinced that the political reality today is one of self-serving elites who use a variety of technological means to manipulate an ignorant, apathetic, alienated, and irresponsible citizenry. When American power is put to use in the world arena, it may be used in the service of a national interest that is defined without very much concern for global economic justice or long-term ecological sanity. It may encourage, for example, the continuation of "hydrocarbon man's" addiction to fossil fuels and a high-tech, high-consumption lifestyle that is neither sustainable nor just. Or American power may be used, as in Latin America, to wage a "war against the poor" through the perpetuation of "low-intensity conflict" that involves illegal disruption of the legitimate economic and political aspirations of small countries we prefer to keep as clients. This course of action may also require, incidentally, deliberate and systematic lying to the American people, from whom the real aims and the true savagery of what is being done in their name are concealed by the "invisible government" which plans and executes these policies in defiance of the ostensible wishes of the Congress and the bulk of the citizenry.[6]

As for religion, its vulnerability to misunderstanding and abuse has always been evident, and there are many indications that the relatively brief triumph of religious tolerance and pluralistic political philosophy in the modern world is not secure. Since the name of God is still being invoked by fundamentalists in several major faith communities to justify all kinds of oppression and forced capitulation to superstitious nonsense, why should one be associated with religion at all? If God is just a possible hypothesis which might give a shot in the arm to the mobilization of people and resources in the fight for human freedom and social justice—but isn't really necessary—why bother? Why bother to jump through all kinds of semantic and conceptual hoops in order to certify a putative "mythopoeic profundity" that may be neither true or efficacious after all?

Perplexed, but not unto Despair

The grounds for despair are many, and it wouldn't be surprising if many people are discouraged thereby, so discouraged that they abandon their commitment to being co-creators with God of an as-yet-unfinished universe. But this reference to the doctrine of co-creatorship is in itself a first step in the direction of the most basic reason of all for cherishing Niebuhr's legacy and trying to live up to it: the reality of God.

I have tried to show that Niebuhr's concept of Christianity's "truth in myths" is a profound witness to his undying trust in the God of the prophets. The truthfulness of such trust can never be proved with mathematical certainty, but it stands alongside the trust and active commitment of a great host of people throughout history who have believed and tried to live in accordance with what the Quakers refer to as "that of God in every person." So just as there is no compelling reason why we must enroll in the household of faith, neither is there a compelling reason why we should not. It remains an option. Indeed, it remains what Niebuhr said it was—a viable option. Biblical faith is still a lens through which we may see the meaning of our lives and the outlines of moral obligation and spiritual experience which challenge those who want to be worthy of the destiny to which God calls us.

Given some of the terrible things now being said and done in the name of religion, there are plenty of reasons to wonder about the value, if not the viability, of any remythologized version of Christian faith. But when some religious people are uttering stupidities and justifying iniquities in the name of God (including a pronouncement of death on Salman Rushdie because he is guilty of violating the sensibilities of a particular faction in one faith community), that is all the more reason to proclaim a different and better understanding of the meaning of faith and of a God-concept compatible with the best human norms of freedom, justice, and love. In this connection, Niebuhr's insights into the true significance of Christianity are still richly edifying.

Something similar can be said about America. We are in a bad time, a time when civic virtue and humane reason have been eclipsed by the glorification of selfishness and cheap, high-consumption goodies which are truly "a mess of pottage" in comparison with a higher concept of human dignity and fulfillment. Niebuhr's optimistic view of America and its role in world affairs is extremely problematic. Given the overriding power of the ethos of acquisitive individualism, and the corruption of our political institutions by the working of that ethos in economic and cultural life, citizens have all too many pretexts for being pessimistically apathetic about politics and half-hearted in their performance of civic obligation. But withdrawal is no solution. Our nation can still profit from Niebuhr's vision of the kind of country we ought to be, and we desperately need the kind of leadership which might be provided by ethically attuned citizens.

Those who conclude that it's futile to try are saying more about themselves—their own weakness and cowardice—than they are about our situation. For it's neither necessary nor honorable to capitulate to despair. It isn't necessary because—in long-range historical perspective—we can see that some things are better now than in Niebuhr's day. Indeed, some of the gloom and turmoil of the present moment result from our realization that the American dream has never been a reality for all our citizens, and we cannot be satisfied with the way things used to be. Moreover, a realistic analysis of the way in which social policy is formulated and history gets made will reveal that the biblical doctrine of the remnant is still very pertinent for us today: what Toynbee referred to as a "creative minority" of savvy, energetic people can accomplish great things in bringing their nation to its senses and ameliorating some of its problems. Incremental social reform is a Sisyphean task, for the great stone of injustice and inhumanity always rolls back down the hill after it has, through much effort, been pushed toward the top. But the effort is not expended in vain, for each time the stone rolls back down, it may not roll back quite as far as it did before, and small increments of genuine progress may be secured.

In any case, as Niebuhr asserted and exemplified in his life, to give up would be ignominious. We must be resigned to the vicissitudes we can't do anything about. But we must know the difference between those mysterious and intractable elements of life and "the things we can do something about," and we should feel honor-bound to respond to the challenge presented by those things.

If there is any substantial truth in the vote of confidence for Reinhold Niebuhr's message I have just cast, it must also be true that he has something to offer as a model of authentic Christian discipleship. For his life is a vindication of an ideal of human fulfillment which involves both reflection and action. He was, after all, a young man from the provinces who worked very hard to acquaint himself with the eternal questions about the meaning of human existence and the answers given by the best thinkers of his culture. And he managed to emerge with a lifelong devotion to co-creatorship which avoided both cynicism and bravado. Whether we buy into the details of his notion of human nature and destiny is less important than our sharing of his conviction that such a moral worldview, and such a conception of selfhood, can be honestly achieved. Niebuhr's thought and life impel us to invest ourselves in a similar intellectual and moral enterprise, and if we follow his example we will revere his legacy and participate in it in the best way possible.

Notes

Introduction

1. See Alasdair MacIntyre, *After Virtue* (2d ed.; Notre Dame, Ind.: University of Notre Dame Press, 1984). MacIntyre's lament is also voiced in Robert Bellah et al., *Habits of the Heart* (Berkeley: University of California Press, 1985).

2. See Jeffrey Stout, *Ethics After Babel* (Boston: Beacon Press, 1988).

3. Every book which deals with Niebuhr's life has something to say about his popularity with students. The best discussion of this can be found in Ronald Stone's recent book, *Professor Reinhold Niebuhr,* which takes as its fundamental assumption that Niebuhr was first and foremost a faculty member at Union Theological Seminary, where he served for four decades.

Chapter 1

1. From now on, the name and significance of the phases of Niebuhr's life refer to his own intellectual growth and to developments in his distinctive contribution to thought contained in his published work during a given period.

2. It is difficult to find a single word which conveys my meaning here without running the risk of misleading the reader. Terms such as "red-blooded" have too many unfortunate connotations, and phrases such as "masculine forcefulness" are too clumsy—so a neologism that is the opposite of "feminism" suggests itself. I can only hope that the discussion which follows does a satisfactory job of communicating the important points I wish to make by analyzing Niebuhr's "masculinism."

3.   Ann Douglas, *The Feminization of American Culture* (New York: Alfred Knopf, 1987).

4.   Richard Fox, *Reinhold Niebuhr: A Biography* (New York: Pantheon Books, 1985), 10.

5.   Fox, 17, 34, 68.

6.   Paul Merkeley, *Reinhold Niebuhr: A Political Account* (Montreal: McGill-Queen's University Press, 1975), 18.

7.   Elisabeth Niebuhr Sifton, "Remembering Reinhold Niebuhr," *World Policy Journal* 10, no. 1 (Spring 1993): 84–85.

8.   Sifton, 85.

9.   Fox, 66. The influence of William James's concept of "the strenuous life" is also evident here.

10.   Fox, 66.

11.   Reinhold Niebuhr, *Leaves from the Notebook of a Tamed Cynic* (Chicago: Willett, Clark and Colby, 1929), 61.

12.   Niebuhr, *Leaves*, 60–61.

13.   Niebuhr, *Leaves*, 124.

14.   Many moralists of the day would have agreed with the Faustian credo expressed by George Bernard Shaw in his preface to *Man and Superman:* "This is the true joy of living, to give yourself utterly to a cause you believe to be a mighty one; to be thoroughly used up before being thrown on the scrapheap; to be a force in Nature instead of a sniveling clod of ailments and grievances, complaining that the world will not devote itself to making you happy."

15.   June Bingham, *Courage to Change* (New York: Scribner's, 1965), 65.

16.   Bingham, 160.

17.   In my opinion, the major secondary sources written by Stone, Merkeley, and Charles Brown offer a better treatment of Reinhold Niebuhr's development and significance as a thinker than Richard Fox's more highly publicized book. But Fox's *Reinhold Niebuhr: A Biography* does contain a number of thought-provoking interpretations of some of Niebuhr's most important ideas, and it certainly presents an unusually intriguing compilation of data and hypotheses about Niebuhr's personal life and his psyche. And some of Fox's most provocative material is contained in essays which are included in the anthologies that have been published since the appearance of the biography. See especially the works edited by Harries, Neuhaus, and Kegley (listed in the bibliography).

18.   Ronald Stone, *Professor Reinhold Niebuhr* (Louisville: Westminster/John Knox Press, 1992), xiii.

19.   From the transcript of a conference whose proceedings are assembled in Richard John Neuhaus, ed., *Reinhold Niebuhr Today,* 125–26. Cuddihy adds: "Preaching was what he loved. He used a few prooftexts of sin as a kind of disedifying discourse to hold people who wouldn't be held by

positive thinking. . . . What he knew was this message and these texts. He broke in, and he was ambitious. He was somewhat ashamed of the gospel. . . . He wasn't ashamed to berate the rich in Detroit, but he was ashamed to berate the Jewish community in New York. . . . The gospel encumbered him with the message of salvation to the Jews, to all people. So he disencumbered the gospel of its universalism, as the message to the Jews; this stood in the way of his success. It had to go."

20.   John Murray Cuddihy, *No Offense* (New York: Seabury Press, 1978), 34. The ad hominem assault continues: "This son of an immigrant Lutheran minister from Wright City, Missouri, had . . . come a long way from his provincial Protestant beginnings. . . . Teaching at Union, he met and married Ursula Keppel-Compton—niece of an Anglican bishop—with full Church of England solemnities. There were to be Niebuhr children, Christopher, who was sent to Groton and Harvard, and Elisabeth, a Chapin and Radcliffe graduate, whose engagement to Charles Proctor Sifton of the law firm of Cadwalader, Wickersham, and Taft was duly made known to the readers of the *New York Times* by 'The Rev. Dr. and Mrs. Reinhold Niebuhr of Stockbridge and New York.'"

21.   Neuhaus, 126.

22.   Neuhaus, 47.

23.   Richard Fox, "Niebuhr's World and Ours," in Neuhaus, 8.

24.   Niebuhr, as quoted in Harold R. Landon, ed., *Reinhold Niebuhr: A Prophetic Voice in Our Time* (Greenwich, Conn.: Seabury Press, 1962), 119.

25.   Fox, 8.

26.   Neuhaus, 47.

27.   Neuhaus, 48. Niebuhr's amiability in everyday contacts may be contrasted, by the way, with Tillich's cold aloofness. I remember an occasion on which a student walked up to Tillich in the lobby at UTS and politely asked him a concise question about something the Grand Theologian had said in a recent lecture, only to be repulsed by an icy stare and a resumption of Tillich's conversation with the "worthwhile" person next to him.

28.   See Richard Fox, "Reinhold Niebuhr: The Living of Christian Realism," in Richard Harries, ed., *Reinhold Niebuhr and the Issues of Our Time* (London: Mowbray, 1986), 9–23. The entire essay is a tribute to Niebuhr's "courage to change," which suggests that June Bingham may have been even more perceptive than she realized in choosing that phrase for the title of her biography of Niebuhr.

29.   Bingham, 31.

30.   Bingham, 30. Someone else remarks that Niebuhr is no different from others in sometimes being wrong; it's just that Niebuhr realizes he is wrong a bit faster than others and is therefore quicker to apologize.

31.   Bingham, 30.

32. I have this quote in my notes from two of the courses I had with Niebuhr. He also refers to it in a charming exchange with Will Scarlett which is recorded in Bingham, 254–55.

33. Reinhold Niebuhr, "Specialists and Social Life," *Detroit Times* (May 5, 1928): 18, as cited in Charles Brown, *Niebuhr and His Age* (Philadelphia: Trinity Press International, 1992), 35.

34. Brown, *Niebuhr and His Age,* 20.

35. Niebuhr, as quoted in Landon, 123.

36. See Harvey Cox, "Theology, Politics and Friendship," *Christianity and Crisis* (Feb. 3, 1986): 17–18.

37. Stone, *Professor Reinhold Niebuhr,* xiii.

38. Bingham, 254–55.

39. *Christian Century* (Dec. 19–26, 1966): 1196–97.

40. *Christian Century* (Dec. 19–26, 1966): 1198.

Chapter 2

1. R. H. Tawney, *Religion and the Rise of Capitalism* (New York: New American Library, 1947), 221.

2. *The Congregationalist,* as quoted in J. Milton Yinger, ed., *Religion, Society, and the Individual* (New York: Macmillan, 1957), 219.

3. Donald B. Meyer, *The Protestant Search for Political Realism* (Berkeley: University of California Press), 39.

4. Henry F. May, *Protestant Churches and Industrial America,* 264.

5. Meyer, 28, 30, 31.

6. Meyer, 43–44.

7. Robert T. Handy, ed., *The Social Gospel in America* (New York: Oxford University Press, 1966), 14.

8. Handy, 14–15, 15.

9. Meyer, 43.

10. Meyer, 58.

11. Kirby Page, *The Abolition of War,* 78–80.

12. Meyer, 35.

13. George Albert Coe, *A Social Theory of Religious Education,* 145, as summarized and interpreted by Meyer, 139–40.

14. As Beckley says, Rauschenbusch believed that something approximating the kingdom of God on earth really could be attained and that Christians certainly ought to strive for nothing less than this goal. See Harlan Beckley, *Passion for Justice* (Louisville: Westminster/John Knox Press, 1992), 309.

15. See Walter Rauschenbusch, *Christianizing the Social Order* (New York: Macmillan, 1912), 90; cf. Meyer, 133. Also note Meyer's criticism of this neat package of beliefs: if social salvation is to be the result of Christians

acting out their prior state of salvation, then salvation can hardly be defined in social terms (Meyer, 136).

16. See especially the chapter "The Kingdom of Evil" in Walter Rauschenbusch, *A Theology for the Social Gospel* (New York: Macmillan, 1917).

17. Walter Rauschenbusch, *Christianity and the Social Crisis* (New York: Macmillan, 1907), 402.

18. Meyer, 63–64.

19. Meyer, 75.

20. Meyer, 21.

21. Meyer, 22, 23.

22. Meyer, 60–61, 62, 63–64, 68.

23. A phrase made famous by Ibsen (especially in *The Wild Ducks*) and rendered even more significant by Shaw's commentary in *The Quintessence of Ibsenism*.

24. Niebuhr, *Does Civilization Need Religion?*, 61, as summarized in Paul Merkeley, *Reinhold Niebuhr: A Political Account*, 29.

25. Richard Fox, *Reinhold Niebuhr: A Biography*, 59.

26. Niebuhr, *Does Civilization Need Religion?*, 61.

27. Merkeley, 31.

28. Merkeley, 31.

28. Merkeley, 35.

30. Merkeley, 53.

31. Merkeley, 55, 18.

32. *Pseudotransformationism* is a word coined by sociologists who conducted a content analysis of religious best-sellers from 1910 to 1955. It refers to the notion that society as a whole can be saved if individuals are spiritually redeemed, one by one. See Louis Schneider and Sanford M. Dornbusch, *Popular Religion* (Chicago: University of Chicago Press, 1958), 96–101.

33. Merkeley, 26, citing Niebuhr, *Leaves*, 146–47.

34. Schneider and Dornbusch, 26–27.

35. Fox, 79.

36. Niebuhr, *Leaves*, 193.

37. Fox, 70.

38. Niebuhr, *Leaves*, 40.

39. Merkeley, 47.

40. Merkeley, 48.

41. Merkeley, 48.

42. As quoted in Ronald H. Stone, *Reinhold Niebuhr: Prophet to Politicians* (Nashville: Abingdon Press, 1972), 49.

43. Fox, 96, 93.

44. Stone, *Prophet to Politicians*, 34.

45. Since this chapter deals only with the period before 1930, this is

not the place to analyze what Niebuhr did and said in regard to race relations later on. But this topic does not come up again until the final chapter, so the reader should be reminded that Reinhold Niebuhr was something of a pioneer in his support for innovative activities directed toward racial justice during these decades. He was a staunch supporter of the Delta Cooperative Farm in Mississippi, the Southern Tenant Farmer's Union, and the Fellowship of Southern Churchmen. He was also an admirer of Martin Luther King, who was greatly influenced by Niebuhr. See Ronald Stone, *Professor Reinhold Niebuhr,* 33.

46. See Ronald H. Stone, "The Contribution of Reinhold Niebuhr to the Late Twentieth Century," in Charles W. Kegley and Robert Bretall, eds., *Reinhold Niebuhr: His Religious, Social, and Political Thought* (2nd ed.; New York: Macmillan, 1956), 62–68.

47. Fox, 94.

48. Charles Brown, *Niebuhr and His Age,* 20.

49. Fox, 94–95.

50. Stone, *Prophet to Politicians,* 27–31; cf. Stone, *Professor Reinhold Niebuhr,* 30–31.

51. Fox, 98, 99.

52. Brown, 25.

53. Reinhold Niebuhr, "The Church and the Industrial Crisis," *Biblical World* 54 (Nov. 1920): 590–92, as cited by Brown, 23–24.

54. Merkeley, 51.

55. Merkeley, 52, 53.

56. Stone, *Prophet to Politicians,* 55.

57. Stone, *Prophet to Politicians,* 55.

58. Fox, 99.

59. Stone, *Prophet to Politicians,* 41.

60. Niebuhr, *Leaves,* 68.

61. Fox, 100.

62. Fox, 100.

63. See Neuhaus, 8.

64. Fox, 166.

65. Neuhaus, 8.

66. Fox, 166.

67. Fox, 166.

68. Reinhold Niebuhr, "How My Mind Has Changed," *Christian Century* (1959–1960), as quoted in Harold E. Fey, ed., *How My Mind Has Changed* (Cleveland: World Publishing, 1961), 117.

69. Stone, *Prophet to Politicians,* 37.

70. Stone, *Prophet to Politicians,* 37. The internal quote is from *Leaves.*

71. *Radical Religion* 1, no. 1 (1936): 39–40.

72. Stone, *Prophet to Politicians,* 36. Stone goes on to say that

Niebuhr's rhetoric sometimes obscures the extent to which he is (as previously noted) "a liberal at heart."

73. See Fox, *Reinhold Niebuhr: A Biography,* 161–66.

74. Fox, 164, 165.

75. Fox, 166.

76. Fox, 31.

77. Fox, 30, 32.

78. Fox, 32.

79. Fox, 84.

Chapter 3

1. Reinhold Niebuhr, *The Nature and Destiny of Man: A Christian Interpretation,* Vol. I: *Human Nature* (New York: Scribner's, 1941), 226–27.

2. Reinhold Niebuhr, *The Irony of American History* (New York: Scribner's, 1952), 155.

3. Niebuhr, *Irony,* 160.

4. Richard Fox, *Reinhold Niebuhr: A Biography,* 177.

5. Niebuhr, *Nature and Destiny,* Vol. I, 61.

6. Reinhold Niebuhr, *The Nature and Destiny of Man: A Christian Interpretation,* Vol. II: *Human Destiny* (New York: Scribner's, 1943), 196.

7. Niebuhr, *Nature and Destiny,* Vol. II, 196–97.

8. Niebuhr, *Nature and Destiny,* Vol. II, 116.

9. Reinhold Niebuhr, *Essays in Applied Christianity,* edited with an introduction by D. B. Robertson (New York: Meridian Books, 1959), 154.

10. Niebuhr, *Essays,* 170.

11. Niebuhr, *Essays,* 171.

12. Niebuhr, *Essays,* 172–73.

13. Niebuhr, *Essays,* 187.

14. Niebuhr, *Essays,* 187. It is characteristic of both Niebuhr and Barth that they could carry on a lengthy debate about serious theological matters, and they disagreed strongly with each other, without becoming personal enemies.

This point is beautifully illustrated in an anecdote recorded in Charles Brown's *Niebuhr and His Age:* "A former student of Niebuhr . . . attended a seminar that Barth held in a coffee place at Celigny on Lake Geneva. Barth, he recalled, sensed that he had studied under Niebuhr, remarking, 'Niebuhr's students always ask the same and the best questions. Why do you always ask these questions?' 'Because,' the student replied, 'you don't give good enough answers.' Barth laughed and admitted that Niebuhr had made telling criticisms of his ethics" (Brown, *Niebuhr and His Age,* 227).

15. Niebuhr, *Nature and Destiny,* Vol. I, 265.

16. Niebuhr, *Nature and Destiny,* Vol. I, 287.

17.   Niebuhr, *Nature and Destiny*, Vol. II, 122.

18.   Daniel Day Williams, "Niebuhr and Liberalism," in Kegley and Bretall, *Reinhold Niebuhr: His Religious, Social, and Political Thought*, 206–7.

19.   See Ronald Stone, "The Contribution of Reinhold Niebuhr to the Late Twentieth Century," in Charles Kegley and Robert Bretall, *Reinhold Niebuhr: His Religious, Social, and Political Thought*, 56–58.

20.   Stone, "The Contribution of Reinhold Niebuhr," 56–58.

21.   Niebuhr, *Nature and Destiny*, Vol. II, 207 (emphasis added).

22.   Niebuhr, *Nature and Destiny*, Vol. II, 292–93. This passage strikes me as a definitive rebuttal to Daniel Day Williams's claim that Niebuhr had an insufficient appreciation for the intrinsic value of the battle against evil in human affairs.

In his essay "Niebuhr and Liberalism" (in Kegley and Bretall, 207), Williams declares that Niebuhr "finds meaning ultimately only in complete victory over evil. Therefore history depends upon something 'beyond history' for its meaning. [But] profound liberalism always regards the struggle with evil as meaningful in itself. . . . Can we not believe in an actual redemptive working of God in history without falling into the utopianism which Niebuhr rightly exposes and rejects?"

The answer, of course, is clear; it is in the affirmative—and I would argue that Niebuhr himself never doubted the moral and spiritual significance of the struggle per se. All he wrote and did in the realm of social and political action is testimony to the fact that he was a happy Sisyphus. He just wanted to make absolutely sure that co-creative activity in pursuit of justice in this wicked world, no matter how relatively successful and no matter how zestfully engaged in, was not confused with the ultimate righteousness and love of God.

23.   Niebuhr, *Nature and Destiny*, Vol. II, 211.

24.   Niebuhr, *Nature and Destiny*, Vol. II, 211–12.

25.   Niebuhr, *Nature and Destiny*, Vol. II, 212.

26.   Reinhold Niebuhr, *An Interpretation of Christian Ethics* (New York: Harper Brothers, 1935), 99, 191, 196; cf. Niebuhr, *Moral Man and Immoral Society* (New York: Scribner's, 1932), 52.

27.   Niebuhr, *Interpretation*, 196, 135, 206–8; Niebuhr, *Moral Man*, 57.

28.   Reinhold Niebuhr, *Reflections on the End of an Era* (New York: Scribner's, 1934), 296.

29.   Niebuhr, *Interpretation*, 201.

30.   Reinhold Niebuhr, *Love and Justice*, edited with an introduction by D. B. Robertson (Philadelphia: Westminster Press, 1957), 230–31.

31.   Niebuhr, *Moral Man*, 52; *Interpretation*, 112, 196–97, 116; Niebuhr, "Christian Faith and Social Action," in John A. Hutchinson,

ed., *Christian Faith and Social Action* (New York: Scribner's, 1953), 235–36, 240, 241.

32.   Niebuhr, "Christian Faith and Social Action," 240.

33.   See Brown, 171, 172.

34.   Brown, 241–42.

35.   Reinhold Niebuhr, *Faith and Politics,* edited with an introduction by Ronald H. Stone (New York: George Braziller, 1968), 144.

36.   Niebuhr, *Nature and Destiny,* Vol. II, 212.

37.   Niebuhr, *Nature and Destiny,* Vol. II, 115.

38.   Niebuhr, *Nature and Destiny,* Vol. II, 212.

39.   In 1966, Niebuhr explained an earlier characterization of the Death-of-God theologians as "stupid" in the following way: "The younger theologians who cheerfully, even blatantly, announced their discovery that 'God is dead' do not seem to realize that all religious affirmations are an expression of a sense of meaning and that a penumbra of mystery surrounds every realm of meaning. Religious affirmations avail themselves of symbols and myths, which express both trust in the meaning of life and an awareness of the mystery of the unknowable that surrounds every realm of meaning." See "Faith as the Sense of Meaning in Human Existence," in Niebuhr, *Faith and Politics,* 3. Cf. note 56, below.

Incidentally, Niebuhr's reverent certitude about the reality of God was manifest in another way that is vital for ethics. The epigraph of this book makes a point proclaimed in one of his most eloquent sermons, which is this: prophetic faith respects the inscrutability of God's purposes in its lack of interest in metaphysical speculation—but its uncertainty in this area is matched by its certainty about God's demands for justice and righteousness in human affairs.

This aspect of Niebuhr's thought is nicely captured in the tribute with which Charles Brown closes his splendid book *Niebuhr and His Age:* "The task of achieving [world community] must be interpreted from the standpoint of a faith which understands the fragmentary and broken character of all historic achievements and yet has confidence in their meaning because it knows their completion to be in the hands of a Divine Power, whose resources are greater than those of men, and whose suffering love can overcome the corruptions of man's achievements, without negating the significance of our striving" (*Niebuhr and His Age,* 251).

40.   Reinhold Niebuhr, "Ten Years That Shook My World," *Christian Century* (Apr. 26, 1939), as cited in Bingham, *Courage to Change,* 19. Cf. Beckley's perceptive statement on the same point: "His method for recovering Christian myths was to test them in light of experience. His editorials in *Radical Religion* and *Christianity and Society* during this period reveal Niebuhr's increasing alarm over the moral failures of communism and, to a lesser extent, dogmatic democratic socialism. Simultaneously, Niebuhr was

increasingly astonished that American democratic liberalism contained resources to produce a tolerable equality of distribution" (Harlan Beckley,
Passion for Justice, 312).

41. See Kegley and Bretall, 9.

42. Reinhold Niebuhr, *Christian Realism and Political Problems* (New
York: Scribner's, 1953), 202.

43. Donald B. Meyer, *The Protestant Search for Political Realism,* 257.

44. See James Gustafson, "Theology in the Service of Ethics: An
Interpretation of Reinhold Niebuhr's Theological Ethics," in Richard Harries, ed., *Reinhold Niebuhr and the Issues of Our Time,* 24–45.

45. Richard Fox, as quoted in Richard John Neuhaus, *Reinhold
Niebuhr Today* (Grand Rapids, Mich.: Eerdmans, 1989), 106.

46. Neuhaus, 111.

47. Neuhaus, 114.

48. Neuhaus, 106.

49. Reinhold Niebuhr, "Intellectual Autobiography," in Kegley and
Bretall, 7.

50. See pp. 86–87.

51. Niebuhr, *Faith and Politics,* 25.

52. Reinhold Niebuhr, *The Essential Reinhold Niebuhr,* edited with an
introduction by Robert McAffee Brown (New Haven, Conn.: Yale University Press, 1986), 237–38.

53. Niebuhr, *The Essential Reinhold Niebuhr,* 241.

54. See Reinhold Niebuhr, *Beyond Tragedy: Essays on the Christian
Interpretation of History* (New York: Scribner's, 1937), ch. 10.

55. Niebuhr, *Irony,* 155.

56. When asked to give his opinion of the Death-of-God theologians
in 1966, Niebuhr said, "I think they are stupid . . . [because] they don't
realize that all religious convictions and affirmations are symbolic," and
because they seem to be in favor of doing away with the symbols that
express "schemes of meaning" without putting anything in their place
(Niebuhr, *The Essential Reinhold Niebuhr,* 230).

57. Kegley and Bretall, 6.

58. H. Richard Niebuhr told this story in a graduate seminar on
Christian Ethics to illustrate the meaning of his concept of "inner history." I
do not know if has ever been told in print.

59. See Niebuhr, *Faith and Politics,* 15–21.

60. Niebuhr, *Beyond Tragedy,* 6.

61. Niebuhr, *Reflections on the End of an Era,* 123ff.; cf. 287–89.

62. One of the most striking documentations of this claim can be
found in a little-known article composed by Niebuhr as a tribute to Henry
Sloan Coffin on the occasion of the latter's retirement as president of Union
Theological Seminary. The "liberal evangelicalism" which Niebuhr praises

here is hardly that of a functionalist who is merely using Christian language to describe a philosophical position that can easily be separated from the biblical mythology in which it is expressed.

63. Niebuhr, *Nature and Destiny,* Vol. II, 109–10.

64. Niebuhr, "The Truth in Myths," in Stone, ed., *Faith and Politics,* 30.

65. Stone, *Faith and Politics,* 10.

66. Reinhold Niebuhr, "How My Mind Has Changed," *Christian Century* (1959–1960), 23.

67. As quoted by Ronald Stone on the basis of a personal interview with Niebuhr. See Stone, *Professor Reinhold Niebuhr,* 70.

68. Niebuhr, *Reflections,* 281–82.

69. Niebuhr, *Reflections,* 294–95.

70. Niebuhr, *Reflections,* 295–96.

71. Niebuhr, *Moral Man,* 277.

72. Niebuhr, *Moral Man,* 81.

73. Dennis McCann, *Christian Realism and Liberation Theology* (Maryknoll, N.Y.: Orbis Books), 31.

74. Niebuhr, *Interpretation,* 158.

75. Niebuhr, *Interpretation,* 159.

76. See McCann, 31–35.

77. See Reinhold Niebuhr, *Justice and Mercy* (sermons and prayers), edited with an introduction by Ursula M. Niebuhr (New York: Harper and Row, 1974), 9.

78. Bronislaw Malinowski, *The Foundations of Faith and Morals* (Folcraft, Pa.: Folcroft Press, 1969), 8.

79. Neuhaus, 125.

80. Neuhaus, 123.

81. Niebuhr, *Justice and Mercy,* 4. Cf. *Leaves,* 81–82.

82. Niebuhr, *Justice and Mercy,* 6. Yet he also insists that the priestly function "must be performed in terms of greater relevance to all the specific problems, personal and social, in which our people stand" (*Justice and Mercy,* 4).

83. William W. Bartley III, "I Call Myself a Protestant," *Harpers* (May 1959): 49–56.

84. Paul Van Buren, *The Secular Meaning of the Gospel* (New York: Macmillan, 1963), 3.

85. See Henry Clark, *The Ethical Mysticism of Albert Schweitzer* (Boston: Beacon Press, 1962), 69–70.

86. When Niebuhr expresses qualms about being too Aristotelian in *Leaves* (which is, after all, his journal from the period before 1928), he is voicing his lingering allegiance to the Social Gospel's reverence for "the claim of the ideal," especially its uneasiness about "compromising one's principles." His mature thought is a wise mixture of idealism and realism

which eschews some of the natural-law rigidities of classical metaphysics without disdaining the place of compromise in the practice of politics.

Chapter 4

1. Reinhold Niebuhr, *Reinhold Niebuhr on Politics,* edited with an introduction by Harry R. Davis and Robert C. Good (New York: Scribner's, 1960), 105.

2. Niebuhr, *Reinhold Niebuhr on Politics,* 105.

3. Niebuhr, *Reinhold Niebuhr on Politics,* 106.

4. Niebuhr, *Reinhold Niebuhr on Politics,* 106.

5. Niebuhr, *Reinhold Niebuhr on Politics,* 106.

6. Niebuhr, *Reinhold Niebuhr on Politics,* 107.

7. Niebuhr, *Nature and Destiny,* Vol. II, 254.

8. Yoder complains that "all of this relevance can only be had at the cost of admitting first that Jesus' way is not *really* for here and now," and for him—as a Christian pacifist—this is an absolutely fatal flaw. See John Howard Yoder, *The Politics of Jesus* (Grand Rapids, Mich.: Eerdmans, 1972), 112 n15. Yet Yoder seems to have a certain admiration for Niebuhr for being honest enough to admit that his understanding of Christian ethics "directly denies Jesus' moral authority," for he declares that "Not until the Jesuits of Pascal's *Provincial Letters* or Reinhold Niebuhr would moralists say straight out that they were doing something other than what Jesus meant" (Yoder, *The Priestly Kingdom* [Notre Dame, Ind.: University of Notre Dame Press, 1984], 203 n8).

9. See Henry Clark, *The Christian Case Against Poverty* (New York: Association Press, 1965), ch. 1.

10. Karen Lebacqz, *Six Theories of Justice* (Minneapolis: Augsburg Press, 1986), 93. The internal quotation is from Daniel Day Williams's essay "Niebuhr and Liberalism" in Kegley and Bretall, *Reinhold Niebuhr: His Religious, Social, and Political Thought,* 210.

11. Niebuhr, *Nature and Destiny,* Vol. II, 247.

12. Niebuhr, *Nature and Destiny,* Vol. II, 248.

13. Niebuhr, *Nature and Destiny,* Vol. II, 248.

14. Niebuhr, *Nature and Destiny,* Vol. II, 244.

15. Reinhold Niebuhr, *The Children of Light and the Children of Darkness* (New York: Scribner's, 1944), 19–20.

16. W. H. Auden, "September 1, 1939," in *Collected Poems* (New York: Random House, 1976).

17. Niebuhr, *Nature and Destiny,* Vol. II, 245.

18. Niebuhr, "Christian Faith and Social Action," 241.

19. Niebuhr, "Christian Faith and Social Action," 241.

20. Niebuhr, *Interpretation,* 46.

21. Niebuhr, *Interpretation,* 156.
22. Class notes, September 27, 1957.
23. Niebuhr, "Christian Faith and Social Action," 241.
24. Niebuhr, *Christian Realism and Political Problems,* 149.
25. Niebuhr, *Christian Realism,* 152.
26. Niebuhr, *Nature and Destiny,* Vol. I, 287.
27. Niebuhr, *Christian Realism,* 151.
28. Niebuhr, *Christian Realism,* 154.
29. Niebuhr, *Christian Realism,* 154.
30. Niebuhr, *Christian Realism,* 159.
31. Niebuhr, *Christian Realism,* 159–60.
32. Niebuhr, *Christian Realism,* 160.
33. Niebuhr, *Nature and Destiny,* Vol. I, 169.
34. Niebuhr, *Nature and Destiny,* Vol. I, 68.
35. Niebuhr, *Nature and Destiny,* Vol. I, 74.
36. Niebuhr, *Nature and Destiny,* Vol. I, 69; cf. Niebuhr, *Faith and Politics,* 132–34.
37. Niebuhr, *Nature and Destiny,* Vol. I, 69.
38. Niebuhr, *Nature and Destiny,* Vol. II, 267; cf. Niebuhr, *Faith and History,* 178.
39. Niebuhr, *Nature and Destiny,* Vol. II, 257.
40. Niebuhr, *Nature and Destiny,* Vol. II, 257.
41. Niebuhr, *Nature and Destiny,* Vol. II, 258.
42. Niebuhr, *Nature and Destiny,* Vol. II, 249.
43. Niebuhr, *Nature and Destiny,* Vol. II, 250.
44. Niebuhr, *Nature and Destiny,* Vol. II, 250.
45. Niebuhr, *Nature and Destiny,* Vol. II, 250.
46. Niebuhr, *Nature and Destiny,* Vol. II, 250–51.
47. Niebuhr, *Nature and Destiny,* Vol. II, 251.
48. Niebuhr, *Nature and Destiny,* Vol. II, 251.
49. Niebuhr, *Nature and Destiny,* Vol. II, 251.
50. Niebuhr, *Nature and Destiny,* Vol. II, 252.
51. Niebuhr, *Nature and Destiny,* Vol. II, 252.
52. Class notes, 11/20/57; cf. Niebuhr, *Children of Light,* 72.
53. Niebuhr, *Nature and Destiny,* Vol. II, 253.
54. "In a monarchy . . . 'respect and obedience' were derived only from the passion of fear. But in a republic . . . the laws had to be obeyed by the people for conscience' sake, not for wrath's. . . . The eighteenth century mind was thoroughly convinced that a popularly based government cannot be supported without *Virtue*" (Gordon S. Wood, *The Creation of the American Republic* [Chapel Hill: University of North Carolina Press, 1969], 66, 68).
55. Niebuhr, *Nature and Destiny,* Vol. II, 259; Niebuhr, *Moral Man,* 4.

56. Niebuhr, *Man's Nature and his Communities*, 22. John Bennett's explanation of this play on words is probably very close to the truth Niebuhr had in mind. The title as it stands "suggests too sharp a contrast between personal and social ethics even for his own thought at the time," for by the time Niebuhr got to New York City he knew perfectly well that "immorality is in man and is not the product of social institutions" (John C. Bennett, "Reinhold Niebuhr's Social Ethics," in Kegley and Bretall, 53).

57. Niebuhr, *Moral Man*, 25.

58. Niebuhr, *Moral Man*, 267, 272.

59. Niebuhr, *Moral Man*, 75.

60. Niebuhr, *Moral Man*, 94.

61. Niebuhr, *Moral Man*, ch. 4.

62. Niebuhr, *Moral Man*, 209.

63. Niebuhr, *Moral Man*, 30–32; 58–60; 36–37.

64. *Christianity and Society* (Winter 1951–52).

65. This is the sort of passage Ernest Lefever has in mind when he describes Niebuhr's attack on "those persons who, in his view, misunderstand our moral responsibility as citizens and as a nation because they fail to understand the realities of politics." (See Lefever's introduction to Reinhold Niebuhr, *The World Crisis and American Responsibility* [New York: Association Press, 1958], 4.)

66. Niebuhr, *Irony*, vii–viii.

67. Donald B. Meyer, *The Protestant Search for Political Realism*, xxii.

68. Meyer, xxii. But Meyer observes that Niebuhr's "sketchy and sporadic" use of the historical evidence did not always prove his thesis very convincingly; indeed, says Meyer, Niebuhr's "extremely cryptic treatment of the still more distant religious roots of the nation" might just as well lead one to see in American life "not so much a case of irony, of men wreaking better than they knew, but of declension, of men losing the thread of wisdom"—and he cites Niebuhr's praise for Abraham Lincoln as an example of this kind of historical outcome. But this, too—this tendency to lose hold of "Lincoln's awareness that 'the Almighty has his own purposes' transcending those of both combatants—is a form of irony which is comparable to the failure of Americans to realize how valuable their empirical bent and their pragmatic instincts are" (Meyer, xxii–xxiii).

69. See William Lee Miller, *Yankee from Georgia* (New York: Time Books, 1978), chs. 12 and 13.

70. Niebuhr, "Christian Faith and Social Action," in Hutchinson, *Christian Faith and Social Action*, 241.

71. Niebuhr, *Nature and Destiny*, Vol. I, 49–50.

72. Niebuhr, "Christian Faith and Social Action," 238–39.

73. Class notes from Niebuhr's course on "Structure of Nations and Empires," April 22, 1959.

74. Class notes, April 22, 1959.

75. Niebuhr, *Moral Man,* 253ff.; Niebuhr, *Love and Justice,* 146–48; Niebuhr, "Christian Faith and Social Action," 231–32.

76. Niebuhr, *Essays,* 186f.

77. Niebuhr, *Reflections,* 186.

78. *Christianity and Society* (Summer 1952): 14.

79. Niebuhr, *Moral Man,* 174, 171, 234.

80. Niebuhr, *Love and Justice,* 146–48. Cf. Herbert Edwards's criticism of Niebuhr in chapter 6.

81. See chapter 3.

82. Niebuhr, *Nature and Destiny,* I, 207.

83. Dale Patrick, "Opening Niebuhrian Thought to the Left," *Christianity and Crisis,* October 19, 1970, 212.

84. Patrick, 213.

85. Bill Kellerman, "Apologist of Power," *Sojourners* (March 1987): 17–18.

86. Kellerman, 18.

Chapter 5

1. *The Democratic Experience* was published from materials which had been prepared for use in courses at Harvard and Barnard in 1962 and 1963, so it actually represents a moment in Niebuhr's thinking when his faith in the exercise of American responsibility in the world arena was buoyed by optimistic hopes concerning the presidency of John F. Kennedy. (See Stone, *Prophet to Politicians,* 204–5.)

2. Since I resist any attempt to denigrate Niebuhr's thought by the use of psychological reductionism, I do not take much stock in Cuddihy's scurrilous attacks on Niebuhr's alleged "opportunism." But Niebuhr himself would have agreed that social location does have some bearing on the ideas one espouses and the activities one undertakes—so it is not irrelevant to bear in mind that from 1939 on Reinhold Niebuhr achieved the status of a celebrity, and the usefulness of his ideas to certain ruling elites served to increase his stature as "an adviser to the Prince(s)." We must also note, following McCann, that Niebuhr's audience changed in the 1940s: many of the "bright young men" who became interested in Niebuhr in the 1930s became influential policymakers in the 1940s. (McCann, *Christian Realism,* 127–28.

3. "Theology and Politics," *Lutheran* 34 (July 9, 1952): 10.

4. "Christian Faith and Political Controversy," *Christianity and Crisis* 12 (July 21, 1952).

5. Reinhold Niebuhr, *Christianity and Power Politics* (New York: Scribner's, 1940), 104–5.

6. Paul Merkeley, *Reinhold Niebuhr: A Political Account,* 173. Speak-

ing of *The Children of Light and the Children of Darkness,* Merkeley goes on to say that "large numbers of admirers of Niebuhr's political leadership did read this small book—in many ways, his most approachable book . . . and, finding that it provided enough theoretical help to meet their own needs as moderate-socialists and enough of a practical programme to meet their needs as New Dealers, ran off with it into the arenas of political argument persuaded that the whole of Niebuhr's doctrine of man was now at their command. The world is full of 'Freudians' who once read *Civilization and Its Discontents,* and of 'Niebuhrian realists' who once read *The Children of Light and the Children of Darkness.*"

    7. Niebuhr, *Reinhold Niebuhr on Politics,* 191–92.

    8. Niebuhr, *Reinhold Niebuhr on Politics,* 191; cf. Merkeley, 170, for a listing of three specific explanations of this point: (1) Niebuhr was still enough of a Marxist to believe that the political institutions actually operate in such a way as to benefit the ruling classes. (2) He warned against believing that "God would not permit Democracy (His cause) to fail. (3) He pointed out that the postwar world will be no better unless we can develop "a more realistic framework for future statesmanship than this manic glorification of our existing institutions and of the national virtues reflected by them."

Merkeley also contends that Niebuhr was actually guilty from time to time of adopting an attitude too uncritical of Roosevelt, Truman, and Kennedy. In words far more judicious than the rhetoric of Cuddihy (yet reminiscent of him) Merkeley concludes (pp. 177–78): "Niebuhr's reputation as a political commentator will always remain colored by the fact that he became a fixture in the liberal establishment in days when men of a reformist bent were, for the most part, genuinely persuaded that problems of social policy were settled in principle in America. Retrospectively, their complacency is difficult to credit, and impossible to excuse. In Niebuhr's case, this lapse is doubly problematical, for it implicated him in the propounding of a variant of that heresy of American exceptionalism which he so vigorously condemned in old-line liberal-idealists."

    9. Stone, *Prophet to Politicians,* 175–77.

  10. Niebuhr, *The Children of Light and the Children of Darkness,* xiii.

  11. Niebuhr, *Children of Light,* 118.

  12. Niebuhr, *Reinhold Niebuhr on Politics,* 183.

  13. Niebuhr, *Reinhold Niebuhr on Politics,* 183.

  14. Niebuhr, *Reinhold Niebuhr on Politics,* 184.

  15. Niebuhr, *Reinhold Niebuhr on Politics,* 185.

  16. Niebuhr, *Reinhold Niebuhr on Politics,* 250–51.

  17. Niebuhr, *Reinhold Niebuhr on Politics,* 314.

  18. "The Conditions of Our Survival," *Virginia Quarterly Review* XXVI, no. 4 (autumn 1950): 481.

  19. Niebuhr, *Reinhold Niebuhr on Politics,* 270–71.

20. Reinhold Niebuhr, *Man's Nature and His Communities* (New York: Scribner's, 1965), 68.

21. Niebuhr, *Man's Nature and His Communities,* 75.

22. Niebuhr, *Man's Nature and His Communities,* 125.

23. Niebuhr, *Nature and Destiny,* Vol. II, 48–49.

24. Niebuhr, *Reinhold Niebuhr on Politics,* 335.

25. Harold R. Landon, ed., *Reinhold Niebuhr: A Prophetic Voice in Our Time,* 104–5.

26. Landon, 106, 108.

27. Niebuhr, *Reinhold Niebuhr on Politics,* 247.

28. Niebuhr, *Reinhold Niebuhr on Politics,* 319.

29. Niebuhr, *Reinhold Niebuhr on Politics,* 253.

30. Niebuhr, *Reinhold Niebuhr on Politics,* 256.

31. Niebuhr, *Reinhold Niebuhr on Politics,* 256.

32. Niebuhr, *Reinhold Niebuhr on Politics,* 257.

33. Niebuhr, *Reinhold Niebuhr on Politics,* 257.

34. Niebuhr, *Reinhold Niebuhr on Politics,* 316–17.

35. Niebuhr, *Reinhold Niebuhr on Politics,* 315–17.

36. Niebuhr, *Reinhold Niebuhr on Politics,* 315–17.

37. Charles Brown, *Niebuhr and His Age,* 169, 184.

38. Personal correspondence from John Bennett, May 8, 1993.

39. Brown, 186.

40. Brown, 166–67.

41. Brown, 171. His optimism on this point was augmented (in early 1955) by his belief that "anti-Americanism abroad was ebbing, [because it was being] replaced by a new prestige resulting chiefly from 'the Supreme Court decision on segregation, the Senate's censure of Senator McCarthy, and increased confidence in President Eisenhower's fervent desire for peace, particularly after he vetoed war measures in the Indo-China crisis'" (p. 170).

42. Brown, 218 n8.

43. Personal correspondence with John Bennett, April 28, 1958.

44. Brown, 168.

45. "The Moral and Spiritual Content of the Atlantic Community," *Five Years of the North Atlantic Alliance: A Symposium* (New York: American Council on NATO, 1954), 25–30.

46. Brown, 216.

47. Personal correspondence with John Bennett, April 28, 1993.

48. Niebuhr, *Reinhold Niebuhr on Politics,* 296, 304.

49. Niebuhr, *Reinhold Niebuhr on Politics,* 309–10.

50. Brown, 213, 239.

51. Niebuhr, *The Democratic Experience,* 75. In a conversation with Hans J. Morgenthau, he even went so far as to make an analogy between

American faith in democracy and Marxist obsession with transferring ownership of the means of production to the workers: "Morgenthau, wouldn't you say that our projection of the ideal of democracy . . . as a universal option for all people is almost in the same category as the Marxist dogma about the socialization of the means of production? This Marxist dogma was not relevant for the industrial nations for which it was designed, but it was relevant to the decaying colonial nations."

And Morgenthau agrees that "they are both dogmas, decaying secular religion, [which proclaim] the last historic echoes of Wilsonianism and Marxist-Leninism" (Reinhold Niebuhr and Hans J. Morgenthau, "The Ethics of War and Peace in the Nuclear Age," *War/Peace Report,* 6, no. 2 [February 1967]: 6).

52. Niebuhr, *Reinhold Niebuhr on Politics,* 309.
53. Niebuhr, *Reinhold Niebuhr on Politics,* 309.
54. Niebuhr, *Reinhold Niebuhr on Politics,* 309.
55. Niebuhr, *Reinhold Niebuhr on Politics,* 309–10.
56. Niebuhr, *Reinhold Niebuhr on Politics,* 311.
57. Brown, 217.
58. Brown, 311.
59. Brown, 311.
60. Stone, *Prophet to Politicians,* 176.
61. Stone, 184.
62. Stone, 188.
63. This list comes from a 1956 article in *The New Leader* entitled "The Seven Great Errors of U.S. Foreign Policy." But since the last fallacy—that of ideological rigidity vis-à-vis Communist China—has no direct bearing on Suez, it is omitted from this discussion. See also Stone, 190f.
64. *Christianity and Crisis* (Jan. 6, 1958), as cited in John C. Bennett, "Niebuhr's Ethic: The Later Years," *Christianity and Crisis* (Apr. 12, 1982): 94.
65. Personal correspondence with John Bennett, April 28, 1993. Bennett adds: "But beyond all of that it seems to me so important that twice I heard him say that he hoped that if we were attacked he would be among the first to be killed because he could not take responsibility for decisions which might follow."
66. Stone, *Prophet to Politicians,* 193.
67. John C. Bennett, "Niebuhr's Ethic: The Later Years," *Christianity and Crisis* (Apr. 12, 1982): 90–91.
68. Stone, 193.
69. John C. Bennett, "Niebuhr's Ethic: The Later Years," *Christianity and Crisis* (Apr. 12, 1982): 90–91.
70. Fox, 288.

71. Brown, *Niebuhr and His Age,* 36.

72. Fox, 288.

73. Stone, 194.

74. John C. Bennett, "Niebuhr's Ethic: The Later Years," *Christianity and Crisis* (Apr. 12, 1982): 92–93. It is also interesting to note that one of Niebuhr's great admirers—Paul Ramsey—at first deplored Niebuhr's failure to support American policy in Southeast Asia, but later admitted his own mistake and praised Niebuhr for being "wiser than he [Ramsey] earlier about the war."

75. Stone, *Prophet to Politicians,* 213.

76. Merkeley, 198.

77. Merkeley, 199.

78. Merkeley, 198.

79. Merkeley, 200.

80. Stone, 213–14.

81. Lefever, 13.

82. Lefever, 4–5.

Chapter 6

1. See Henry Clark, *The Church Under Thatcher* (London: Society for the Promotion of Christian Knowledge, 1993).

2. Niebuhr professes admiration for "vocational pacifism" (i.e., the personal witness of a conscientious objector who knows that his actions will not eliminate war, yet refuses to participate in order to protest against war's inhumanity). But Niebuhr has little use for the kind of pacifism which believes that the renunciation of violence by a fairly large number of individuals can be effective in preventing its use and the lamentable loss of life that results. Pacifists complain that critics either damn their position with faint praise or attribute to it a set of naive expectations which are not really a part of their thinking. Stanley Hauerwas even goes so far as to argue that a proponent of just war theory is incapable of understanding pacifism and therefore has no right to object to it. (Stanley Hauerwas, "Can a Pacifist Think About War?" [unpublished paper], Ethikon Institute's Jerusalem Conference on War and Peace, Jan. 4–7, 1993.

When I reflect on my own lack of sympathy with pacifism—or, to be more honest, my horror at the thought of leaving relatively innocent and helpless people unprotected from the savagery wrought by the bad guys of this wicked world—I am persuaded that Hauerwas might conceivably have a point. The only brand of pacifist thought which strikes me as worthy of serious attention is a newly developed theory of which Niebuhr could have known nothing—namely, the strategy of "civilian-based resistance" now being advocated by theorists such as Gene Sharp and George Crowell, and by certain "green" politicians in Europe. See Gene Sharp, *National Security Through Civilian-Based Defense* (Omaha: Civilian-based Defense Association, 1985); and George Crowell, "The Case for Nonviolent Civilian Defense Against External Aggression," a paper originally prepared for a conference on "The Ethics of Nonviolence" organized by the Institute of Philosophy of the Soviet Academy of Sciences.

3. See Sharp; Crowell.

4. Beverly Harrison, *Making the Connections* (Boston: Beacon Press, 1985), 27.

5. Harrison, 28.

6. Harrison, 58–59.

7. Harrison, 63.

8. Rubem Alves, "Ideology of the Establishment," *Christianity and Crisis* (Sept. 17, 1973): 175. One of the features of Niebuhrian thought that is under attack in this article is his failure to understand and appreciate the validity of the kind of utopian thought which "believes that somewhere, somehow, God is doing his thing; he is overthrowing the existing order. Therefore, it is necessary to debunk our man-made realities [of which the world postulated by Christian Realism is a prime example]."

9. Cornel West, *Prophetic Fragments* (Grand Rapids, Mich.: Eerdmans, 1988), 144–52.

10. See especially Michael Novak, *The Spirit of Democratic Capitalism* (New York: Simon and Schuster, 1982), ch. XIX, and "Reinhold Niebuhr: Model for Neoconservatives," *Christian Century* (Jan. 22, 1986). Novak is right about one thing, though: American opinion "needs Niebuhr again," not least because of his realism about human nature and because of his admonitions to self-criticism (which is especially needed, says Novak, by America's "New Class").

11. William Lee Miller, "In Strange Company," *New Republic* (Apr. 21, 1982): 27–28.

12. See John C. Bennett, "Niebuhr's Ethic: The Later Years," *Christianity and Crisis* (Apr. 12, 1982); Charles Brown, *Niebuhr and His Age,* chs. 7–9.

13. Michael Novak's attempt to claim Niebuhr as the patron saint of modern American neoconservatism also fails in reference to his thinking on economic policy. Chapter XIX of Novak's *The Spirit of Capitalism,* for example, makes a futile attempt to turn Niebuhr into a disciple of Adam Smith by tracing the evolution of Niebuhr's disillusionment with Marxism. He is correct in showing how Niebuhr came to see the folly of the Marxist prejudice against private property along with the pragmatic benefits of the market's reliance upon pecuniary self-interest instead of altruism or a command economy—but the very passages Novak quotes show that Niebuhr did not forget about the importance of equality as an element in a worthy

concept of justice. He doesn't even come close to demonstrating that Niebuhr's awareness of the errors of Marxism constitutes a blanket endorsement of laissez-faire capitalism.

14. When I say "we" throughout the rest of this chapter, it is not the so-called "royal we" (which would distance the writer—defined as "expert"—from his readers). On the contrary, it is a "we" which is meant to convey the assumption that both parties (writer and readers) have a common concern—namely, to figure out what is valuable, what is rather unimportant, and what may be dangerous in the legacy of Reinhold Niebuhr.

15. Dennis McCann, *Christian Realism and Liberation Theology,* 125.

16. McCann, *Christian Realism,* 127.

17. Judith Plaskow, *Sex, Sin, and Grace* (Washington, D.C.: University Press of America, 1980), 63.

18. Plaskow, 63–65.

19. Plaskow, 86.

20. Plaskow, 87.

21. Aurelia Takacs Fule, "Being Human Before God: Reinhold Niebuhr in Feminist Mirrors," paper presented at the Reinhold Niebuhr Centenary Symposium, McGill University, Montreal, Canada, September 26–28, 1992, page 12.

22. Fule, 12.

23. Herbert Edwards, "Niebuhr, 'Realism,' and Civil Rights in America," *Christianity and Crisis* (Feb. 3, 1986): 12. Comparing Niebuhr's attempts to be "100% American" with Martin Luther King, Jr.'s attempts not to conform to stereotyped notions about Negroes while at Crozer Theological Seminary, Edwards adds: "Like King, Niebuhr overcompensated, becoming more American, more patriotic, than other Americans. In fact, he became an Anglophile, . . . at a time when England was the greatest imperial power in the world, controlling more 'colored' or 'nonwhite' populations than any other nation."

24. Edwards, 12.

25. Edwards, 12.

26. See Dideri Mattijsen, ed., *Church, Society, and Change* (Den Haag: CIP-gegevens Konicklijke Bibliotheek, 1985), 136–38.

27. Harrison, 59.

28. Harrison, 59.

29. L. Katherin Harrington, "Reinhold Niebuhr and Economic Philosophy," paper prepared for a seminar on Reinhold Niebuhr and the Legacy of Niebuhrianism, University of Southern California, 1992, 40.

30. M. M. Thomas, "A Third World View of Christian Realism," *Christianity and Crisis* (Feb. 3, 1986): 8–9.

31. Thomas, 9.

32. Thomas, 9.

33. Thomas, 10. On this particular point, Thomas may have been even closer to an important truth than he realized, yet less fair to the moral thrust of Niebuhr's thinking. The fact is, Niebuhr does appear to have been something of an apostle of "productive justice"—i.e., the belief that technology can create such enormous economic productivity that even the least advantaged citizens of a modern country will have "enough" to live in good health (Howard Richards, "Productive Justice," in William Aiken and Hugh LaFollette, eds., *World Hunger and Moral Obligation*).

In a 1961 sermon on "Covetousness," he shows the influence of this historical moment by declaring that technological transfer is a crucial part of bringing about global economic justice: "Wealth and poverty are on the whole not due to exploitation, although there is always exploitation of the weak by the strong. It is a matter of technical competence. . . . We are not good enough to share everything that comes out of technical competence, but we must be good enough and wise enough to share the competence, the skill by which the abundance of things can be produced or created" (Niebuhr, *Justice and Mercy*, 68).

34. Thomas, 10.

35. West, 151.

36. Edwards, 14.

37. Edwards, 14.

38. Edwards, 14.

39. Edwards, 15.

40. Edwards, 15.

41. Ronald Stone, "The Contribution of Reinhold Niebuhr to the Late Twentieth Century," in Kegley and Bretall, eds., *Reinhold Niebuhr: His Religious, Social, and Political Thought*, 78–79.

42. John Bennett maintains that Niebuhr always sounded better when commenting on social and political issues than he appears to be when judged only in the light of passages from his writings singled out for criticism by his attackers. This is something which is felt by almost anyone who sees a writer whom he admires suffering "attack by proof-texting." Personal correspondence with John Bennett, May 8, 1993.

43. Niebuhr, "Gunnar Myrdal, *An American Dilemma*," *Christianity and Society* 9 (Summer 1944): 42.

44. Charles Brown, *Niebuhr and His Age*, 108.

45. Brown, 118–20.

46. See Niebuhr, *Moral Man and Immoral Society*, 46–47. John Bennett is of the opinion that what Niebuhr said on these pages constitutes both an admission of the principal feminist argument about oppression and a refutation of the detailed complaints about Niebuhr's insensitivity sometimes advanced by feminist writers. Cf. pp. 65 and 117–18.

47. It is this line of thinking, in fact, which might lead some observers to say that Niebuhr is insufficiently aware of the ambiguities of all human attempts to fight against injustice or in other ways seek a better world. Psychologists such as Ernest Becker and Otto Rank would say that fear of insignificance (in Niebuhr's terms, "finitude") inevitably drives human beings to invest too much power in their leaders, who inevitably become murderous tyrants. But this line of reasoning complains that Niebuhr does not have *enough* awareness of the virulence of pride, not that he puts too much emphasis on it.

48. Niebuhr, "The Sin of Racial Prejudice," *The Messenger* 13 (February 3, 1948): 6.

49. Fule, "Being Human Before God," 14.

50. Niebuhr, *Moral Man in Immoral Society*, 261–62.

51. Plaskow, *Sex, Sin, and Grace*, 87.

52. Susan Dunfee, as quoted by Fule, 11.

53. Reinhold Niebuhr, "Norman Thomas," *Christianity and Crisis* (Jan. 11, 1965): 271.

54. "The Test of Christian Faith Today," *Christianity and Crisis* (Oct. 28, 1959): 1240.

55. See note 33 above.

56. Niebuhr, "The Abundance of Things Man Possesses," *The Messenger* 20 (August 16, 1955): 7.

57. See Daniel Bell, *The End of Ideology*.

58. Brown, *Niebuhr and His Age*, 193.

59. Chapter XIX of *The Spirit of Democratic Capitalism* is a futile attempt to show that Niebuhr was the intellectual and spiritual heir of neo-conservatism. It is futile because all it demonstrates is that Niebuhr saw the folly of the Marxist prejudice against private property along with the pragmatic benefits of the market's reliance upon pecuniary self-interest instead of altruism or a command economy. Novak is correct, for example, in pointing out that Niebuhr understood the notion of the pragmatic functions of self-interest in Adam Smith's portrait of the free-market system. But the very passages Novak quotes show that Niebuhr had not forgotten about the utility of equality as a shaper of justice. He doesn't even come close to demonstrating that Niebuhr's awareness of the errors of Marxism constitutes a blanket endorsement of laissez-faire capitalism.

William Lee Miller points out: "Niebuhr was always a man of the democratic left. He was never a conservative, neo- or otherwise." See "In Strange Company," *The New Republic* (Apr. 21, 1982): 27.

60. "Ideology in the Social Struggle," *Christianity and Society* XI, 2 (Spring 1946): 9.

61. "The Character of Ideology," *Christianity and Society* XII, 3 (Summer 1947): 5.

62. *Christianity and Society* XVIII, 2 (Spring 1953): 4–5.
63. Brown, 190.
64. Brown, 192.
65. Personal correspondence with the author, May 8, 1993.
66. Stone, *Prophet to Politicians,* 76.
67. Stone, 76.
68. William Lee Miller, "In Strange Company," *The New Republic* (Apr. 21, 1982): 27.
69. Cited in Gary J. Dorrien, "Economic Democracy," *Christianity and Crisis* (Sept. 10, 1990): 274.

Chapter 7

1. It could be argued that Niebuhr himself foresaw the reverse dimension of this problem, articulating it in these words: "But the final mystery of human sin cannot be understood if it is not recognized that the greatest teachers of this Reformation doctrine of the sinfulness of all men used it on occasion as the instrument of an arrogant will-to-power against theological opponents" (Niebuhr, *Nature and Destiny,* Vol. 1, 202).
2. West, 150.
3. This is one of the greatest assets of "situation ethics" rightly understood—that is, understood as "summary rule-agapism," an approach which requires one to take traditional prescriptions and proscriptions quite seriously and to act in accordance with them unless there are very sure and specific reasons for thinking that another course of action might be more loving in the sense that it would lead to better consequences for those likely to be affected.

See Joseph Fletcher's "Reply to My Critics," *The Situation Ethics Debate,* which clarifies his position in an important way. It is in this essay that he defines his concept of situation ethics as summary rule-agapism, which he sees as a "Golden Mean" between Pharisaic legalism and the antinomianism—or act-agapism—with which situation ethics is often confused.

4. Niebuhrians may be in the position of the unfortunate woman described by Sartre in his discussion of "bad faith." (See Mary Warnock, *Existentialist Ethics* [New York: St. Martin's Press, 1967], 29–33. As Simone de Beauvoir has observed, "Sartre forged the concept of bad faith to account for what goes on in the subconscience.)

Sartre describes the experience of a woman who wakes up to find a strange man in her bed and then feels absolutely amazed by what has happened. As she tries to remember exactly what transpired on the previous evening, she recalls that she certainly had no intention of allowing herself to be seduced by a man she scarcely knew. She wonders how he could possibly have interpreted her animated conversation as a sign of interest in him. She had made no protest, it is true, when he held her hand and gazed intently into her eyes, but how could he have attributed any significance to such a trivial indication of friendly sentiments? And she had not wanted to be so rude as to rebuke him for the tender words he had spoken so softly in her ear, but—why should that have encouraged him to think that she might be willing to let him come home with her? As for the fact that she actually had invited him to come into her flat when the evening was over—well, it was a meaningless gesture of gratitude for an enjoyable evening, and she had said that he would have to leave in only a few minutes.

Yes. As Sartre observes, any woman who acts that way (and then denies any responsibility at all for what took place) is kidding herself. To behave and to think this way is to exhibit "bad faith"—i.e., a refusal to be honest about what one really intends and to acknowledge accountability for the consequences.

In like fashion, the greatest fear of the Christian Realist probably ought to be the possibility that he or she is acting in bad faith in performing sociocultural analysis and in reaching the conclusions about ethical behavior and social policy he or she actually comes up with. What if in teaching our students and parishioners to practice Christian Realism in a similar fashion, we may (sometimes? frequently? almost always?) be perpetuating grievous error and iniquity? If so, it would be better to have a millstone tied around our necks and to be cast into the sea.

5. See especially William Greider, *Who Will Tell the People?* (New York: Simon and Schuster, 1992).

6. See Jack Nelson-Pallmeyer, *War Against the Poor* (Maryknoll, N.Y.: Orbis Books, 1989).

Bibliography

Auden, W. H. *Collected Poems*. New York: Random House, 1976.

Beckley, Harlan. *Passion for Justice*. Louisville: Westminster/John Knox Press, 1992.

Bellah, Robert, et al. *Habits of the Heart*. Berkeley: University of California Press, 1985.

Bingham, June. *Courage to Change*. New York: Scribner's, 1965.

Brown, Charles. *Niehbuhr and His Age*. Philadelphia: Trinity Press International, 1992.

Clark, Henry. *The Christian Case Against Poverty*. New York: Association Press, 1965.

————. *The Church Under Thatcher*. London: Society for the Promoting of Christian Knowledge, 1993.

————. *The Ethical Mysticism of Albert Schweitzer*. Boston: Beacon Press, 1962.

Cox, Harvey G., ed. *The Situation Ethics Debate*. Philadelphia: Westminster Press, 1968.

Cuddihy, John Murray. *No Offense*. New York: Seabury Press, 1978.

Douglas, Ann. *The Feminization of American Culture*. New York: Alfred Knopf, 1987.

Durkin, Kenneth. *Reinhold Niebuhr*. London: Geoffrey Chapman, 1989.

Fey, Harold E., ed. *How My Mind Has Changed*. Cleveland: World Publishing, 1961.

Fletcher, Joseph. *Situation Ethics*. Philadelphia: Westminster Press, 1966.

Fox, Richard. *Reinhold Niebuhr: A Biography*. New York: Pantheon Books, 1985.

Fule, Aurelia Tokacs. "Being Human Before God: Reinhold Niebuhr in Feminist Mirrors." Paper presented at the Reinhold Niebuhr Centenary Symposium, McGill University, Montreal, Canada, September 26–28, 1992.

Greider, William. *Who Will Tell the People?* New York: Simon and Schuster, 1992.

Handy, Robert T., ed. *The Social Gospel in America.* New York: Oxford University Press, 1966.

Harries, Richard, ed. *Reinhold Niebuhr and the Issues of Our Time.* London: Mowbray, 1986.

Harrison, Beverly. *Making the Connections.* Boston: Beacon Press, 1985.

Hutchison, John A., ed. *Christian Faith and Social Action.* New York: Scribner's, 1953.

Kegley, Charles, and Robert Bretall, eds. *Reinhold Niebuhr: His Religious, Social, and Political Thought.* New York: Macmillan, 1956.

Landon, Harold R., ed. *Reinhold Niebuhr: A Prophetic Voice in Our Time.* Greenwich, Conn.: Seabury Press, 1962.

Lebacqz, Karen. *Six Theories of Justice.* Minneapolis: Augsburg Press, 1986.

McCann, Dennis P. *Christian Realism and Liberation Theology.* Maryknoll, N.Y.: Orbis Books, 1982.

MacIntyre, Alasdair. *After Virtue.* 2d ed. Notre Dame, Ind.: University of Notre Dame Press, 1984.

Malinowski, Bronislaw. *The Foundation of Faith and Morals.* Folcraft, Pa.: Folcraft Press, 1969.

Mattijsen, Dideri, ed. *Church, Society, and Change.* Den Haag: CIP-gegevens Konicklijke Bibliotheek, 1985.

Merkeley, Paul. *Reinhold Niebuhr: A Political Account.* Montreal: McGill-Queen's University Press, 1975.

Meyer, Donald B. *The Protestant Search for Political Realism.* Berkeley: University of California Press, 1960.

Miller, William Lee. *Yankee from Georgia.* New York: Time Books, 1978.

Morganthau, Hans J. "The Political Conscience of Reinhold Niebuhr." *Esquire,* December 1983, p. 399.

Nelson-Pallmeyer, Jack. *War Against the Poor.* Maryknoll, N.Y.: Orbis Books, 1989.

Neuhaus, Richard John. *Reinhold Niebuhr Today.* Grand Rapids, Mich.: Eerdmans, 1989.

Niebuhr, Reinhold. *Beyond Tragedy: Essays on the Christian Interpretation of History.* New York: Scribner's, 1937.

———. *The Children of Light and the Children of Darkness.* New York: Scribner's, 1944.

———. *Christian Realism and Political Problems.* New York: Scribner's, 1953.

———. *Christianity and Power Politics.* New York: Scribner's, 1940.

———. *The Contribution of Religion to Social Work.* New York: Columbia University Press, 1932.

————. *The Democratic Experience: Past and Prospects.* (With Paul E. Sigmund.) New York: Praeger, 1969.

————. *Discerning the Signs of the Times.* New York: Scribner's, 1946.

————. *Does Civilization Need Religion?* New York: Macmillan, 1927.

————. *Essays in Applied Christianity.* Edited with an introduction by D. B. Robertson. New York: Meridian Books, 1959.

————. *The Essential Reinhold Niebuhr.* Edited with an introduction by Robert McAffee Brown. New Haven, Conn.: Yale University Press, 1986.

————. *Faith and Politics.* Edited with an introduction by Ronald H. Stone. New York: George Braziller, 1968.

————. *An Interpretation of Christian Ethics.* New York: Harper and Brothers, 1935.

————. *The Irony of American History.* New York: Scribner's, 1952.

————. *Justice and Mercy.* (Sermons and prayers.) Edited with an introduction by Ursula M. Niebuhr. New York: Harper and Row, 1974.

————. *Leaves from the Notebook of a Tamed Cynic.* Chicago: Willett, Clark and Colby, 1929.

————. *Love and Justice.* Edited with an introduction by D. B. Robertson. Philadelphia: Westminster Press, 1957.

————. *Man's Nature and His Communities.* New York: Scribner's, 1965.

————. *Moral Man in Immoral Society.* New York: Scribner's, 1932.

————. *A Nation So Conceived: Reflections on the History of America from Its Early Visions to Its Present Power.* (With Alan Heimert.) New York: Scribner's, 1963.

————. *The Nature and Destiny of Man: A Christian Interpretation.* Volume I: *Human Nature* (1941). Volume II: *Human Destiny* (1943). New York: Scribner's.

————. *A Pious and Secular America.* New York: Scribner's, 1958.

————. *Reflections on the End of an Era.* New York: Scribner's, 1934.

————. *Reinhold Niebuhr on Politics.* Edited with an introduction by Harry R. Davis and Robert C. Good. New York: Scribner's, 1960.

————. *A Reinhold Niebuhr Reader.* Edited with an introduction by Charles C. Brown. Philadelphia: Trinity Press, 1992.

————. *Reinhold Niebuhr: Theologian of Public Life.* Edited with an introduction by Larry Rasmussen. London: Collins, 1959; Minneapolis: Augsburg Fortress Press, 1991.

————. *The Self and the Dramas of History.* New York: Scribner's, 1955.

————. *The Structure of Nations and Empires.* New York: Scribner's, 1959.

————. *The World Crisis and American Responsibility.* Edited with an introduction by Ernest W. Lefever. New York: Association Press, 1958.

————. *Young Reinhold Niebuhr: His Early Writings, 1911–1931.* Edited with an introduction by William G. Chrystal. St. Louis: Eden, 1977.

———— and Hans J. Morganthau. "The Ethics of War and Peace in the Nuclear Age." *War/Peace Report,* 6, no. 2 (February 1967): 3–8.

Novak, Michael. *The Spirit of Democratic Capitalism.* New York: Simon and Schuster, 1982.

Plaskow, Judith. *Sex, Sin, and Grace.* Washington, D.C.: University Press of America, 1980.

Rauschenbusch, Walter. *Christianity and the Social Crisis.* New York: Macmillan, 1907.

————. *Christianizing the Social Order.* New York: Macmillan, 1912.

————. *A Theology for the Social Gospel.* New York: Macmillan, 1917.

Schneider, Louis, and Sanford M. Dornbusch. *Popular Religion.* Chicago: University of Chicago Press, 1958.

Sifton, Elisabeth Niebuhr. "Remembering Reinhold Niebuhr." *World Policy Journal,* 1, no. 1 (Spring 1993): 83–90.

Stone, Ronald H. *Professor Reinhold Niebuhr.* Louisville: Westminster/John Knox Press, 1992.

————. *Reinhold Niebuhr: Prophet to Politicians.* Nashville: Abingdon Press, 1972.

Stout, Jeffrey. *Ethics After Babel.* Boston: Beacon Press, 1988.

Tawney, R. T. *Religion and the Rise of Capitalism.* New York: New American Library, 1947.

Welch, Sharon D. *The Feminine Ethic of Risk.* Minneapolis: Fortress Press, 1990.

West, Cornel. *Prophetic Fragments.* Grand Rapids, Mich.: Eerdmans, 1988.

Van Buren, Paul. *The Secular Meaning of the Gospel.* New York: Macmillan, 1963.

Wood, Gordon S. *The Creation of the American Republic.* Chapel Hill: University of North Carolina Press, 1969.

Yinger, J. Milton, ed. *Religion, Society, and the Individual.* New York: Macmillan, 1957.

Yoder, John Howard. *The Politics of Jesus.* Grand Rapids, Mich.: Eerdmans, 1972.

————. *The Priestly Kingdom.* Notre Dame, Ind.: University of Notre Dame Press, 1984.

Index

DATE DUE

DUE	RETURNED

KING PRESS NO 306